ISLAM IN FOCUS

In the name of God, Most Gracious, Most Merciful.
Praise be to God, the Cherisher and Sustainer of the Worlds;
Most Gracious, Most Merciful; Master of the Day of Judgment. You do we worship, and Your aid we seek. Show us
the straight way, the way of those on whom You have bestowed Your Grace, those whose (portion) is not wrath, and
who go not astray.

ISLAM IN FOCUS

HAMMUDAH ABDALATI

AMERICAN TRUST PUBLICATIONS

DEDICATION

With Genuine Humility, I Acknowledge Your Aid, O GOD!
In The True Spirit Of Islam, I Appreciate Your Grace, O GOD!
WITH All My Heart, I Thank You, O GOD!

Without Your Guidance And Love,
This Work Would Not Have Been Possible.
Were It Not For Your Help And Cause,
This Humble Contribution Would Have Never Become A Reality.

And If It Is Worth Dedicating,
Please Bless It With Your Acceptance;

It Is Dedicated To You, O GOD!

Hammudah Abdalati

ACKNOWLEDGEMENTS

The publishers acknowledge their deep gratitude to the World Assembly of Muslim Youth for their financial support and encouragement; to the Muslim Students Association of the United States and Canada for their initiative in organizing Muslim scholars; to the North American Islamic Trust for their leadership in publication of works of Islamic scholarship and to Dr. M. Zahirul Hassan for his proofreading.

CONTENTS

Chapter III

Chapter IV

Chapter V

APPENDIX I   **Appendix I**

Appendix II

Appendix III

FOREWORD

The purpose of this work is simply to acquaint the average reader with the basic teachings of Islam. It will be obvious that there is no intention to present the depth or breadth of Islam in this book. What is intended, however, is to provide the common but literate person with a proper insight into the subject and help him to appreciate the principles which Islam stands for. Once he develops the initial interest, he can pursue the course of deeper knowledge on his own.

The Muslims of the Western Hemisphere, especially those young among them who reside in remote areas, do face complex problems. All the surrounding circumstances are unfavorable as far as Islam is concerned. Radio comments and television shows, news items and magazine articles, motion pictures and even school textbooks, all seem to misrepresent Islam and not always innocently. Besides, certain overenthusiastic groups try to exploit the condition of these Muslims in the hope that they may become converts to this denomination or that sect. On the other hand, there are many temptations in life to divert the attention of people and turn their interest away from the right course of religion. This is harmful enough; but it is more so in the case of the young Muslims and is still much more in the case of Islam, the religion that is poorly understood in this part of the world. It is true that some Muslim parents try to provide their children with religious guidance and instruction; but of what good are these limited efforts and how effective can they be in this high-pressure environment?

What happens then? What is the result of this difficult situation? It must be admitted, in all honesty, that the picture looks gloomy but not hopeless. Some Muslims, who are innocent victims of their high-pressure environment, become indifferent and self-contained. They feel ashamed, afraid, or suspicious of their surroundings. Consequently, they cannot possibly make any valuable contribution to their society or derive any significant benefit from it. Others flow with the tide of society to become fashionable and acceptable. These, too, will neither contribute to nor benefit from the society in which they live. Such "Muslims" may even become destructive and disgraceful, for they will be without effective religious morals.

Along with these indifferent, withdrawn, and indulgent Muslims, there are others who may not be better in any way. They are probably fascinated by what seems to be a high degree of effective organization of certain religious groups or by the wide social circulation fostered by certain secular fraternities. Such individuals are, for the most part, marginal people and mere joiners. They may even be viewed as souls lost in the "lonely crowd" so characteristic of modern society. They join not because they have become thoroughly indoctrinated in the faith of this or that particular group. Nor is it because they have developed an unselfish love for humanity. Rather, they join because they do not properly appreciate their own Islamic heritage. As a result of this and of their living in non-Muslim environments, they may not acquire the necessary knowledge and courage to stand out as Muslims. If such "Muslims" have any real interest in religion, they will not deviate from the path of Islam, which stands for the highest level of religious evolution and human aspiration. Moreover, if they do really care for the spiritual and moral welfare of mankind, they will find the greatest satisfaction within the framework of Islam. So, whenever they join any other group they can only show a superficial interest and will settle for poor substitutes. The result is that they lose the spiritual contact with their fellow Muslims and remain marginal in their new circles of association.

When the ultimate consequences of the total situation are analyzed, they will be found deplorable and harmful to all parties concerned. A loss to the Muslim platform is a greater loss to all other worthy platforms. The true Muslim can contribute most effectively to the realization of responsible citizenship and universal peace, mutual understanding and human brotherhood, freedom of conscience and maintenance of human dignity. All these principles are part and parcel of Islam. They are enjoined upon the Muslim and entrusted to him. If a Muslim, who is supposed to stand for these principles, is lost or grows indifferent, it means that humanity at large will be deprived of his valuable contributions. This is no small loss.

The Muslims have good reasons to believe that their Book, the Glorious Qur'an, is the Master Book of Revelation and the Standard of Religious Truth. They also believe that Islam has come to reaffirm the Eternal Divine Message and settle the past religious disputes so that man may embark upon creative constructive activities in all walks of life. This does not mean that the Muslims set themselves apart from or above the rest of mankind. They try neither to impose Islam nor to classify the human race into inferior and superior ranks. They do not entertain the concept of favored and condemned nations or endorse the doctrine of the Chosen and the Gentile. Rather, they are commissioned to convey the Divine Message to mankind and to make their indispensable contribution to humanity. In other words, the Muslims cannot afford to be indifferent, exclusive, or arrogant. It is their solemn duty to open wide their minds to all the realities of life and stretch far their arms to all people of whatever class, creed, race, or nationality. The good which they can do and the services they can render will fully materialize only when they put Islam into practice and associate with other people in the kind, humane spirit of Islam.

In view of all these circumstances, we are trying to make a fresh introduction to Islam. It is not our intention to cause the Muslims to become blind fanatics or narrow-minded people because Islam is strongly opposed to such things. Our hope is to re-acquaint these Muslims and their like with the truth of Islam and provide them with a spiritual insight into the universe and a moral approach to the human condition. If this is realized, it will make them responsible citizens of their respective countries, honorable members of the human race, and, above all else, God-minded people.

Does the picture I have drawn here mean a pessimistic outlook on the future of Islam in the modern world? Or is it a brave confession of the despair and helplessness to which the Muslims may seem subject? Or is it a reflection of the expected outcome of a losing spiritual battle the Muslims are fighting in the New World? Certainly not. Pessimism and despair are contrary to the spirit of Islam, and helplessness is incompatible with faith in God. The future of Islam is the future of humanity, and if humanity has any future-- which I believe it has--there is a great and bright future in store for Islam. The spiritual battle which the Muslims are fighting today is not a losing battle, although the progress appears to be slow. If the Muslims, for any reason, lose their spiritual battle, humanity will suffer irreparable losses.

The significance of this preface, then, is to draw a realistic picture of the situation which is confronting the Muslims of the New World. It is to warn parents and children alike of the dangers that are approaching and of the losses that must be prevented. Moreover, it is to remind all those who are genuinely interested in the spiritual well-being of humanity that they have to be alert and take a fresh attitude toward humanity and its problems.

To Allah's care we leave our Muslim brethren, and in Him do we have infinite confidence that our endeavors will not be in vain; 'I only desire reform to the best of my power; and my success (in the task) can only come from God. In Him I trust, and unto Him I look.' (Qur'an, 11:88).

HAMMUDAH ABDALATI

PREFACE

TO THE SECOND EDITION

This book was first conceived in response to certain urgent needs of both Muslim and non-Muslim readers in North America. It was prepared under pressures of different sorts and degrees. As a result, many essential and desirable features were, of necessity, left out. But in spite of that, the book was well received and proved to be helpful, thank God, الْحَمْدُ لِلَّه

The encouraging, appreciative comments of the readers, the genuine interest of many Muslim groups, the active support of Islamic centers and the continued need for this kind of service have made it morally necessary to keep the book available for wide circulation. Thus the need arose for a revised edition.

And once again, an effort is made in response to this moral necessity. The goal of the revision is essentially to achieve greater clarity of ideas and more simplicity of expression. The basic approach and contents of the first edition will remain the same. Addition and deletion of any material will be minimal. One deeply regrets the fact that time does not allow us a more elaborate revision to make full use of the new experiences and the valuable suggestions of many concerned readers. However, it is still a great source of joy that the book will be in circulation to continue the initial service to Islam, the Muslims, and all truth seekers of whatever persuasions.

If this modest effort is successful, it is by God's grace and guidance. But if it falls short of the readers' expectations, we can only pray and hope that God will forgive our imperfect judgements.

رَّبَّنَا عَلَيْكَ تَوَكَّلْنَا ، وَإِلَيْكَ أَنَبْنَا ، وَإِلَيْكَ الْمَصِيرُ

Our Lord! In You only do we trust; upon You alone do we depend; unto You we turn in repentance; and with You rests our ultimate destination. (Qur'ān, 60:4)

CHAPTER I
THE IDEOLOGICAL
FOUNDATION OF ISLAM
Allah (God)

Knowledge of God and belief in Him constitute the very foundation of Islam. The subject is so vital that it calls for a thorough and clear discussion. For the purpose of clarity some simple demonstrations will be used. This may sound boring or too simple for those who already know something about the subject. Such informed persons are invited to have patience and show appreciation of the importance of the matter.

There are individuals who like to doubt the concept of God in the name of science, or because of a lack of experience and understanding. The attitude of such people reflects an uneasy mentality, although they claim to be learned intellectuals. My concern will not be with their claims; rather it will be with their true position. This will explain why a great deal of the discussion is designed in a simple shape as if it were directed mainly to children, and not to adults. On the other hand, a major objective of this work is to convey

---

[1]The question of God's existence has preoccupied the great minds for many centuries. Those who believe in God seem to agree that the limited finite human intelligence cannot prove the existence of the Infinite Boundless God Who is. It can only illustrate or demonstrate His existence to the satisfaction of the curious human mind. Those who deny God claim to rely on science, philosophy, or special theories of knowledge. Their arguments are sometimes inapplicable, sometimes irrelevant, always complex, and often incomprehensible. However, the developed free mind will find its way to God. Failure to find the way does not mean that there is no way. Denial of reality does not make it unreal. For an interesting comparative view see, for example, Jacques Maritain, *Approaches to God*. (New York: The Macmillan Company, 1954); Muhammad Zafrulla Khan, *Islam: Its Meaning For Modern Man*. (New York: Harper & Row, 1962); John Hick, ed., *The Existence of God*. (New York: The Macmillan Company, 1964).

the true concept of God in Islam to the young Muslims. Another consideration here is that the concept of God in Islam is distorted in the minds of many non-Muslims who are so-called believers in God and advocates of religion.

For these reasons some simple and perhaps elementary demonstrations are used in this presentation. Yet the simplicity of some arguments here may provoke profound thinking in many adults. If it does so, it will prove to be a desirable and creative simplicity, which itself is a distinct characteristic of Islam.

As we look around in our environments, we see that every family has a head; every school has a principal; every city or town has a mayor; every province state has a premier governer; and every nation has a head of state. Moreover, we know beyond doubt that every product is the work of a certain producer, and that every beautiful art is the creation of some great artist. All this is obvious, yet it does not satisfy the hunger for knowledge and the curiosity of man about the great things in the world. One often wonders at the beauties of nature with its scenic charms and marvels; the almost endless horizons in the sky and their far-reaching expansions; the ceaseless succession-of day and night in the most orderly manner; the course of the sun, the moon, and the great stars; the world of animate and inanimate objects, the continuous process and evolution of man generation after generation. One often wonders because one would like to know the maker and maintainer of all these things with which we live and which we immensely enjoy.

Can we find an explanation of the great universe? Is there any convincing interpretation of the secret of existence? We realize that no family can function properly without a responsible head, that no city can prosperously exist without sound administration, and that no state can survive without a chief of some kind. We also realize that nothing comes into being on its own. Moreover, we observe that the universe exists and functions in the most orderly manner, and that it has survived for hundreds of thousands of years. Can we, then, say that all this is accidental and haphazard? Or can we attribute the existence of man and the whole world to mere chance?

If man were to come into being by accident or by sheer chance, his entire life would be based on chance, and his whole existence would be meaningless. But no sensible man can conceive of his life as meaningless, and no rational being would leave his existence at the mercy of fluctuating chance. Every reasonable human being tries to make his life as meaningful as possible and set for himself a model of conduct according to some design. Individuals, groups and nations do plan their course of action, and every careful plan produces some desired effects. The fact of the matter is that man does engage in planning of one sort or another, and can appreciate the merits of good planning.

Yet man represents only a very small portion of the great universe. And if he can make plans and appreciate the merits of planning, then his own existence and the survival of the universe must also be based on a planned policy. This means that there is a Designing Will behind our material existence, and that there is a Unique Mind in the world to bring things into being and keep them moving in order. The marvellous wonders of our world and the secrets of life are too great to be the product of random accident or mere chance.

In the world, then, there must be a Great Force in action to keep everything in order. In the beautiful nature there must be a Great Artist who creates the most charming pieces of art and produces everything for a special purpose in life. This Force is the strongest of all forces, and this Artist is the greatest of all artists. The true believers and deeply enlightened people recognize this Artist and call Him Allah or God. They call Him God because He is the Creator and the Chief Architect of the world, the Originator of life and the Provider of all things in existence. He is not a man because no man can create or make another man. He is not an animal, nor is He a plant. He is neither an idol nor is He a statue of any kind because none of these things can make itself or create anything else. He is not a machine. He is neither the sun nor is He the moon or any other star, because these things are controlled by a great system, and are themselves made by someone else. He is different from all these things, because He is the Maker and Keeper of them all. The maker of anything must be different from and greater than the thing which he makes. We also know that nothing can come to life on its own, and that the marvellous world did not create itself or come into existence by accident. The continuous changes in the world prove that it is made, and everything which is made must have a maker of some sort.

The Maker and Sustainer of the world, the Creator of and Provider for man, the Active Force and Effective Power in nature are all one and the same, and that is known to be Allah or God. This is the Secret of all secrets and the Most Supreme of all beings. The Holy Qur'ān, the True Book of God says:[2]

---

[2] Good literary works cannot be fully translated into any other language. This is more so in the case of the Qur'ān, the Book that challenged (and still does) the native masters of the Arabic language and literature and proved their inability to produce anything even remotely similar to the shortest chapter of the Book. It is impossible, therefore, to reproduce the meaning, beauty, and fascination of the Qur'ān in any other form. What appears here, then, is not

It is God Who has made the night for you, that you may rest therein, and the day to see. Verily God is full of Grace and Bounty to men. Yet most men give no thanks. Such is God, your Lord, the Creator of all things. There is no god but He; why then do you turn away from Him. Thus are turned away those who deny the Signs of God. It is God Who has made for you the earth as a resting place and the sky as a shelter, and has given you shape and made your shapes beautiful, and has provided for you sustenance of things good and pure; such is God your Lord. So glory to God, the Lord of the worlds! He is the Living (One); There is no god but He: call upon Him, giving Him sincere devotion. Praise be to God, Lord of the worlds (Qur'ān, 40:61-65).

It is God Who has subjected the sea to you, that ships may sail through it by His command, that you may seek of His Bounty, and that you may be grateful. And He has subjected to you, as from Him, all that is in the heavens and on earth. Behold; in that there are Signs indeed for those who reflect (Qur'ān, 45:12-13).

The Supreme Master of the whole world and the Creator of everything is Allah (God). Because He is so Great and different from the other beings, man can know Him only by reflection and through meditation. He exists at all times, and His great power is in action everywhere in the world. Man has to believe in His existence because everything in the world proves that He exists. Belief in God and His great power alone can provide mankind with the best possible explanation of many mysterious things in life. This is the safest way to true knowledge and spiritual insight, the right path to good behavior and sound morals, the surest guide to happiness and prosperity.

Once man believes that God exists he must know His attributes and names. Generally speaking every perfection and absolute goodness belong to Him, and no defect or wrong applies to Him. In specific terms, one should know and believe the following:

1. God is only One, has no partner or son, and neither gives birth, nor is He born. He is eternally besought by all and has no beginning or end, and none is equal to Him (Qur'ān, 112:1-5).

2. He is the Merciful and the Compassionate, the Guardian and the True Guide, the Just and the Supreme Lord, the Creator and the Watchful, the First and the Last, the Knowing and the Wise, the Hearing and the Aware, the Witness and the Glorious, the Able

the Qur'ān proper or its perfect translation even if such were possible. Rather, it is a human interpretation in a different language that falls far short of the forcefulness of the original Book of God. For these reasons, no quotation marks will be inserted in any strict fashion in what appears here as translation.

and the Powerful (Qur'ān, for example, 57:1-6; 59:22-24).

3. He is the Loving and the Provider, the Generous and the Benevolent, the Rich and the Independent, the Forgiving and the Clement, the Patient and the Appreciative, the Unique and the Protector, the Judge and the Peace (Qur'ān, for example, 3:31; 11:6; 35:15; 65:2-3).

Each one of these names and attributes of God is mentioned in various places in the Holy Qur'ān. We all enjoy the care and mercy of God Who is so Loving and Kind to His creation. If we try to count His favors upon us, we cannot, because they are countless (Qur'ān, 14:32-34; 16:10-18).

God is High and Supreme, but He is very near to the pious thoughtful people; He answers their prayers and helps them. He loves the people who love Him and forgives their sins. He gives them peace and happiness, knowledge and success, life and protection. He welcomes all those who want to be at peace with Him and never rejects any of them. He teaches man to be good, to do the right and to keep away from the wrong. Because He is so Good and Loving, He recommends and accepts only the good and right things. The door of His mercy is always open to any who sincerely seek His support and protection (Qur'ān, 2:186; 50:16).

The Love of God for His creatures is immense and beyond human imagination. We cannot measure or count His favors. He creates us and takes good care of us, not only from the time of our birth onward, but even long before that. He makes us in the best form of creation and gives us all the senses and faculties that we need for our growth. He helps us when we cannot help ourselves, and provides for us and for our dependents. He creates in man the mind to understand, the soul and conscience to be good and righteous, the feelings and sentiments to be kind and humane.

By His mercy we gain true knowledge and see the real light. Because He is Merciful He creates us in the most beautiful shape and provides us with the sun and the moon, the land and the sea, the earth and the skies, the plants and the animals. He is the Creator of all these things and many others for our benefit and use. He makes things that are of service to us in this life, and gives man dignity and intelligence, honor and respect, because man is the best of all created things and is God's viceroy on earth. The mercy of God gives us hope and peace, courage and confidence. It enables us to remedy our griefs and sorrows, to overcome our difficulties and obtain success and happiness. Indeed, the mercy of God relieves the distressed, cheers the afflicted, consoles the sick, strengthens the desperate, and comforts the needy. In short, the mercy of God is active everywhere all the time in every aspect of our lives. Some people may fail to recognize it only because they take it for granted. But it is real and we can feel it with our hearts and appreciate it with our minds.

The Loving Merciful God never forgets us or lets us down or ignores our sincere calls upon Him. By His Mercy and Love He has shown us the Right Way and sent to us messengers and teachers, books and revelations—all are meant for our help and guidance. The Last Messenger from God is Muhammad, and the most genuine existing book of God is the Qur'ān. From the traditions of Muhammad and the teachings of the Qur'ān, we learn about the Forgiving God. If a person commits a sin or does something wrong, then he is violating the Law of God, committing a grave offense against God and abusing his own dignity and existence. But if he is sincere and wishes to repent, regrets his wrong deeds and wants to turn to God, faithfully seeks pardon from God and honestly approaches Him, then God will certainly accept him and forgive him. Even those who reject God or His Oneness are assured of forgiveness, should they realize their erroneous attitude and resolve to come back to God. In this connection the Qur'ān says:

God forgives not that partners should be set up with Him; but He forgives anything else, to whom He pleases; to set up partners with God is to devise a sin most heinous indeed (Qur'ān, 4:48, 116).

Say: 'O My servants who have transgressed against their souls! Despair not of the Mercy of God: for God forgives all sins: For He is Most Forgiving, Most Merciful. Turn to your Lord (in repentance) and submit to Him, before the penalty comes on you; after that you shall not be helped. And follow the Best of the courses revealed to you from your Lord, before the penalty comes on you—of a sudden while you perceive not!' (Qur'ān, 39:53-54).

In return for all these great favors and kindness God does not need anything from us, because He is the Needless and the Independent. He does not ask us to pay Him back, for we cannot reward Him or value His immeasurable favors and mercy. What He commands us to do, however, is only to be good, to be thankful and appreciative, to follow His recommendations and enforce His Law, to be the proper manifestation of His goodness and excellent attributes, to be His honest agents and true representatives on earth. He does not want to enslave us, because He is the One Who grants us dignity and honor. He does not wish to subjugate us, because He is the One Who emancipates us from fear and superstitions. He does not desire to humiliate us because He is the One Who creates us and exalts our ranks above all other beings. So whatever rules and prescriptions He passes unto us are designed for our own benefit and good. They are meant to help us to enjoy our lives with one another in peace and kindness, in brotherhood and cooperation. They are destined to make us attain His most pleasant company and adopt the surest approach to eternal happiness.

There are various ways to know God, and there are many things to tell about Him. The great wonders and impressive marvels of the world are like open books in which we can read about God. Besides, God Himself comes to our aid through the many messengers and revelations He has sent down to man. These messengers and revelations tell us everything we need to know about God. So by reflecting on nature, by hearing the words of the messengers, and by reading the divine revelations we can gain most convincing knowledge about God and find the Straight Path to Him.

To complete this portion of discussion, some representative verses of the Qur'ān may be rendered as follows: Allah bears witness that there is no god but He—and so do the angels and those possessed of knowledge—Maintainer of Justice; there is no god but He, the Mighty, the Wise (Qur'ān 3:19). Allah is the Creator of all things, and He is the Guardian over all things. To Him belong the keys of the heavens and the earth (39:63-64). Allah originates Creation; then He repeats it; then to Him shall you be brought back (30:12). To Him belongs whatever is in the heavens and the earth. All are obedient to Him. It is He Who originates the Creation, then repeats it, for it is most easy for Him. His is the most exalted state in the heavens and the earth. He is the Mighty, the Wise (30:27-28).

The Meaning of Islam

The word Islam is derived from the Arabic root "SLM" which means, among other things, peace, purity, submission and obedience. In the religious sense the word Islam means submission to the Will of God and obedience to His Law. The connection between the original and the religious meanings of the word is strong and obvious. Only through submission to the Will of God and by obedience to His Law can one achieve true peace and enjoy lasting purity.

Some outsiders call our religion "Mohammedanism" and address the believers in Islam as "Mohammedans". The Muslims both reject and protest the use of these words. If our faith is classified as Mohammedanism and if we are called Mohammedans, there will be seriously wrong implications. This misnomer implies that the religion takes its name after a mortal being, namely, Muhammad and that Islam is no more than another "ism" just like Judaism, Hinduism, Marxism, etc.

7

Another wrong implication of this misnomer is that outsiders might think of the Muslims, whom they call Mohammedans, as worshippers of Muhammad or as believers in him in the same way as Christians, for example, believe in Jesus. A further wrong implication is that the word Mohammedanism may mislead the outsider and make him think that the religion was founded by Muhammad and therefore takes its name after the founder. All these implications are seriously wrong or at best misleading. Islam is not just another "ism". Nor do Muslims worship Muhammad or look upon him the same way as Christians, Jews, Hindus, Marxists, etc., look upon their respective leaders. The Muslims worship God alone. Muhammad was only a mortal being commissioned by God to teach the word of God and lead an exemplary life. He stands in history as the best model for man in piety and perfection. He is a living proof of what man can be and of what he can accomplish in the realm of excellence and virtue. Moreover, the Muslims do not believe that Islam was founded by Muhammad, although it was restored by him in the last stage of religious evolution. The original founder of Islam is no other than God Himself, and the date of the founding of Islam goes back to the age of Adam. Islam has existed in one form or another all along from the beginning and will continue to exist till the end of time.

The true name of the religion, then, is Islam and those who follow it are Muslims. Contrary to popular misconceptions, Islam or submission to the Will of God, together with obedience to His Law, does not mean in any way loss of individual freedom or surrender to fatalism. Anyone who thinks or believes so has certainly failed to understand the true meaning of Islam and the concept of God in Islam. The concept of God in Islam describes Him as the Most Merciful and Gracious, and the Most Loving and most concerned with the well-being of man, and as Full of Wisdom and care for His Creatures. His Will, accordingly, is a Will of Benevolence and Goodness, and whatever Law He prescribes must be in the best interest of mankind.

When the civilized people abide by the laws of their countries, they are considered sound citizens and honest members of their respective societies. No responsible person would say that such people lose their freedom by their obedience to the Law. No rational being would think or believe for a moment that such law-abiding people are fatalists and helpless. Similarly, the person who submits to the Will of God, which is a good Will, and obeys the Law of God, which is the best Law, is a sound and honest person. He is gaining protection of his own rights, showing genuine respect for the rights of others, and enjoying a high degree of responsible, creative freedom. Submission to the good Will of God, therefore, does not take away or curtail individual freedom. On the contrary, it gives freedom of a high degree in abundant measures. It frees the mind from superstitions and fills it with truth. It frees the soul from sin and wrong and quickens it with goodness and purity. It frees the self from vanity and greed, from envy and tension, from fear and insecurity. It frees man from subjugation to false deities and low desires, and unfolds before him the beautiful horizons of goodness and excellence.

Submission to the good Will of God, together with obedience to His beneficial Law, is the best safeguard of peace and harmony. It enables man to make peace between himself and his fellow men on the one hand, and between the human community and God on the other. It creates harmony among the elements of Nature. According to Islam, everything in the world, or every phenomenon other than man is administered by God-made Laws. This makes the entire physical world necessarily obedient to God and submissive to His Laws, which, in turn, means that it is in a state of Islam, or it is Muslim. The physical world has no choice of its own. It has no voluntary course to follow on its own initiative but obeys the Law of the Creator, the Law of Islam or submission. Man alone is singled out as being endowed with intelligence and the power of making choices. And because man possesses the qualities of intelligence and choice he is invited to submit to the good Will of God and obey His Law. When he does choose the course of submission to the Law of God, he will be making harmony between himself and all the other elements of Nature, which are by necessity obedient to God. He will be consistent with the truth and in harmony with all the other elements of the universe. But if he chooses disobedience he will deviate from the Right Path and will be inconsistent. Besides, he will incur the displeasure and punishment of the Law-Giver.

Because Islam means submission to the Good Will of God and obedience to His Beneficial Law, and because this is the essence of the message of all God-chosen messengers, a Muslim accepts all the prophets previous to Muhammad without discrimination. He believes that all those prophets of God and their faithful followers were Muslims, and that their religion was Islam, the only true universal religion of God (Qur'ān, 2:128-140; 3:78-85; 17:42-44; 31:22; 42:13).

To sum up this discussion, it may be helpful to reproduce my statement which appeared in the *Observer Dispatch* (O.D.) of Utica on December 4, 1972. The statement shows how much distoriton and confusion there is in this regard. The partial overlapping and repetition may be forgiven because of the extreme sensitivity of the issue and the need to reiterate the Islamic point of view.

A particular news item (O.D., Nov. 25) is alarming. It invites sympathy for the misinformed public and pity for many a school teacher or man of the pulpit. It calls upon every man of good will and conscience to stand up to his moral obligations.

Marcus Eliason reported from Israeli-occupied Jordan that "The Moslems," among other things, "worship Abraham as Ibrahim..."

It is incredible in this day and age, in this small world of ours, to read in fresh print that the Muslims worship Ibrahim. It is more incredible yet that this news comes from sources presumably knowledgeable and is passed on to a public entitled to know.

For centuries, many Westerners held and propagated the idea that the Muslims worshipped Muhammed, whose religion was called Mohammedanism and whose followers were known in the West as Mohammedans. Then it somehow became apparent to those Westerners that the Muslims worshipped Allah, a "deity of sorts." And now this new discovery that they worship Abraham as Ibrahim.

The fact is that the Muslims never worshipped Muhammad or any other human being. They have always believed that Muhammad was a mortal like the numerous prophets before him, and it is the highest tribute to humanity that a man could achieve the most exalted status of prophethood.

The Muslims believe that Muhammad was the last, not the only prophet, who reinforced and immortalized the eternal message of God to mankind. This message was revealed by God to many prophets of different nations at different times, including Abraham, Ishmael, Isaac, David, Moses, Jesus, and Muhammad (peace be upon them). What is more important is that the Muslims believe in them without discrimination against any.

Because of their universal outlook and cosmopolitan orientation, the Muslims sorrowfully consider it an unfortunate misnomer to call them Mohammedans and their faith Mohammedanism. The implications are distasteful and for good reasons. The Muslims do not think of themselves as a racial or ethnic group with any exclusive monopolies. Their religion is not named after a man or place; it is transcendent and atemporal.

The proper name of the religion is Islam and its followers are properly called Muslims. In the religious context, the word Islam means submission to the will of God and obedience to God's Law. The will of God is defined by the Koran as good and compassionate, and His law as the most beneficent and equitable. Any human being who so submits and obeys is, therefore, a Muslim in a moral state of Islam. It is in this sense that the Koran calls Abraham and all authentic prophets Muslims and designates their religions by one and the same title, namely Islam. Hence, the Muslim is not only a follower of Muhammad exclusively; he also follows Abraham,

10

Moses, Jesus, and the rest of God's messengers.

Finally, the word Allah in Islam simply but most emphatically means the One and only Eternal God, Creator of the universe, Lord of all lords, and King of all kings. The only unforgivable sin in Islam is the belief in any deity besides or other than God. The most common daily prayer among Muslims is: "In the name of God, the most compassionate, the most merciful."

The Fundamental Articles Of Faith In Islam

The true, faithful Muslim believes in the following principal articles of faith:

1. He believes in One God, Supreme and Eternal, Infinite and Mighty, Merciful and Compassionate, Creator and Provider. This belief, in order to be effective, requires complete trust and hope in God, submission to His Will and reliance on His aid. It secures man's dignity and saves him from fear and despair, from guilt and confusion. The reader is invited to see the meaning of Islam as explained above.

2. He believes in all the messengers of God without any discrimination among them. Every known nation had a warner or messenger from God. These messengers were great teachers of the good and true champions of the right. They were chosen by God to teach mankind and deliver His Divine message. They were sent at different times of history and every known nation had one messenger or more. During certain periods two or more messengers were sent by God at the same time to the same nation. The Holy Qur'ān mentions the names of twenty-five of them, and the Muslim believes in them all and accepts them as authorized messengers of God. They were, with the exception of Muhammad, known as "national" or local messengers. But their message, their religion, was basically the same and was called ISLAM, because it came from One and the Same Source, namely, God, to serve one and the same purpose, and that is to guide humanity to the Straight Path of God. All the messengers with no exception whatsoever were mortals, human beings, endowed with Divine revelations and appointed by God

to perform certain tasks. Among them Muhammad stands as the Last Messenger and the crowning glory of the foundation of prophethood. This is not an arbitrary attitude, nor is it just a convenient belief. Like all the other Islamic beliefs, it is an authentic and logical truth. Also, it may be useful to mention here the names of some of the great messengers like Noah and Abraham, Ishmael and Moses, Jesus and Muhammad, may the peace and blessings of God be upon them all. The Qur'ān commands the Muslims thus:

We believe in God, and the revelation given to us, and to Abraham, Ishmael, Isaac, Jacob and the Tribes; and that which was given to Moses and Jesus, and that which was given to all prophets from their Lord. We make no discrimination between one and another of them, and we bow to God (2:136, cf. 3:84; 4:163-165; 6:84-87).

3. The true Muslim believes, as a result of article two, in all the scriptures and revelations of God. They were the guiding light which the messengers received to show their respective peoples the Right Path of God. In the Qur'ān a special reference is made to the books of Abraham, Moses, David and Jesus. But long before the revelation of the Qur'ān to Muhammad some of those books and revelations had been lost or currupted, others forgotten, neglected, or concealed. The only authentic and complete book of God in existence today is the Qur'ān. In principle, the Muslim believes in the previous books and revelations. But where are their complete and original versions? They could be still at the bottom of the Dead Sea, and there may be more Scrolls to be discovered. Or perhaps more information about them will become available when the Christian and Jewish archaeologists reveal to the public the complete original findings of their continued excavations in the Holy Land. For the Muslim, there is no problem of that kind. The Qur'ān is in his hand complete and authentic. Nothing of it is missing and no more of it is expected. Its authenticity is beyond doubt, and no serious scholar or thinker has ventured to question its genuineness. The Qur'ān was made so by God Who revealed it and made it incumbent upon Himself to protect it against interpolation and corruption of all kinds. Thus it is given to the Muslims as the standard or criterion by which all the other books are judged. So whatever agrees with the Qur'ān is accepted as Divine truth, and whatever differs from the Qur'ān is either rejected or suspended. God says: 'Verily We have, without doubt, sent down the Qur'ān; and We will assuredly guard it (15:9; cf. 2:75-79; 5:13-14, 41, 45, 47; 6:91; 41:43).

4. The true Muslim believes in the angels of God. They are purely spiritual and splendid beings whose nature requires no food or drink or sleep. They have no physical desires of any kind nor material needs. They spend their days and nights in the service of God. There are many of them, and each one is charged with a certain duty. If we cannot see the angels with our naked eyes, it does not necessarily deny their actual existence. There are many things in the world that are invisible to the eye or inaccessible to the senses, and yet we do believe in their existence. There are places we have never seen and things like gas and ether that we could not see with our naked eyes, smell or touch or taste or hear; yet we do acknowledge their existence. Belief in the angels originates from the Islamic principle that knowledge and truth are not entirely confined to the sensory knowledge or sensory perception alone (16:49-50; 21:19-20. See also the references in article two above).

5. The true Muslim believes in the Last Day of Judgement. This world will come to an end some day, and the dead will rise to stand for their final and fair trial. Everything we do in this world, every intention we have, every move we make, every thought we entertain, and every word we say, all are counted and kept in accurate records. On the Day of Judgement they will be brought up. People with good records will be generously rewarded and warmly welcomed to the Heaven of God, and those with bad records will be punished and cast into Hell. The real nature of Heaven and Hell and the exact description of them are known to God only. There are descriptions of Heaven and Hell in the Qur'ān and the Traditions of Muhammad but they should not be taken literally. In Heaven, said Muhammad, there are things which no eye has ever seen, no ear has ever heard, and no mind has ever conceived. However, the Muslim believes that there definitely will be compensation and reward for the good deeds, and punishment for the evil ones. That is the Day of Justice and final settlement of all accounts.

If some people think that they are shrewd enough and can get away with their wrong doings, just as they sometimes escape the penalty of the mundane laws, they are wrong; they will not be able to do so on the Day of Judgement. They will be caught right on the spot defenceless, without any lawyer or counsel to stand in their behalf. All their deeds are visible to God and counted by His agents. Also, if some pious people do good deeds to please God and seem to get no appreciation or acknowledgement in this temporary world, they will eventually receive full compensation and be widely acknowledged on That Day. Absolute Justice will be done to all.

Belief in the Day of Judgement is the final relieving answer to many complicated problems of our world. There are people who commit sins, neglect God and indulge in immoral activities, yet they seem to be "superficially" successful in business and prosperous in life. And there are virtuous and God-minded people, yet they seem to be getting less rewards for their sincere efforts and more suffering in the present world. This is puzzling and incompatible with the Justice of God. If the guilty people can escape the mundane law unharmed and, in addition, be more prosperous, what is, then, left for the virtuous people? What will promote the cause of morality and goodness? There must be some way to reward goodness and arrest evil. If this is not done here on this earth—and we know that it is not done regularly or immediately—it has to be done some day, and that is the Day of Judgement. This is not to condone injustice or tolerate mischief in this world. It is not to sedate the deprived or comfort their exploiters. Rather, it is to warn the deviants from the Right Path and remind them that the Justice of God shall run its full course sooner or later (see, for example, the previous references).

6. The true Muslim believes in the timeless knowledge of God and in His power to plan and execute His plans. God is not indifferent to this world nor is He neutral to it. His knowledge and power are in action at all times to keep order in His vast domain and maintain full command over His creation. He is Wise and Loving, and whatever He does must have a good motive and a meaningful purpose. If this is established in our minds, we should accept with good Faith all that He does, although we may fail to understand it fully, or even think it is bad. We should have strong Faith in Him and accept whatever He does because our knowledge is limited and our thinking is based on individual or personal considerations, whereas His knowledge is limitless and He plans on a universal basis.

This does not in any way make man fatalist or helpless. It simply draws the demarcation line between what is God's concern and what is man's responsibility. Because we are by nature finite and limited, we have a finite and limited degree of power and freedom. We cannot do everything, and He graciously holds us responsible only for the things we do. The things which we cannot do, or things which He Himself does, are not in the realm of our responsibility. He is Just and has given us limited power to match our finite nature and limited responsibility. On the other hand, the timeless knowledge and power of God to execute His plans do not prevent us from making our own plans in our own limited sphere of power. On the contrary, He exhorts us to think, to plan and to make sound choices, but if things do not happen the way we wanted or planned them, we should not lose Faith or surrender ourselves to mental strains and shattering worries. We should try again and again, and if the results are not satisfactory, then we know that we have tried our best and cannot be held responsible for the results, because what is beyond our capacity and responsibility is the affair of God alone. The Muslims call this article of Faith the belief in 'Qadaa' and 'Qadar', which simply means, in other words, that the Timeless Knowledge of God anticipates events, and that events take place according to the exact Knowledge of God (Qur'ān, for example, 18:29; 41:46; 53:33-62; 54:49; 65:3; 76:30-31).

7. The true Muslim believes that God's creation is meaningful and that life has a sublime purpose beyond the physical needs and material activities of man. The purpose of life is to worship God. This does not simply mean that we have to spend our entire lives in constant seclusion and absolute meditation. To worship God is to know Him; to love Him; to obey His commandments; to enforce His law in every aspect of life; to serve His cause by doing the right and shunning the evil; and to be just to Him, to ourselves, and to our fellow human beings. To worship God is to "live" life not to run away from it. In brief, to worship God is to imbue ourselves with His Supreme Attributes. This is by no means a simple statement, nor is it an oversimplification of the matter. It is most comprehensive and conclusive. So if life has a purpose and if man is created to serve that purpose, then he cannot escape the responsibility. He cannot deny his existence or ingore the vital role he has to play. When God charges him with any responsibility, He provides him with all the required assistance. He endows him with intelligence and power to choose his course of conduct. Man, thus, is strongly commended by God to exert his utmost to fully serve the purpose of his existence. Should he fail to do that, or misuse his life or neglect his duties, he shall be responsible to God for his wrong deeds (see 21:17-18; 51:56-58; 75:37).

8. The true Muslim believes that man enjoys an especially high-ranking status in the hierarchy of all the known creatures. He occupies this distinguished position because he alone is gifted with rational faculties and spiritual aspirations as well as powers

of action. But the more his rank excels, the more his responsibility grows. He occupies the position of God's viceroy on earth. The person who is appointed by God to be His active agent, must necessarily have some power and authority, and be, at least potentially, endowed with honor and integrity. And this is the status of man in Islam; not a condemned race from birth to death, but a dignified being potentially capable of good and noble achievements. The fact that God chose His messengers from the human race shows that man is trustworthy and capable, and that he can acquire immense treasures of goodness (2:30-34; 6:165; 7:11; 17:70-72, 90-95).

9.   The true Muslim believes that every person is born "Muslim". This means that the very course of birth takes place in accordance with the Will of God, in realization of His plans and in submission to His Commands. It also means that every person is endowed with spiritual potentialities and intellectual inclinations that can make him a good Muslim, if he has the right access to Islam and is left to develop his innate nature. Many people can readily accept Islam if it is properly presented to them, because it is the Divine formula for those who want to satisfy their moral and spiritual needs as well as their natural aspirations, those who want to lead a constructive and sound life, whether personal or social, national or international. This is so because Islam is the universal religion of God, the Maker of human nature, Who knows what is best for human nature (30:30; 64:1-3; 82:6-8).

10.   The true Muslim believes that every person is born free from sin and all claims to inherited virtue. He is like a blank book. When the person reaches the age of maturity he becomes accountable for his deeds and intentions, if his development is normal and if he is sane. Man is not only free from sin until he commits sin, but he is also free to do things according to his plans on his own responsibility. This dual freedom: freedom from sin and freedom to do effective things, clears the Muslim's conscience from the heavy pressure of Inherited Sin. It relieves his soul and mind from the unnecessary strains of the Doctrine of Original Sin.

This Islamic concept of freedom is based upon the principle of God's justice and the individual's direct responsibility to God. Each person must bear his own burden and be responsible for his own actions, because no one can expiate for another's sin. Thus, a Muslim believes that if Adam had committed the First Sin, it was his own responsibility to expiate for that sin. To assume that God was unable to forgive Adam and had to make somebody else expiate for his sin, or to assume that Adam did not pray for pardon or prayed for it but it was not granted, would be extremely unlikely and contrary to God's mercy and justice as well as to His attribute of forgiveness and power to forgive. To assume the said hypothesis, would be an audacious defiance of common sense and flagrant violation of the very concept of God (see the references in article nine above; Qur'an, 41:46; 45:15; 53:31-42; 74:38; the Concept of Sin below):

On this rational basis as well as on the authority of the Qur'ān, the Muslim believes that Adam realized what he had committed and prayed to God for pardon, as any other sensible sinner would. It is also on the same basis, the Muslim believes, that God, the Forgiving and Merciful, granted Adam pardon (2:35-37; 20:117-122). Hence, the Muslim cannot possibly accept the doctrine that Adam with the whole human race had been condemned and unforgiven until Jesus came to expiate for their sins. Consequently, the Muslim cannot entertain the dramatic story of Jesus' death on the cross just to do away with all human sins once and for all.

Here the reader must be cautioned against any wrong conclusions. The Muslim does not believe in the crucifixion of Jesus by his enemies because the basis of this doctrine of crucifixion is contrary to Divine mercy and justice as much as it is to human logic and dignity. Such a disbelief in the doctrine does not in any way lessen the Muslim's reverence for Jesus, or degrade the high status of Jesus in Islam, or even shake the Muslim's belief in Jesus as a distinguished prophet of God. On the contrary, by rejecting this doctrine the Muslim accepts Jesus but only with more esteem and higher respect, and looks upon his original message as an essential part of Islam. So let it be stated, again, that to be a Muslim a person must accept and respect all the prophets of God without any discrimination. The general status of Jesus in Islam will be further discussed in a later chapter.

11. The true Muslim believes that man must work out his salvation through the guidance of God. This means that in order to attain salvation a person must combine Faith and action, belief and practice. Faith without action is as insufficient as action without Faith. In other words, no one can attain salvation until his Faith in God becomes dynamic in his life and his beliefs are trans-

lated into reality. This is in complete harmony with the other Islamic articles of Faith. It shows that God does not accept lip service, and that no true believer can be indifferent as far as the practical requirements of Faith are concerned. It also shows that no one can act on behalf of another or intercede between him and God (see, for example, the Qur'ān, 10:9-10; 18:30; 103:1-3).

12. The true Muslim believes that God does not hold any person responsible until He has shown him the Right Way. This is why God has sent many messengers and revelations, and has made it clear that there would be no punishment before giving guidance and sounding the alarm. So, a person who has never come across any Divine revelations or messenger, or a person who is insane is not held responsible to God for failing to obey the Divine instructions. Such a person will be responsible only for not doing what his sound common sense tells him to do. But the person who knowingly and intentionally violates the Law of God or deviates from His Right Path will be punished for his wrong deeds (4:165; 5:16 & 21; 17:15).

This point is very important for every Muslim. There are many people in the world who have not heard of Islam and have no way of knowing about it. Such people may be honest and may become good Muslims, if they find their way to Islam. If they do not know and have no way of knowing, they will not be responsible for failing to be Muslims. Instead, the Muslims who can present Islam to such people will be the ones responsible for failing to invite them to Islam and show them what Islam is. This calls upon every Muslim throughout the globe not only to preach Islam in words but also—and more importantly—to live it in full (see, for example, the Qur'ān, 3:104; 16:125).

13. The true Muslim believes that in human nature, which God created, there is more good than evil, and the probability of successful reform is greater than the probability of hopeless failure. This belief is derived from the fact that God has tasked man with certain assignments and sent messengers with revelations for his guidance. If man were by nature a hopeless case, impossible to reform, how could God with His absolute wisdom assign him responsibilities and invite him to do or shun certain things? How could God do that, if it were all in vain? The fact that God cares for man and takes a stand in his interest proves that man is neither helpless nor hopeless, but is more appreciative of and inclined to good than otherwise. Surely with sound

Faith in God and due confidence in man miracles can be worked out, even in our own times. To understand this properly, one has to carefully study the relevant passages in the Qur'ān and reflect on their meanings.

14. The true Muslim believes that Faith is not complete when it is followed blindly or accepted unquestioningly unless the believer is reasonably satisfied. If Faith is to inspire action, and if Faith and action are to lead to salvation, then Faith must be founded on unshakable convictions without any deception or compulsion. In other words, the person who calls himself a Muslim because of his family traditions, or accepts Islam under coercion or blind imitation is not a complete Muslim in the sight of God. A Muslim must build his Faith on well-grounded convictions beyond any reasonable doubt and above uncertainty. If he is not certain about his Faith, he is invited by God to search in the open book of Nature, to use his reasoning powers, and to reflect on the teachings of the Qur'ān. He must search for the indisputable truth until he finds it, and he will certainly find it, if he is capable and serious enough (see, for example, the Qur'ān, 2:170; 43:22-24).

This is why Islam demands sound convictions and opposes blind imitation. Every person who is duly qualified as a genuine and earnest thinker is enjoined by Islam to employ his faculties to the fullest extent. But if a person is unqualified or uncertain of himself, he should pursue his thinking only as far as his limits can take him. It will be quite in order for such a person to rely only on the authentic sources of religion, which are sufficient in themselves, without applying to them any critical questioning of which he is incapable. The point is that no one can call himself a true Muslim unless his Faith is based on strong convictions and his mind is clear from doubts. Because Islam is complete only when it is based on strong convictions and freedom of choice, it cannot be forced upon anybody, for God will not accept this forced faith. Nor will He consider it a true Islam if it does not develop from within or originate from free and sound convictions. And because Islam insures freedom of belief many non-Muslim groups lived and still live in the Muslim countries enjoying full freedom of belief and conscience. The Muslims take this attitude because Islam forbids compulsion in religion. It is the light which must radiate from within, because freedom of choice is the cornerstone of responsibility. This does not exempt the parents from responsibility for their children. Nor does it condone their being indifferent to the spiritual welfare of their dependents. In fact, they must do everything possible to help them to build a strong inspiring faith.

To establish Faith on sound grounds, there are various parallel avenues. There is the Spiritual approach which is based mainly on the Qur'ān and the Traditions of Muhammad. There is also the rational approach which eventually leads to Faith in the Supreme Being. This is not to say that the Spiritual approach lacks sound rationality. Nor is the rational approach deprived of inspiring spirituality. Both approaches, in fact, complement one another and may well become in a state of lively interaction. Now if a person is sufficiently equipped with sound rational qualities, he may resort to the rational approach or to the Spiritual approach or to both, and may be confident that his conclusion will be right. But if a person is incapable of profound inquiry or is uncertain of his reasoning powers, he may confine himself to the Spiritual approach and be contented with the knowledge he can derive from the authentic sources of religion. The point is that whether one uses the Spiritual approach or the rational technique or both, one will in the end come to Faith in God. All these avenues are equally important and accepted by Islam, and when properly channeled, lead to the same end, namely Faith in the Supreme Being (Qur'ān, 5:16-17; 12:109; 18:30; 56:80).

15. The true Muslim believes that the Qur'ān is the word of God revealed to Muhammad through the agency of the Angel Gabriel. The Qur'ān was revealed from God piece by piece on various occasions to answer certain questions, solve certain problems, settle certain disputes, and to be man's best guide to the truth of God and eternal happiness. Every letter in the Qur'ān is the word of God, and every sound in it is the true echo of God's voice. The Qur'ān is the First and most authentic Source of Islam. It was revealed in Arabic. It is still and will remain in its original and complete Arabic version, because God has made it His concern to preserve the Qur'ān, to make it always the best guide for man, and to safeguard it against corruption (cf. 4:82; 15:9; 17:9; 41:41-44; 42:7, 52-53).

In testimony to God's conservation, the Qur'ān is the only Scripture in human history that has been preserved in its complete and original version without the slightest change in style or even punctuations. The history of recording the Qur'ān, compiling its chapters and conserving its text is beyond any doubt not only in the minds of the Muslims but also in the minds of honest and serious scholars. This is a historical fact which no scholar from any faith—who respects his knowledge and integrity—has ever questioned. As a matter of fact, it is Muhammad's standing miracle that if all mankind were to work together they could not produce the like of one Qur'anic chapter (2:22-24; 11:13-14; 17:88-89).

16. The true Muslim believes in a clear distinction between the Qur'ān and the Traditions of Muhammad. The Qur'ān is the word of God whereas the Traditions of Muhammad are the practical interpretations of the Qur'ān. The role of Muhammad was to convey the Qur'ān as he received it, to interpret it, and to practice it fully. His interpretations and practices produced what is known as the Traditions of Muhammad. They are considered the Second Source of Islam and must be in complete harmony with the First Source, namely the Qur'ān, which is the Standard and the Criterion. If there be any contradiction or inconsistency between any of the Traditions and the Qur'ān, the Muslim adheres to the Qur'ān alone and regards everything else as open to question because no genuine Tradition of Muhammad can ever disagree with the Qur'ān or be opposed to it.

Remarks

In this discussion of the cardinal articles of Faith in Islam, we have deliberately differed from the Traditional view on the subject. We did not confine them to five or six articles. Instead, we tried to include as many Principles as was possible. But it should be pointed out here that all the articles of Faith mentioned above are based upon and derived from the teachings of the Qur'ān and the Traditions of Muhammad. More verses from the Qur'ān and many parts of the Traditions could have been quoted to show the foundation of these articles of Faith. This was not done because of the limitations of space. However, the Qur'ān and the Traditions of Muhammad are available references for any detailed study.

We have also kept to a minimum the use of Western terminology and technical language like predestination, fatalism, free will, and so on. This was done deliberately because we wanted to avoid confusion and technicalities. Most of the technical terms used in religion among non-Arabic speaking people lead to misunderstanding, when applied to Islam, and give wrong impressions. It would be impossible to serve the purpose of this work if foreign religious terms were adopted and applied to Islam. If we were to use the alien religious terminology here, we would have had to add many qualifications and comments to clarify the picture of Islam. This also would have required much more space which we could not possibly afford under the circumstances. So, we tried to explain things in ordinary simple language, and this same course will be followed in the remainder of the book.

CHAPTER II

THE BASIC CONCEPTS
OF ISLAM

The Concept of Faith (Iman)

Some people may think that man becomes a Muslim when he confesses belief in the Oneness of the True God and in Muhammad as His Last Messenger. But this is far from the full meaning of Faith. The full meaning of Faith in Islam is not, by any means, something nominal or mere formality. Faith in Islam is a state of happiness acquired by virtue of positive action and constructive conceptions as well as dynamic and effective measures.

The Holy Qur'an and the Traditions of Muhammad define these required measures and establish the standards which build up a meaningful Faith. Thus, the true believers are:

1. Those who believe in God, His angels, His Books as completed by the Qur'an, His messengers with Muhammad being the Last of them all, the Day of Final Judgement, the absolute knowledge and wisdom of God.

2. Those who trust God always and enjoy unshakable confidence in Him.

3. Those who spend in the way of God of what He has given them in the form of wealth, life, health, knowledge, experience, and so on.

4. Those who observe their daily prayers regularly as well as the weekly and annual congregations.

5. Those who pay their religious taxes (alms or Zakah) to the rightful beneficiaries (individuals or institutions), the *minimum* of which is two and a half percent of the annual "net" income, or of the total value of stocks if in business—after discounting all expenses and credits.

6. Those who enjoin the right and good, and combat the wrong and evil by all lawful means at their disposal.

7. Those who obey God and His Messenger Muhammad; and feel increasing strength of faith when the Qur'an is recited, and humility of heart when God's name is mentioned.

8. Those who love God and His Messenger most, and love their fellow men sincerely for the sake of God alone.

9. Those who love their near and distant neighbors and show genuine kindness to their guests, especially the strangers.

10. Those who say the truth and engage in good talk, or else abstain.

It is clear that the very meaning of Faith makes Islam penetrate deeply and constructively into every aspect of life. According to Islam, true Faith has a decisive effect on the spiritual and material lot of man, and also on his personal and social behaviour as well as his political conduct and financial life. To show how the Qur'an describes the true believers, here are some examples. The Qur'an contains numerous references like these:

They only are the true believers whose hearts feel submissive (and humble) when God is mentioned; and when the revelations of God are recited unto them, they (the revelations) increase and strengthen their Faith; and who trust in their Lord, establish the prayer (as enjoined on them) and spend of what We have bestowed on them (in the cause of God). Those are they who are in truth believers. For them are (high) grades (of honor) with their Lord, and a bountiful provision (Qur'an, 8:2-4).

And the believers, men and women, are protecting (and allied) friends of one another; they enjoin the right and forbid the wrong, and they establish worship and they pay the poor-due, and they obey God and His Messenger. As for these, God will have mercy on them; verily God is Mighty, and Wise. God promises the believers, men and women, Gardens under which rivers flow, to dwell therein, and beautiful mansions in Gardens of everlasting bliss. But the greatest bliss is the Good Pleasure of God. That is the supreme felicity (Qur'an, 9:71-72).

The true believers are those only who believe in God and His Messenger (Muhammad) and afterward doubt not, but strive with their wealth and their lives for the cause of God. Such are the sincere (Qur'an, 49:15).

Besides these Qur'anic references, there are many relevant

Traditions of Muhammad. For example, he says:

None of you can be a true believer unless he loves for his fellow believer what he loves for himself.

Three qualities are the sign of sound faith, and he who acquires them can really feel the sweet taste of Faith. They are (1) to love God and His Messenger most of all, (2) to love his fellow man for the sake of God alone, and (3) to resent and resist returning to disbelief as much as he does being cast into fire.

He who believes in God and the Last Day of Judgement is forbidden to cause any harm to his neighbor, is to be kind to his guests—especially the strangers, and is to say the truth or else abstain.

There are many verses and traditions like the ones cited above. But it should be borne in mind, however, that the given quotations are not and cannot be the exact words of the Qur'an and Muhammad as they sound in the Arabic Text. The reason for that is simple. No interpreter, however learned and masterful he may be, can ever convey the spiritual power and charming appeal of the Qur'an through any language. The Qur'an is—and so God made it— inimitable, and it is beyond human imagination and power to produce anything like it. What is true of the Qur'an in this respect is also true of the Traditions of Muhammad to a certain extent, because, after the Qur'an, his words are the most conclusive and eloquent[1].

The Concept of Righteousness (Birr)

Islam always warns against superficial concepts and rituals, against lifeless formalities and non-effective beliefs. In one representative verse God explains the full meaning of righteousness as follows:

It is not righteousness that you turn your faces (in prayer) towards East or West; but it is righteousness to believe in God and the Last Day, and the Angels and the Book, and the Messengers; to spend of your wealth—in spite of your love for it—for your kin, for orphans, for the needy, for the wayfarer, for those who ask, and for the ransom of slaves; to be steadfast in prayer and practice regular charity; to fulfill the contracts which you have made; and to be firm and patient, in pain and adversity, and throughout

[1] See note 2 in chapter I above.

all periods of panic. Such are the people of truth, the God-minded (Qur'an, 2:177).

In this verse there is a beautiful and clear description of the righteous man. He should obey all the salutary regulations, and should make his sincere motive the love of God and the love of his fellow man for the sake of God. Here we have four elements: (i) our Faith should be true and sincere, (ii) we must be prepared to show it in deeds of charity and kindness to our fellow man, (iii) we must be good citizens by supporting charitable institutions and social organizations, and (iv) we must be steadfast and unshakable in all circumstances.

It is clear, therefore, that righteousness is not merely a matter of void utterances. It must be founded on strong Faith and constant practice. It must cover the person's thinking and action and extend to his inside and outside life, to his individual and common affairs. When the Islamic principle of righteousness is established, it provides the individual with peace in all circumstances, the society with security on all levels, the nation with solidarity, and the international community with hope and harmony. How peaceful and enjoyable life can be when people implement the Islamic Concept of Righteousness! What can be more reassuring than faith in the Beneficent Creator and investing in such good worthy causes? What can be more humane than relieving the deep anxieties of the subjugated, alleviating the sufferings of the exploited, and responding to the needs of the helpless? What is more methodical and honest than the fulfillment of commitments, the preservation of clear conscience, and the maintenance of integrity? And what is more spiritually joyful than doing all this regularly, as a matter of course, and for the love of God?

The Concept of Piety (Taqwa)

What has been said about faith and righteousness is generally true of piety. Again, it is not a matter of convenient claims and oral confessions. It is much more serious. As always, the Qur'an is our best source, and when it speaks of the pious it describes them as those who believe in the Unseen (which is taught by God), are steadfast in prayer, and spend of what We have provided for them; and who believe in the Revelation sent to you (Muhammad), and sent before your time, and (in their hearts) have the assurance of the Hereafter. They are on true guidance from their Lord, and it is these who will prosper (Qur'an, 2:3-5). The pious are those who spend (freely in the way of God) whether in prosperity or in adversity; who restrain anger and pardon (all men;—for God loves those who do good; and those who—having done something to be ashamed of, or wronged their own souls—earnestly bring God into mind, and ask for forgiveness for their sins,—and who can forgive sins except God?—and are never obstinate in persisting knowingly in (the wrong) they have done. For such the reward is forgiveness from their Lord, and Gardens with rivers flowing underneath,—an eternal dwelling. How excellent a recompense for those who work (and strive)! (Qur'an, 3:134-136).

In these verses we find that piety requires a proper use of the mind by grasping the truth of God and life, a proper use of wealth by spending in the way of God under all circumstances and a proper use of the spiritual as well as the physical abilities of man by observing the prayer. It also demands a high degree of self-control over one's anger and emotions, a moral capacity for forgiveness and patience, and a conscious urge to make the sinner return to God in regret and repentance. To be pious is to be a man of true and fine convictions, of determination and character, of will and courage and, above all, to be a man of God. Piety, righteousness and meaningful Faith are interrelated and all pour into one channel. They lead to Islam and build up the true Muslim.

The Concept of Prophethood

The Merciful and Loving God has sent many prophets at different times of history. Every known nation has had one prophet or more. All the prophets of God were men of good character and high honor. They were prepared and chosen by God to deliver His Message to mankind. Their honesty and truthfulness, their intelligence and integrity are beyond doubt. They were infallible in that they did not commit sins or violate the Law of God. But as mortals, they might have made unintentional mistakes in some human affairs and decisions. Their private judgment were not necessarily always right.

The sending of these prophets from God is a clear manifestation of a strong link between Heaven and Earth, between God and man. It means that man is reformable and in him there is much good. The purpose of prophethood is to confirm what man already knows or can know, and to teach him what he does not or cannot know by his own means. It is also to help man to find the Straight Path of God, and to do the right and shun the wrong. Prophethood is an eloquent expression of God's love for His creations and His will to guide them to the right way of belief and behavior. It is an emphasis of His justice to man, because He shows him true guidance first, and then holds him responsible for his deeds. He gives warnings through His prophets, and if man fails to see the dangers of his wrong deeds, his behavior becomes punishable. This is in complete accord with God's love and justice, and the worth and capability of man of being responsible to his Lord.

The Source of prophethood and the Sponsor of all the prophets are One and the Same: it is God. Their aim is to serve God, to acquaint man with God and His Divine teachings, to establish truth and goodness, to help man to realize the true purpose of his existence and help him to conduct his life in a purposeful way. It is on this basis that the Muslims make no discrimination among the prophets and accept their teachings as consistent and complementary. And this is the reason why the Muslims believe in all the Divine Books and accept all the prophets of God as already mentioned.

The Concept of Life [2]

Life is a brilliant demonstration of God's wisdom and knowledge, a vivid reflection of His art and power. He is the Giver and Creator of life. Nothing comes to existence by chance, and nobody creates himself or anybody else. Life is a dear and cherishable asset, and no sensible or normal person would like to lose it by choice. Even those who feel so desperate and take their lives by committing slow suicide, try in the last minute to regain their existence and wish to capture a second chance to live. Life is given to man by God, and He is the only Rightful One to take it back; no one else has the right to destroy a life. This is why Islam forbids all kinds of suicide and self-destruction, and recommends patience and good Faith when a dear soul passes away. When a murderer is executed in punishment, his life is taken away by the right of God and in accordance with His Law.

When God gives life to man, it is not in vain that He endows him with unique qualities and great abilities. Nor is it in vain that He charges him with certain obligations. God means to help man to fulfill the purpose of life and realize the goal of existence. He means to help him to learn the creative art of living and enjoy the good taste of life according to the Divine guidance. Life is a trust from God, and man is a trustee who should handle his trust with honesty and skill, with mindfulness of God and with consciousness of responsibility to Him.

---

[2]In connection with this concept, see below the Concept of the Universe.

Life may be likened to a journey starting from a certain point and ending at a certain destination. It is a transitory stage, an introduction to the Eternal Life in the Hereafter. In this journey man is a traveller and should be concerned with only what is of use to him in the Future Life. In other words, he should do all the good he can and make himself fully prepared to move any minute to Eternity. He should consider his life on this earth as a chance provided for him to make the best of it while he can, because when his time to leave comes he can never delay it for one second. If his term expires, it will be too late to do anything about it or extend it. The best use of life, therefore, is to live it according to the teachings of God and to make it a safe passage to the Future Life of Eternity. Because life is so important as a means to an ultimate end, Islam has laid down a complete system of regulations and principles to show man how to live it, what to take and what to leave, what to do and what to shun, and so on. All men come from God, and there is no doubt that they shall return to Him. In one of His comprehensive statements Prophet Muhammad wisely advised man to consider himself a stranger in this life or a traveller passing by the world.

The Concept of Religion

Throughout history religion has been abused and misunderstood. Some people use it as a means of exploitation and suppression, as a pretext for prejudice and persecution. Some other people use it as a source of power and domination over the elite and the masses alike. In the name of religion unjustifiable wars have been launched, freedom of thought and conscience has been oppressed, science has been persecuted, the right of the individual to maturity has been denied, and man's dignity and honor have been flagrantly debased. And in the name of religion an injustice has been inflicted upon humanity with the result that religion itself has suffered many losses.

These are historical facts which no one can deny. But is this the proper function of religion or the right approach to religion? Could this be the purpose of religion? The indisputable answer is an emphatic no. There are many religions in the world, and each one claims to be the one and only true religion. Each religion is supposed to have come from God for the right guidance of man. But these claims contradict each other and have caused dissensions among people and vehement reactions to religion—instead of welding mankind into one universal brotherhood under the One Universal Benevolent God. This situation makes any neutral observer confused and perhaps averse to all kinds of religion.

The Islamic concept of religion is unique in the broadest sense of the word. It is true that genuine religion must come from God for the right guidance of man. And it is equally true that human nature and major human needs are basically the same at all times. This conception leads to one conclusion, and that is: There is only one true religion coming from the One and the Same God, to deal with the outstanding human problems of all times. This religion is ISLAM. But it should be borne in mind that Islam was not taught by Prophet Muhammad alone. On the contrary, Islam had been taught by all the prophets before Muhammad, and the true followers of Abraham and Moses as well as those of Jesus and the rest were all called MUS-LIMS. So Islam has been, and will continue to be, the true universal religion of God, because God is One and Changeless, and because human nature and major human needs are fundamentally the same, irrespective of time and place, of race and age, and of any other considerations.

Bearing this in mind, the Islamic concept maintains that religion is not only a spiritual and intellectual necessity but also a social and universal need. It is not to bewilder man but to guide him. It is not to debase him but to elevate his moral nature. It is not to deprive him of anything useful, or to burden him, or to oppress his qualities but to open for him inexhaustible treasures of sound thinking and right action. It is not to confine him to narrow limits but to launch him into wide horizons of truth and goodness. In short, true religion is to acquaint man with God as well as with himself and the rest of the universe. This is by no means an oversimplification of the function of religion. Here is what it means.

When the purpose of true religion is carefully examined, it will be found that religion satisfies the spiritual and moderate material needs of man. It unties his psychological knots and complexes, sublimates his instincts and aspirations, and disciplines his desires and the whole course of life. It improves his knowledge of God—the Highest Truth in the universe, and of his own self. It teaches him about the secrets of life and the nature of man and how to treat them, about good and evil, about right and wrong. It purifies the soul from evil, clears the mind from doubts, strengthens the character and corrects the thinking and convictions of man. All this can be achieved only when man faithfully observes the spiritual duties and physical regulations introduced by religion.

On the other hand, true religion educates man and trains him in hope and patience, in truthfulness and honesty, in love for the right and good, in courage and endurance, all of which are required for the mastery of the great art of living. Moreover, true religion insures man against fears and spiritual losses, and assures him of

God's aid and unbreakable alliance. It provides man with peace and security and makes his life meaningful.

That is what true religion can do for humanity, and that is the concept of religion in Islam. Any religion which fails to bear these fruits is not Islam or, rather, is not religion at all, and any man who fails to draw these benefits from religion is not religious or God-minded. God is absolutely true when He says in the Holy Qur'an: Verily the religion with God is Islam. Nor did the People of the Book dessent therefrom except through envy of each other, after knowledge had come to them. But if any deny the Signs of God, God is swift in calling to account (Qur'an, 3:19). And if anyone desires a religion other than Islam, never will it be accepted of him; and in the Hereafter he will be in the ranks of those who have lost (all spiritual good) (Qur'an, 3:85).

The Concept of Sin

One of the major troublesome areas of human existence is the problem of sin or evil in the world. It is commonly believed that sin started with Adam and Eve during their life in the Garden of Eden. That event led to the Fall and has ever since branded the human race with guilt, stigma, and bewilderment.

Islam has taken a unique position on the whole issue, a position which is not shared by any other religion we know. The Qur'an states that Adam and Eve were directed by God to reside in the Garden of Eden and enjoy its produce as they pleased, assured of bountiful supplies and comfort. But they were warned not to approach a particular tree so that they would not run into harm and injustice. Then Satan intrigued them to temptation and caused them to lose their joyful state. They were expelled from the Garden and brought down to earth to live, die, and be taken out again at last for the Final Judgment. Having realized what they had done, they felt shame, guilt, and remorse. They prayed for God's mercy and were forgiven (Qur'an, 2:35-38; 7:19-25; 20:117-123).

This symbolic event is significantly revealing. It tells that the human being is imperfect and ever wanting even if he were to live in paradise. But committing a sin or making a mistake, as Adam and Eve did, does not necessarily deaden the human heart, prevent spiritual reform or stop moral growth. On the contrary, the human being has enough sensibility to recognize his sins and shortcomings. More importantly, he is capable of knowing where to turn and to whom he should turn for guidance. Much more important is the fact that God is ever prepared to respond to the sincere calls of those who seek His aid. He is so Gracious and Compassionate that His Forgiveness is Encompassing and His Mercy all-Inclusive (Qur'an, 7:156). One last revealing reading of the event is that discrimination on the basis of sex and hereditary guilt or sin are alien to the spirit of Islam.

The idea of Original Sin or hereditary criminality has no room in the teachings of Islam. Man, according to the Qur'an (30:30) and to the Prophet, is born in a natural state of purity or *fitrah*, that is, Islam or submission to the will and law of God. Whatever becomes of man after birth is the result of external influence and intruding factors. To put the matter in terms of modern thought, human nature is malleable; it is the socialization process, particularly the home environment, that is crucial. It plays a decisive role in the formation of human personality and the development of moral character. This does not deny to the individual the **freedom** of choice or exempt him from responsibility. Rather, it is a relief from that heavy burden of hereditary criminality or instinctual sin.

God, by definition, is Just, Wise, Merciful, Compassionate, and Perfect. He has created man by breathing into him of His own Spirit (Qur'an, 15:29; 32:9; 66:12). Since God is the absolute infinite good and His Spirit the absolute perfect one; since man, through creation, received of the Spirit of God, then man was bound to retain at least some portion of this good Spirit of the Creator. This may account for the good dispositions of man and his spiritual longings. But, on the other hand, God created man to worship Him, not to be His equal, rival, the perfect incarnation or absolute embodiment of His goodness. This means that no matter how much good and perfect man may be, by the grace of creation, he is still far short of the goodness and perfection of the Creator. Man is not without such qualities, to be sure. But they are limited and proportionate to man's finite nature, capacity, and responsibility. This may explain the imperfection and fallibility of man.

However, imperfection and fallibility are not the equivalent of sin or synonymous with criminality—at least not in Islam. If man is imperfect he is not left helpless or deserted by God to fall victim to his shortcomings. He is empowered by revelations, supported by reason, fortified by the freedom of choice, and guided by various social and psychological dispositions to seek and achieve relative perfection. The constant gravitation between the forces of good and evil is the struggle of life. It gives man something to look forward to, ideals to seek, work to do, and roles to play. It makes his life interesting and meaningful, not monotonous and stagnant. On the other hand, it pleases God to see His servants in a state of spiritual and moral victory.

According to the moral scale of Islam, it is not a sin that man is imperfect or fallible. This is part of his nature as a finite limited creature. But it is a sin if he has the ways and means of relative perfection and chooses not to seek it. A sin is any act, thought, or will that (1) is deliberate, (2) defies the unequivocal law of God, (3) violates the right of God or the right of man, (4) is harmful to the soul or body, (5) is committed repeatedly, and (6) is normally avoidable. These are the components of sin which is not innate or hereditary. It is true, however, that man has the potential capacity of sin latent in him; but this is not greater than his capacity of piety and goodness. If he *chooses* to actualize the potential of sin instead of the potential of goodness, he will be adding a new external element to his pure nature. For this added external element man alone is responsible.

In Islam, there are major and minor sins as there are sins against God and sins against both God and man. All sins against God, except one, are forgivable if the sinner sincerely seeks forgiveness. The Qur'an has stated that truly God does not forgive the sin of *shirk* (polytheism, pantheism, trinity, etc.). But He forgives sins other than this and pardons whom He wills. Yet if the polytheist or atheist comes back to God, his sin will be forgiven. Sins against men are forgivable only if the offended pardon the offender or if the proper compensations and/or punishments are applied.

In conclusion, sin is acquired not inborn, emergent not built-in, avoidable not inevitable. It is a deliberate conscious violation of the unequivocal law of God. If man does something that is truly caused by natural instincts or absolutely irresistible drives and uncontrollable urges, then such an act is not a sin in Islam. Otherwise, God's purpose will be pointless and man's responsibility will be in vain. God demands of man what lies within the human possibilities and reaches.

The Concept of Freedom

Freedom, both as a concept and as a value, has been denied many individuals, groups, and nations. It has been often misunderstood and abused. The fact is that in no human society can man be free in the absolute sense of the word. There must be some limitations of one sort or another, if the society is to function at all.

Apart from this general idea, Islam teaches freedom, cherishes it, and guarantees it for the Muslim as well as for the non-Muslim. The Islamic concept of freedom applies to all voluntary activities of man in all walks of life. As already stated, every man is born free on the *fitrah* or in a pure state of nature. This means that man is born free from subjugation, sin, inherited inferiority, and ancestral hinderance. His right of freedom is sacred as long as he does not deliberately violate the Law of God or desecrate the rights of others.

One of the main objectives of Islam is to emancipate the mind from superstitions and uncertainties, the soul from sin and corruption, the conscience from oppression and fear, and even the body from disorder and degeneration.

The course which Islam has enjoined on man to realize this goal includes profound intellectual endeavors, constant spiritual observances, binding moral principles, and even dietary regulations. When man follows this course, religiously, he cannot fail to reach his ultimate goal of freedom and emancipation.

The question of freedom with regard to belief, worship, and conscience is also of paramount importance in Islam. Every man is entitled to exercise his freedom of belief, conscience, and worship. In the words of the Qur'an, God says: Let there be no compulsion in religion. Truth stands out clear from Error. Whoever rejects Evil and believes in God has grasped the strongest bond that never breaks. And God knows and hears all things (Qur'an, 2:256).

Islam takes this attitude because religion depends upon faith, will, and committment. These would be meaningless if induced by force. Furthermore, Islam presents the Turth of God in the form of an opportunity and leaves the choice for man to decide his own course. The Qur'an says: The Truth is from your Lord. Let him who will, believe, and let him who will, disbelieve (Qur'an, 18:29).

The Islamic concept of freedom is an article of faith, a solemn command from the Supreme Creator. It is built on the following fundamental principles. First, man's conscience is subject to God only, to Whom every man is directly responsible. Secondly, every human being is personally responsible for his deeds and he alone is entitled to reap the fruits of his work. Thirdly, God has delegated to man the responsibility to decide for himself. Fourthly, man is sufficiently provided with spiritual guidance and endowed with rational qualities that enable him to make responsible, sound choices. Such is the foundation of the Islamic concept of freedom and such is the value of freedom in Islam. It is a natural right of man, a spiritual privilege, a moral prerogative, and, above all, a religious duty. Within the framework of this Islamic concept of freedom, there is no room for religious persecutions, class conflict, or racial prejudice. The individual's right of freedom is as sacred as his right of Life; freedom is the equivalent of Life itself.

The Concept of Equality

One basic element in the value system of Islam is the principle of equality or, better yet, equity. This value of equality is not to be mistaken for or confused with identicalness or stereotype. Islam teaches that, in the sight of God, all men are equal, but they are not necessarily identical. There are differences of abilities, potentials, ambitions, wealth, and so on. Yet none of these differences can by itself establish a status of superiority of one man or race to another. The stock of man, the color of his skin, the amount of wealth he has, and the degree of prestige he enjoys have no bearing on the character and personality of the individual as far as God is concerned. The only distinction which God recognizes is the distinction in piety, and the only criterion which God applies is the criterion of goodness and spiritual excellence. In the Qur'ān, God says:

O mankind, verily We have created you from a single (pair) of a male and a female, and have made you into nations and tribes, that you may know each other. Verily the most honored of you in the sight of God is the most righteous (49:13).

The differences of race, color, or social status are only accidental. They do not affect the true stature of man in the sight of God. Again, the value of equality is not simply a matter of constitutional rights or gentlemen's agreement or condescending charity. It is an article of faith which the Muslim takes seriously and to which he must adhere sincerely. The foundations of this Islamic value of equality are deeply rooted in the structure of Islam. It stems from basic principles such as the following: (1) All men are created by One and the Same Eternal God, the Supreme Lord of all. (2) All mankind belong to the human race and share equally in the common parentage of Adam and Eve. (3) God is just and kind to all his creatures. He is not partial to any race, age, or religion. The whole universe is His dominion and all people are His creatures. (4) All people are born equal in the sense that none brings any possession with him, and they die equal in the sense that they take back nothing of their worldly belongings. (5) God judges every person on the basis of his own merits and according to his own deeds. (6) God has conferred on man, man as such, a title of honor and dignity.

Such are some of the principles behind the value of equality in Islam. When this concept is fully utilized, it will leave no place for prejudice or persecutions. And when this Divine ordinance is fully implemented, there will be no room for oppression or suppression. Concepts of chosen and gentile peoples, words such as privileged and condemned races, expressions such as social castes and second-class citizens will all become meaningless and obsolete.

The Concept of Brotherhood

Another fundamental element in the value system of Islam is the value of human brotherhood. This value also is founded on the same principles which have been discussed in connection with freedom and equality. Besides those foregoing principles, human brotherhood in Islam is based on an unshakable belief in the Oneness and Universality of God the worshipped, the unity of mankind the worshippers, and the unity of religion the medium of worship. For the Muslim, God is One, Eternal and Universal. He is the Creator of all men, the Provider for all men, the Judge of all men, and the Lord over all men. To Him, social status, national supermanship, and racial origin are insignificant. Before Him, all men are equal and brothers of one another.

The Muslim believes in the unity of mankind with regard to the source of creation, the original parentage, and the final destiny. The source of creation is God Himself. The original common parentage is that of Adam and Eve. To this first parentage, every human being belongs and of it he partakes. As for the final destiny, there is no doubt in the Muslim's mind that it will be to God, the Creator, to Whom all men shall return.

The Muslim believes in the unity of God's religion. This means that God does not confine His religion or favors to any particular nation, race, or age. It further means that there can be no contradiction or fundamental differences in the Religion of God. When all this is interpreted properly, it will leave no ground for pretended supremacy or presumptuous exclusivity. And when it is imparted into the human mind, it will provide man with a clear concept and a solid basis of human brotherhood. Because the Muslim believes in the Oneness of God, the unity of mankind, and the unity of religion, he believes in all the Messengers and Revelations of God without discrimination[3].

The Concept of Peace

To appreciate how Islam approaches the question of peace, one has only to consider a few elementary facts about Islam. Peace and Islam are derived from the same root and may be considered synony-

---

[3]See the discussion of the Articles of Faith above.

mous. One of God's names is Peace. The concluding words of the daily prayers of every Muslim are words of peace. The greeting of the Muslims when they return to God is peace. The daily salutations among the Muslims are expressions of peace. The adjective "Muslim" means, in a sense, peaceful. Heaven in Islam is the abode of peace.

This is how fundamental and dominant the theme of peace is in Islam. The individual who approaches God through Islam cannot fail to be at peace with God, with himself, and with his fellow men. Taking all these values together, putting man in his proper place in the cosmos, and viewing life in the Islamic perspective, men of good faith and principles cannot fail to make our world a better world, to regain human dignity, to achieve equality, to enjoy universal brotherhood, and to build a lasting peace[4].

The Concept of Community

The word community has acquired certain connotations, some of which are romantic and nostalgic, some derogatory and reactionist. But since we intend to deal with the basics, we shall confine our discussion to the most fundamental meanings of the word community.

In one basic sense, the concept community means "all forms of relationship that are characterized by a high degree of personal intimacy, emotional depth, moral commitment, social cohesion, and continuity in time . . . It may be found in . . . locality, religion, nation, race, occupation, or (common cause). Its archetype . . . is the family" (Nisbet, pp. 47-8)[5].

In another basic sense, a community is a comprehensive group with two chief characteristics: (1) it is a group within which the individual can have most of the activities and experiences that are important to him. (2) The group is bound together by a shared sense of belonging and a feeling of identity (Broom & Selznick, p. 31)[6].

The historical master trend has been a movement from those intimate, deep, moral relationships of community to those impersonal, formal utilitarian relationships of mass society. The movement has been designated by different phases and marked by far-reaching consequences.

From this historical trend, one can infer certain conclusions. First, this historical evolution has not been totally negative or com-

---

[4]See the discussion of War and Peace below.

[5]Robert Nisbet, *The Sociological Tradition* (New York: Basic Books, 1966).

[6]L. Broom & P. Selznick, *Sociology: A Text with Adapted Readings* (New York: Harper & Rowe, 1968).

pletely positive and constructive. Both negative and positive consequences have affected different people in different degrees. Secondly, modern society is far from perfect, there is a great task yet to be performed. Thirdly, the human condition is not a lost cause or a hopeless case. True, there are crises and travail, but the situation is not entirely out of control. Finally, mankind has grown more interdependent and human societies more intertwined. Whatever happens in one segment of society is bound to affect the rest. We should keep this in mind when we discuss the Islamic concept of community.

It should be generally correct to state that the Islamic concept of community has certain unique characteristics. Such unique characteristics relate to the foundation or basis of the community, its historic mission and purpose, its status among other communities, its identity, and its continuity.

The community in Islam is not founded on race, nationality, locality, occupation, kinship, or special interests. It does not take its name after the name of a leader or a founder or an event. It transcends national borders and political boundaries. The foundation of the community in Islam is the principle which designates submission to the will of Allah, obedience to His law and commitment to His cause. In short, an Islamic community is present only when it is nourished and fostered by Islam.

The Islamic community has a historic mission far beyond mere survival, sheer power, breeding, or physiological continuity. Such a mission is described in the Holy Qur'an as follows:

Let there be a community (or ummah) among you, advocating what is good, demanding what is right, and eradicating what is wrong. These are indeed the successful (3:104). You are the best community ever raised, you enforce what is right, fight what is wrong, and believe in Allah (3:110).

The historic role of the Islamic Community is to be the true embodiment of the virtuous, the wholesome, and the noble. A truly Islamic community is the alert guardian of virtue and the bitter enemy of vice. What is required of the community at large is likewise required of every individual member. This is because the whole community is an organic entity and every individual is accountable to Allah. The role of the individual Muslim is best described by the statement of the Prophet:

Whoever of you sees something wrong must seek to rectify it by action or deed; if he cannot, let him try to change it by word; if he cannot, let his *feelings* of disapproval and condemnation intensify and this is the minimal degree of faith. As we can see, this description is very significant and comprehensive. In this age of revolutionary media, no one in his right mind can underestimate the power of concerted actions, or the power of communicable words, or the power of feelings.

The historic role of the Islamic community is further restated in the Qur'anic verse (2:143)

We have made you a middle nation, a well-integrated community, a balanced *ummah*, so that you may be witnesses over other people and the Messenger a witness over you.

Such a role of witnessing is both highly significant and extremely demanding. It means that the community of Islam must be exemplary. It must set the highest standards of performance and be the reference point for others. It must avoid excesses and extravagances, static rigidity and instant evaporation. To strike a middle course of action, to be steadfast and consistent, to know what to accept and what to reject, to have principles and at the same time remain adaptable is probably the hardest test of the human character and social viability. But this is the role of the Islamic community and the historic mission of Muslims. And it is this very criterion that qualifies the Muslim as the best human community ever to evolve.

The identity of the Islamic community centers upon the principles of consistent balance, exemplary conduct, unity of purpose, reciprocity of feelings, solidarity, and equity. Numerous are the statements of the Qur'ān and Sunnah to this effect (for example 4:135, 21:92, 23:52).

With regard to the continuity of the Islamic community, certain points are noteworthy. It is the duty of Muslims to do everything within their means to insure that continuity. The rules of marriage and inheritance, the duties of *Zakah* and *Hajj*, the mutual rights and obligations of kin, the individual conscientiousness and social belonging—all these are oriented to the healthy continuity of the community of Islam. On the other hand, Allah has pledged to protect this continuity in several ways. First, He has pledged to preserve the Qur'an and protect its purity (15:9).

This means that there shall always be a community to follow the Qur'ān; the Qur'ān shall not be without followers even though there may be followers of other books. Secondly, Islam itself is a continuity. Whenever a nation deviated from the path of Allah, He restated His word, reaffirmed His truth, and commissioned new prophets or reformers to carry on. Thirdly, Allah has issued a strong warning to the effect that if Muslims turned away from the right path, they would be the losers; Allah would replace them by other people unlike the failing Muslims (47:38).

Again, the believers are warned that if any of them turns back from his Faith, soon will God produce people whom He will love and they will love Him,—humble toward the believers and mighty against the disbelievers, fighting in the way of God and never afraid of reproaches (Qur'an, 5:57).

The Concept of Morality

The concept of morality in Islam centers around certain basic beliefs and principles. Among these are the following: (1) God is the Creator and Source of all goodness, truth, and beauty. (2) Man is a responsible, dignified, and honorable agent of his Creator. (3) God has put everything in the heavens and the earth in the service of mankind. (4) By His Mercy and Wisdom, God does not expect the impossible from man or hold him accountable for anything beyond his power. Nor does God forbid man to enjoy the good things of life. (5) Moderation, practicality, and balance are the guarantees of high integrity and sound morality. (6) All things are permissible in principle except what is singled out as obligatory, which must be observed, and what is singled out as forbidden, which must be avoided. (7) Man's ultimate responsibility is to God and his highest goal is the pleasure of his Creator.

The dimensions of morality in Islam are numerous, far-reaching, and comprehensive. The Islamic morals deal with the relationship between man and God, man and his fellow men, man and the other elements and creatures of the universe, man and his innermost self. The Muslim has to guard his external behavior and his manifest deeds, his words and his thoughts, his feelings and intentions. In a general sense, his role is to champion what is right and fight what is wrong, seek what is true and abandon what is false, cherish what is beautiful and wholesome and avoid what is indecent. Truth and virtue are his goal. Humbleness and simplicity, courtesy and compassion, are his second nature. To him, arrogance and vanity, harshness and indifference, are distasteful, offensive, and displeasing to God.

More specifically, the Muslim's relationship with God is one of love and obedience, complete trust and thoughtfulness, peace and appreciation, steadfastness and active service. This high-level morality will, undoubtedly, nourish and reinforce morality at the human level. For in his relationship with his fellow men, the Muslim must show kindness to the kin and concern for the neighbor, respect for the elderly and compassion for the young, care for the sick and support for the needy, sympathy for the grieved and cheer for the depressed, joy with the blessed and patience with the misguided, tolerance toward the ignorant and forgiveness of the helpless, disapproval of the wrong and rise above the trivial. Moreover, he must respect the legitimate rights of others as much as he does his own. His mind must be occupied with constructive ideas and serious pursuits; his heart must beat with compassionate feelings and good will; his soul must radiate with peace and serenity; his counsel must be sincere and courteous.

The Muslim's moral obligation is to be a vivid example of honesty and perfection, fulfill his commitments and perform his tasks well, seek knowledge and virtue by all possible means, correct his mistakes and repent his sins, develop a good sense of social consciousness and nourish a feeling of human response, provide for his dependents generously without extravagance and meet their legitimate needs. Nature and the world are the field of exploration and the object of enjoyment for the Muslim. He must utilize their elements and ponder their marvels, read them as signs of God's greatness and preserve their beauty, explore their wonders and discover their secrets. But whether he uses them for utility or for sheer enjoyment, he must avoid waste and excess. As a responsible agent of God and a conscientious trustee, he must always be mindful of others who share the world with him and who will succeed him in the future.

The moral principles of Islam are sometimes stated as positive commitments which must be fulfilled and sometimes as negative prescriptions which must be avoided. Whether they are stated positively or negatively, they are designed to build in the human being a sound mind, a peaceful soul, a strong personality, and a healthy body. There is no doubt that these are necessary requirements of the general welfare and prosperity of mankind. And to help man to satisfy these requirements Islam has, among other things, laid down the following regulations:

1. To bear witness to the Oneness of God and the Messengership of Muhammad in a meaningful commital way;

2. To observe the daily prayers regularly;

3. To pay the religious tax which is known as alms or the poor-due (zakah);

4. To keep the fast of the Holy Month of Ramadan;

5. To make a pilgrimage to the Holy City of Mecca at least once in his lifetime.

The moral and social implications of these regulations will be discussed later in detail.

Besides these positive measures, there are others which may be called preventive and precautionary ones. To protect man from insanity and degeneration, from weakness and indulgence, from indecency and temptation, Islam has prohibited certain things pertaining to food, drinking, recreation, and sex. Among these are the following:

1. All kinds of intoxicating wines, liquors, and spirits (Qur'an, 2: 219; 4:43; 5:93-94);

2. The meat and products of swine (pork, bacon, ham, lard), of wild animals that use claws or teeth to kill their victims (tigers, wolves, leopards, etc.), of all birds of prey (hawks, vultures, crows, etc.), of rodents, reptiles, worms and the like, of dead animals and birds that are not slaughtered properly (Qur'an, 2:172-173; 5:4-6);

3. All forms of gambling and vain sports (Qur'an, 2:219; 5:93-94);

4. All sexual relations out of wedlock and all manners of talking, walking, looking and dressing in public that may instigate temptation, arouse desire, stir suspicion, or indicate immodesty and indecency (Qur'an, 23:5-7; 24:30-33; 70:29-31).

This Act of Prohibition is introduced by God for the spiritual and mental well-being of man as well as for the moral and material benefit of humanity. It is not an arbitrary action or a self-imposed intrusion from God. On the contrary, it is a sign of God's interest in the welfare of humanity and an indication of His good care for man.

When God prohibits certain things, it is not because He wants to deprive man of anything good or useful. It is because He means to protect man and allow him to develop a good sense of discrimination, a refined taste for the better things in life, and a continued interest in higher moral values. To achieve this, good care must be taken of man's spirit and mind, soul and body, conscience and sentiments, health and wealth, physique and morale. Prohibition, therefore, is not deprivation but enrichment, not suppression but discipline, not limitation but expansion.

To show that all prohibitions are acts of mercy and wisdom, two Islamic principles are worth mentioning in this connection. First, extraordinary circumstances, emergencies, necessities and exigencies allow the Muslim to do what is normally forbidden. As long as these circumstances exist and to the extent that he cannot help the situation, he is not to blame if he fails to observe the moral rules of God (see Qur'an, 2:173; 5:4). Secondly, God has inscribed for Himself the rule of mercy: any who do evil out of ignorance, but thereafter repent and amend their conduct, will be forgiven; surely, God is Merciful and Oft-forgiving (Qur'an, 6:54).

In a remarkable, typical passage, the Qur'an has laid down the grounds and philosophy of sound moral conduct. The passage may be rendered as follows:

O Children of Adam! Wear your beautiful apparel at every time and place of prayer; eat and drink, but waste not by excess, for God loves not the wasters. Say: 'Who has forbidden the beautiful gifts of God, which He has produced for His servants, and the things, clean and pure, (which He has provided) for sustenance?' Say: 'They are, in the life of this world, for those who believe, (and) purely for them on the Day of Judgement.' Thus do We explain the Signs in detail for those who understand. Say: 'The things that my Lord has indeed forbidden are: shameful deeds, whether open or secret, sins and trespasses against truth or reason; assigning of partners to God—and saying things about God of which you have no knowledge' (Qur'an, 7:31-33).

The range of morality in Islam is so inclusive and integrative that it combines at once faith in God, religious rites, spiritual observances, social conduct, decision making, intellectual pursuits, habits of consumption, manners of speech, and all other aspects of human life. Because morality is such an integral part of Islam, the moral tone underlies all the passages of the Qur'ān and the moral teachings are repeatedly stressed in various contexts throughout the Holy Book. This makes it difficult to devise any reasonably brief classification of these moral teachings according to their citations in the Qur'ān. Every principle is mentioned many times in various contexts. It appears either as a single significant principle or as an element of a total system of morality, which itself is an element of a complete religious supersystem.

In view of this, the following passages must be taken only as representative selections from the Qur'ān, rendered and interpreted by human endeavors which, inevitably, fall short of the perfection of the original and complete version of the Book.

Serve God, and join not any partners with Him; and do good;—to parents, kinsfolk, orphans, the needy ones, neighbors who are near, neighbors who are strangers, the companion by your side, the wayfarer (you meet), and what your right hands possess (captives, slaves, animals, birds, etc.): For God loves not the arrogant, the vainglorious;— (Nor) those who are niggardly or enjoin niggardliness on others, or hide the bounties which God has bestowed on them; for We have prepared for those who resist Faith a punishment that steeps them in contempt; (Nor) those who spend of their substance, (out of hypocrisy) just to be seen of men, but have no faith in God and the Last Day. If any take the Evil One for their intimate, what a dreadful intimate he is! (4:36-38).

Say (O Muhammad): 'Come, I will rehearse what God has (really) prohibited you from'; join not anything as equal with Him; be good to your parents; kill not your children on a plea of want;— for We provide sustenance for you and for them;— come not nigh to the orphan's property, except to improve it, until he attains the age of full strength; give measure and weight with full justice;— no burden do We place on any soul, but that which it can bear; and whenever you speak, speak justly, even if a near relative is concerned; and fulfill the Covenant of God. Thus does He Command you, that you may remember. Verily, this is My Way, leading straight; follow it; follow not (other) paths: They will scatter you about from His Right Path. Thus does He command you, that you may be righteous (6:151-153).

God commands justice, the doing of good, and kindness to kith and kin; and He forbids all shameful deeds, and injustice and rebellion: He instructs you, that you may receive admonition. Fulfill the Covenant of God when you have entered into it, and break not your oaths after you have confirmed them; indeed you have made God your surety; for God knows all that you do—whoever works righteousness, man or woman, and has Faith, verily, to him will We give a new Life, a life that is good and pure, and We will bestow on such (workers) their reward according to the best of their actions (16:90-91, 97).

Invite (all) to the Way of your Lord with wisdom and beautiful preaching; and argue with them in ways that are best and most gracious; for your Lord knows best, who have strayed from His Path, and who are truly guided (16:125).

Who is better in speech than one who calls (others) to God, works righteousness, and says: 'I am one of those who bow in Islam'. Nor can Goodness and Evil be equal. Repel (Evil) with what is best. Then the one between whom and you there was hatred will become as it were your friend and intimate! (41:33-34).

Whatever is given to you (here) is (only) a convenience of this Life. But that which is with God is better and more lasting. (It is.) For those who believe and put their trust in their Lord; those who avoid the greater crimes and shameful deeds, and, when they are angry even then forgive; those who hearken to their Lord, and establish regular prayer; who (conduct) their affairs by mutual consultation; who spend out of what We bestow on them for sustenance; and those who, when an oppressive wrong is inflicted on them, (are not cowed but) help and defend themselves. The recompense for an injury is an injury equal to it (in degree), but if a person forgives and makes reconciliation, his reward is due from God, for God loves not those who do wrong. But indeed if any do help and defend themselves after a wrong (done) to them, against such (persons) there is no cause of blame. The blame is only against those who oppress men with wrong doing and insolently transgress beyond bounds through the land, defying right and justice. For such (oppressors and transgressors) there will be a penalty grievous. But indeed if any show patience and forgive, that would truly be an exercise of courageous will and resolution in the conduct of affairs (42:36-43).

If any do wish for the transitory things (of this Life), We readily grant them such things as We will, to such persons as We will, but in the end have We provided Hell for them where they will burn, disgraced and rejected.

And those who do wish for the (things of) the Hereafter, and strive therefor with all due striving, and have Faith,—they are the ones whose striving is appreciable (by God.)

Of the bounties of your Lord We bestow freely on all these as well as those: the bounties of your Lord are not closed (to anyone)...

Take not with God another object of worship: or you (man!) will sit in disgrace and destitution.

Your Lord has decreed that you worship none but Him, and that you be kind to parents. Whether one or both of them attain old age in your life, say not to them a word of contempt, nor repel them, but address them in terms of honor.

And out of kindness, lower to them the wing of humility, and say: 'My Lord! bestow on them Your mercy even as they cherished me in childhood.'

Your Lord knows best what is in your hearts. If you do deeds of righteousness, verily He is Most Forgiving to those who turn to Him again and again (in true penitence).

And render to the kindred their due rights, as (also) to those in want, and to the wayfarer. But squander not (your wealth) in the manner of a spendthrift. Verily spendthrifts are brothers of the Evil Ones; and the Evil One is to his Lord ungrateful.

And even if you have to turn away from them (the said people), in pursuit of the Mercy from your Lord which you do expect, yet speak to them words of easy kindness.

Make not your hand tied (like a niggard's) to your neck, nor stretch it forth to its utmost reach (like an irresponsible squanderer, if you choose either way), you will become blameworthy and destitute (respectively).

Verily your Lord does provide sustenance in abundance for whom He pleases, and He provides in a just measure; for He does know and regard all His servants.

Kill not your children for fear of want. We shall provide sustenance for them as well as for you. Verily the killing of them is a great sin.

Nor come nigh to adultery; for it is a shameful deed and an evil, opening the road (to other evils).

Nor take life—which God has made sacred—except for just cause. And if anyone is slain wrongfully, We have given his heir authority (to demand equal punishment or to forgive). But let him not exceed bounds in the matter of taking life; for he is helped (by the Law).

Come not nigh to the orphan's property except to improve it, until he attains the age of full strength; and fulfill (every) engagement: for (every) engagement will be enquired into (on the Day of Reckoning).

Give full measure when you measure, and weigh with a balance that is straight. That is the most fitting and the most advantageous in the final determination.

And pursue not that of which you have no knowledge (idle and useless curiosity); for every act of hearing, or of seeing or of (feeling in) the heart will be enquired into (on the Day of Reckoning).

Nor walk on the earth with arrogance; for you cannot rend the earth asunder, nor reach the mountains in height.

Of all such things the evil is hateful in the sight of your Lord. These are among the (precepts of) wisdom, which your Lord has revealed to you. Take not, with God, another object of worship, lest you should be thrown into Hell, blameworthy and rejected (17:18-39).

We bestowed wisdom on Luqman: 'Show your gratitude to God'. Any who is grateful does so to the profit of his own soul. But if any are ungrateful, verily God is free of all needs, worthy of all praise. . . . And We have enjoined on man (to be good) to his parents. In travail upon travail did his mother bear him, and in years twain was his weaning. (Hear the command), show gratitude to Me and to your parents. To Me is your final Goal. But if they strive to make you join in worship with Me things of which you have no knowledge (or do any wrong), obey them not; yet bear them company in this life with justice (and consideration), and follow the way of those who turn to Me (in love). In the end the return of you all is to Me,

and I will tell you the truth (and meaning) of all that you did. . . .
O my Son! (said Luqman): Establish regular prayer, enjoin what is
just (and right) and forbid what is wrong; and bear with patient constancy whatever betide you; for this is firmness (of purpose) in (the
conduct of) affairs. And swell not your cheek (for pride) at men, nor
walk in insolence through the earth; for God loves not any arrogant
boaster. And be moderate in your pace, and lower your voice; for the
harshest of sounds without doubt is the braying of the ass (31:12-19).

O you who believe! Intoxicants and gambling . . . are an
abomination, of Satan's handiwork. Avoid such (abomination), so
that you may prosper. Satan's plan is only to excite enmity and
hatred between you, with intoxicants and gambling, and hinder you
from the rememberance of God and from prayer. Will you not then
abstain? (5:93-94).

But seek, with that which God has bestowed on you, the Home
of the Hereafter. Nor forget your portion in this world. But do you
good, as God has been good to you, and seek not mischief in the
land; for God loves not the mischief makers (28:77).

These selections can be supported by many others from the
Qur'ān and the Traditions of Muhammad. In themselves they are
sufficient to portray the fundamental morals of Islam. These Islamic
morals are unique in their nature under all circumstances. They are
introduced by God not simply to be admired occasionally but to be
enforced and effective. They are meant to help the individual to
develop his personality and cultivate his character in the most wholesome manner, to strengthen his bonds and consolidate his association
with God, the Source of all Goodness. Never were the Islamic morals
designed to intimidate the individual and make him passive or indifferent. One example will illustrate the point. If a Muslim is
wronged or oppressed, he has the free choice either to resist and
retaliate in an equal measure or to forgive and entrust God with the
results of his deed. He knows that he is authorized to take either
action, and he equally knows that it is better for him to forgive. So
when he forgives, he does so with his own free choice for the love of
God. Similarly, when he retaliates he is not violating the Law or
acting unjustly; he is defending his rights, an attitude which is a
sacred duty in itself, and is helping the rightful authorities to establish order and justice. If Islam were to demand absolute forgiveness
as some other creeds do in theory, many undisciplined people would
be tempted to do wrong and exceed all limits. Likewise, if Islam were
to demand only retaliation, as some other creeds ruthlessly teach,
there would be no room for mercy and patience nor for spiritual
reform and moral maturity, in which case many fine qualities of man

would subside and many moral potentials may never be actualized.

It is common knowledge that the people who are taught to forgive under all circumstances do not, and probably cannot, practice their teachings, because it is not in the interest of humanity in the long run, nor is it in the interest of morality itself. Likewise, the people who are taught to practice stern retaliation have little or no respect for human virtues and care less for moral values as universal rules. But Islam, the Divine foster of human nature, has given the right answers to human problems. To those wrong doers who are looking for a second chance, who may improve or benefit by granting them pardon, forgiveness is recommended and preferable. But against those who might misunderstand the motives of forgiveness or be tempted to pursue the wrong course, equal retaliation is authorized. Thus, the attitude of the Muslim in either case is sound and beneficial When he forgives, he pleases God, retains the upper hand and contributes to the reformation of the delinquent. And when he retaliates, he defends the right, establishes order and justice, and helps to arrest evil. Now, which is sound morality? The attitude of the person who is a ruthless avenger indiscriminately? Or the attitude of a Muslim who makes room for mercy and forgiveness, and who allows for extraordinary circumstances? And who is morally sound? The person who forgives because he knows that he is not allowed to retaliate? Or a Muslim who forgives while he is fully aware that he can lawfully retaliate? Which is real forgiveness? The one resulting from external compulsion and prohibition not to act otherwise? Or the one resulting from freedom of choice and freedom of action? It is no wonder that the moral principles of Islam are sound, unique, and adaptive. They are the instructions of God, the Source of all goodness and morality.

The Concept of the Universe

In the foreword, we briefly discussed the position of the Muslims and the future of Islam in the Western Hemisphere. In this part, we shall discuss the position of man in the contemporary world, the general human situation, and the Islamic concept of the universe or world view. This will reaffirm the concepts that have already been discussed, add some new ideas, and tie together the various dimensions of the subject in a summary recapitulatory fashion.

The present human situation is alarming, to say the least. It demands concern and active response on the part of all people of good will and God-mindedness. But this does not, and should not, lead to despair or resignation. The spirit of hope is, and has always been, an integral part of Islam (see, e.g., Qur'ān, 12:87; 65:3).

The problems and crises of modern times are not entirely unique or peculiar. It is true that they are difficult, complex, and agonizing. Perhaps this is even more so now than ever before. But the difference, however, between this age and those of yester centuries is basically a difference of degree rather than of kind. The ever-increasing complexity of our contemporary predicaments may be largely due to a similar, proportionate rise in our expectations and capacities.

For many centuries and in numerous regions of the globe, the chief source of the most difficult crises has essentially been a kind of inflexible, exclusive, and intolerant attitude toward the unfamiliar the different, and the foreign. This orientation fostered racism, elitism, bigotry, prejudice, and a whole host of other equally distasteful attitudes.

Few people can really deny that humanity is facing an unusual crisis. This present human crisis seems to emanate from a serious imbalance between our external, outward, material explorations and our internal, inward, moral gropings Nothing is simpler than calling for the maintenance of an equilibrium, advocating a "middle range," or crusading for the "golden means." Yet nothing has been harder to attain. In the past, utterances such as man cannot live by bread alone were sometimes so distorted as to connote disregard for man's material welfare. Similarly, trust in God has been misunderstood; it is often taken to mean helpless fatalism or categorical denial of human free will and self-realization. An overemphasis on spirituality and resignation is bound to give rise to a counter emphasis on materialism, rationalism, "free will", and so on. Stressed beyond certain limits, spirituality may become superstition, and confusion. Likewise, a counter stress may turn materialism into laxity, free will into libertinism, and rationalism into sheer vanity. The intellectual history of the last few centuries demonstrates these tendencies only too well.

Over the years of recent decades, the spiritual scale tipped up and down. In the sixties, and now in the seventies, the news-making events are those of the unsurpassed, unprecedented, outerspace explorations. Equally sensational are the unprecedented explorations in the inward, internal realms of being, however faddish, cultic, or neurotic they may seem to be.

The rise of these two unprecedented and unbalanced types of exploration is exceptionally alarming. The reason probably lies in the fact that the two types do not seem to relate to each other, let alone converge. There is no apparent reciprocity, mutual reinforcement, or crossfertilization. Besides, their precarious, unbalanced existence is a constant threat to the majority of people. It may very well drive them into ambivalence and confusion which may, in turn, intensify the problems of society and harden the lot of modern man. But such a precarious course can be changed if the outward scientific explorations and the inward moral gropings are somehow reconciled. Man does not live by bread alone. That is true enough. But neither does he live by prayers only. He is both a political or materialistic animal and a religious explorer of the holy.

As already mentioned, the contemporary world is clearly baffled by numerous problems. But it is equally baffled by the conflicting diagnoses and prescriptions to cope with these problems. Some people sing along with the popular lyric, "What the world needs now is love. . .etc." Some call for a human rebirth. Others turn to Marxism, Humanism, Satanism, or Scientism as the ultimate solution. Still more are awaiting the arrival of some future Savior. Yet this long list does not even include the indifferent, the hopeless, and the apathetic who may in fact outnumber the optimist clubs combined. But it seems that the greatest need today is the pressing need for "understanding." What man needs most of all is to understand himself and his nature, his potentials and limitations, his place in the universe and relationships with its elements.

The question now is how can Islam help man to understand himself, unclog his mind, and clear his blurred vision? To try an answer to this question, it will be necessary to keep in mind the basic concepts of Islam which have been discussed and to elaborate further some elements of its value system. This analysis will hopefully show how they may relate to modern man in his contemproary predicament, and how they may help him to find his way through.

The principle of "moderation" is most characteristic of Islam. It is probably best expressed in the way Islam views human nature, the meaning of life, and the idea of God. Islam does not subscribe to the one-sided "humanistic" philosophy, which almost deifies man and recognizes nothing beyond. Neither does Islam endorse the equally one-sided verdict that human nature is inherently vicious, wicked, or sinful, Islam rejects the idea that life is nasty, brutal, short, and miserable. But it equally rejects the idea that life is an end in itself, pleasurable, and carefree. Islam does give life a positive meaning, a purpose. It would devalue life on earth *only* relative to the Hereafter. It is not concerned exclusively with the here and now, the instant hedonism, and the immediate pleasures. Nor does it completely bypass the here and now in pursuit of a future paradise in a hereafter. It addresses itself to both the human condition here on earth and the human destiny in the Hereafter. Such concern is, of course, proportionate; it values each phase of existence according to its relative effect on the general well-being of man (Qur'ān, 7:33;

17:18-21; 28:77; 57:20-21).

In the Qur'ān, there is a passage (2:27-39) which is typical of so many others. This passage contains some of the fundamental principles of Islam, and represents the foundations of the world view of Islam. Outstanding among these principles are the following:

1. The world is a becoming entity, created by the will of a Designer and sustained by Him for meaningful purposes. Historical currents take place in accordance with His will and follow established laws. They are not directed by blind chance, nor are they random and disorderly incidents.

2. Man also is created by God and is commissioned to be God's viceroy on earth. He is so chosen to cultivate the land and enrich life with knowledge, virtue, purpose, and meaning. And to achieve this goal, everything in the earth and the heavens is created *for* him and is made subservient to him. Life on this planet is not a prison for man; his coming into the world was not an arbitrary punishment for previously committed sins. Nor was he expelled from another world and cast out into this one. His existence was no mere chance or undesigned occurrence.

3. Knowledge is the unique faculty of man and is an integral part of his personality and his being. It is knowledge that qualifies man to be the viceroy of his Creator and entitles him to command the respect and allegiance even of the angels of God.

4. The first phase of life on earth began not in sin or rebellion against the Creator. The "Fall" from the Garden of Eden and what followed thereafter—the remorse of Adam and Eve, their repentance, God's forgiveness of and compassion for them, the enmity between man and Satan—all this was no surprise to the Creator. Nor was it an accident in the course of events. It was too meaningful to be accidental. Rather, it seems to have been designed to discipline the first man, to give him actual experience of fall and rise, moral defeat and triumph, straying from and reconciliation with the Creator. In this way, man would become better prepared for life and more enlightened to face its uncertainties and trying moments.

5. Eve was not the weaker party of the first human couple. She neither tempted Adam to eat of the forbidden tree nor was she alone responsible for the expulsion from the Garden of Eden. Both Adam and Eve were equally tempted and equally responsible; both were remorseful, repented, and were blessed with the forgiveness and compassion of God. This is significant as it liberates Eve from the

curse that has followed her and her sex throughout the ages, and acquits her of the charge that she alone bears all or most of the responsibility for the Fall. Furthermore, it declares in no uncertain terms that the belief in the moral inferiority of women is unfounded and the double standard is totally unjustifiable. Here, as elsewhere, the Qur'ān makes it very clear that both man and woman are equally capable of virtue and weakness, equally sensitive, and equally meritorious[7].

6.　Man is a free agent endowed with a free will. This is the essence of his humanity and the basis of his responsibility to his Creator. Without man's relative free will life would be meaningless and God's covenant with man would be in vain. Without human free will, God would be defeating His own purpose and man would be completely incapable of bearing any responsibility. This, of course, is unthinkable.

7.　Life emanates from God. It is neither eternal nor an end in itself, but a transitional phase, after which all shall return to the Creator.

8.　Man is a responsible agent. But responsibility for sin is borne by the actual offender alone. Sin is not hereditary, transferable, or communal in nature. Every individual is responsible for his own deeds. And while man is susceptible to corruption, he is also capable of redemption and reform. This does not mean that Islam prefers the individual to the group. Individualism means little or nothing when severed from social context. What it means is that the individual has different sets of roles to play. He must play them in such a way as to guard his moral integrity, preserve his identity, observe the rights of God, and fulfill his social obligations.

9.　Man is a dignified honorable being. His dignity derives from the fact that he is infused with the spirit of his Creator. What is more important is that such dignity is not confined to any special race, color, or class of people. It is the natural right of man, every man, the most honorable being on earth.

10.　The passage, finally, points to the deep-seated roots of the Oneness of God and the unity of mankind. It shows, further, that man's highest virtues are piety and knowledge, that when such knowledge is acquired and invested according to the divine guidance, man's blissful destiny will be assured and his life will be serene.

---

[7]See the Concept of Sin above.

CHAPTER III

THE APPLICATION OF FAITH

In this chapter we propose to deal with the major exercises of Faith as laid down by Islam. They are Prayers (Salah), Fasting (Sawm), Alms–giving or "Charity" (Zakah) and Pilgrimage (Hajj). The way God has enjoined these exercises makes them serve all spiritual purposes and satisfy human needs. Some of them are daily; some weekly; some monthly; some bi-annually; some annually; and some are required as a minimum once in a lifetime. So they embrace all the days of the week, all the weeks of the month, all the months of the year, and all the years of life, and they, above all, mark the whole course of life with a Divine touch.

It has already been mentioned that Faith without action and practice is a dead end, as far as Islam is concerned. Faith by nature is very sensitive and can be most effective. When it is out of practice or out of use, it quickly loses its liveliness and motivating power. The only way to enliven Faith and make it serve its purpose is practice. Practice provides Faith with nourishment, survival and effectiveness. In return, Faith inspires man to be constant in his devotion and persistent in his practice. This is because the inter-relationship between Faith and practice is very strong, and their interdependence is readily understandable. A person without Faith has no real source of inspiration and, consequently, has no worthy objectives to attain or even aspire to. The life of such a person is meaningless, and he lives from day to day, which is no life at all. On the other hand, the person who confesses Faith but does not practice it is a self-deceiving person, and in fact has no Faith, in which case he is no more than a helpless straying wanderer.

The interrelationship between Faith and practice in Islam

has vivid reflections on the entire setup of the religion and manifests the deep philosophy of its teachings. Islam does not recognize any kind of separation between soul and body, spirit and matter, religion and life. It accepts man the way God has created him and recognizes his nature as composed of soul and body. It does not neglect his spiritual nature; else he would be like any animal. Nor does it underestimate his physical needs; else he would be an angel, which he is not and cannot be. According to Islam, man stands in the center of the stream of creation. He is not purely spiritual because the purely spiritual beings are the angels, nor is he beyond that, because the Only Being beyond that is God alone. He is not entirely material or physical, because the only beings of this class are the animals and other irrational creatures. So being of such a complementary nature, man has parallel demands and parallel needs: spiritual and material, moral and physical. The religion which can help man and bring him close to God is the religion which takes into consideration all these demands and needs, the religion which elevates the spiritual status and disciplines the physical desires. And this is the religion of Islam. To oppress either side of human nature, or upset the balance, or lean to one direction only, would be an abusive contradiction to human nature as well as an irresponsible defiance of the very nature in which God has created man.

Because Islam grants complete recognition of human nature as it is, and takes deep interest in the spiritual as well as the material well-being of man, it does not consider religion a personal affair or a separate entity from the current general course of life. In other words, religion has no value unless its teachings have effective imprints on the personal and public course of life. On the other hand, life is meaningless, if it is not organized and conducted according to the Divine Law. This explains why Islam extends its sense of organization to all walks of life: individual and social behavior, labor and industry, economics and politics, national and international relations, and so on. It also demonstrates why Islam does not recognize "secularism" or separation of religion from man's daily transactions. The interaction between true religion and meaningful life is vital. And this is why Islam penetrates into all walks of life to conduct all human activities in a sound and wholesome manner, acceptable to God and benevolent to man.

As a result of this necessary correspondence between true religion and daily life, Islam does not attend to the doctrine of "six days for me or the world and one day for the Lord". This doctrine amounts to nothing in the long run, and makes the liveliness of religion turn pale and faint. Besides, it shows serious injustice to God on man's part and afflicts detrimental injuries on the latter's soul. It is a serious negligence of the spiritual and moral needs which are as important as, if not greater than, the material desires. It is a dangerous disruption of the nature of man, and any such imbalance is a symptom of degeneration. Similarly, if man earmarks six days for monkery or exclusive meditation and one day for himself, he would be better in no way. The balance would still be upset. The natural and logical course, then, is the course which Islam has offered. Being of a complementary nature and standing in the center of the stream of creation, man will plunge into serious troubles, if he neglects either his soul or his body, or if he lets either one outweigh the other. To nourish both, to foster both in a well-balanced and sound manner is the hardest test of man's sense of justice and integrity as well as of his willpower and truthfulness. And to help man to pass this test, Islam has come to his rescue with the regular exercises of Faith.

The Prayers (Salah)

The Purpose of Prayer

Prayer constitutes one pillar of Islam and is considered the Foundation of Religion. Any Muslim who fails to observe his prayers and has no reasonable excuse is committing a grave offense and a heinous sin. This offense is so grave because it is not only against God, which is bad enough, but is also against the very nature of man. It is an instinct of man to be inclined to adore the great beings, and to aspire to lofty goals. The greatest being and the loftiest goal of all is God. The best way to cultivate in man a sound personality and actualize his aspirations in a mature course of development is the Islamic Prayer. To neglect prayer is to oppress the good qualities in human nature and unjustifiably deny it the right to adore and love, the right to aspire and ascend, the right to excel in goodness and achieve noble aims. Such oppression and denial constitute a very serious and destructive offense. Here lies the significance and vitality of prayer in the life of man.

It should always be borne in mind that God does not need man's prayer, because He is free of all needs. He is only interested in our prosperity and well-being in every sense. When He emphasizes the necessity of prayer and charges us with any duty, He means to help us; because whatever good we do is for our own benefit, and whatever offence we commit is against our own souls. Here, too, man is the center of gravity, and his common interest is the main concern. The benefit which man can derive from the Islamic prayer is immeasurable, and the blessing of prayer is beyond imagination. This is not just a "theory" or conventional assumption; it is a fascinating fact and a spiritual experience. Here is an explanation of the effectiveness of the Islamic prayer:—

1. It strengthens the belief in the Existence and Goodness of God and transmits this belief into the innermost recesses of man's heart.

2. It enlivens this belief and makes it constructive in the practical course of life.

3. It helps man to realize his natural and instinctive aspirations to greatness and high morality, to excellence and virtuous growth.

4. It purifies the heart and develops the mind, cultivates the conscience and comforts the soul.

5. It fosters the good and decent elements in man, and supresses the evil and indecent inclinations.

When we analyze the Islamic prayer and study its unique nature, it will reveal to us that it is not merely a physical motion or a void recital of the Holy Book. It is a matchless and unprecedented formula of intellectual meditation and spiritual devotion, of moral elevation and physical exercise, all combined. It is an exclusively Islamic experience where every muscle of the body joins the soul and the mind in the worship and glory of God. It is difficult for anyone to impart in words the full meaning of the Islamic prayer, yet it can be said that it is:—

1. A lesson in discipline and willpower;

2. A practice in devotion to God and all worthy objectives;

3. A vigilant reminder of God and constant revelation of His Goodness;

4. A seed of spiritual cultivation and moral soundness;

5. A guide to the most upright way of life;

6. A safeguard against indecency and evil, against wrong deviation and stray;

7. A demonstration of true equality, solid unity, and brotherhood;

8. An expression of thankfulness to God and appreciation of Him;

9. A course of inner peace and stability;

10. An abundant source of patience and courage, of hope and confidence.

This is the Islamic prayer, and that is what it can do for man. The best testimony to this statement is to experience the prayer and avail oneself of its spiritual joys. Then one will know what it really means.

The Conditions of Prayer

The offering of prayer is obligatory upon every Muslim, male or female, who is:

1. Sane and responsible;

2. Relatively mature and in the age of puberty, normally about fourteen. (Children should be advised by parents to start practice at the age of seven and strongly urged by the age of ten);

3. Free from serious sickness and, in the case of women, free from menstruation and confinement due to child birth and nursing. The maximum period of both is ten and forty days, respectively. In these circumstances women are exempt from prayers completely.

Prayer is not valid unless the following requirements are fulfilled:

1. Performing the ablution (Wudu'),which will be explained later;

2. Purity of the whole body, the clothes worn on it, and the ground used for prayer from all kinds of dirt and impurity;

3. Dressing properly in such a way as to meet the moral regulations aimed at covering the private parts. For the male, the body should be covered at least from the navel to the knees. For the female, the whole body should be covered except the face, the hands and the feet. For both, transparent clothes must be avoided in prayer;

4. Declaring the intention of prayer (Niyyah) by both heart and tongue whenever possible;

5. Facing the right direction of "Qiblah", the direction of the Ka'bah at Mecca. There are many ways to decide the right direction. If a person has no means of telling, he whould follow his best judgement.

The Kinds of Prayer

The following are the various kinds of prayer:
1. Obligatory (Fard), which includes the five daily prayers, the Friday's noon congregation and the funeral prayer. Failure to observe these prayers is a serious and punishable sin, if there is no reasonable excuse.

2. Supererogatory (Wajib and Sunnah), which includes the prayers accompanying the obligatory services, and the congregations of the two great festivals (Eeds). Failure to observe these is a harmful negligence and a reproachable conduct.

3. Optional prayer which includes all voluntary prayers at any time of the day or the night. Two periods have a special preference: the later part of the night until just before the breaking of the dawn and the mid-morning period.

The Times of Prayer

Every Muslim, male or female, must offer at least five daily prayers in time, if there is no lawful reason for exemption, combination, or temporary delay, They are:

1. The Early Morning Prayer (Salatu-l-Fajr), which may be offered any time after the dawn and before sunrise, a total period of about two hours.

2. The Noon Prayer (Salatu-z-Zuhr)[1]. This prayer may be offered anytime after the sun begins to decline from its Zenith until it is about midway on its course to setting. For example, if the sun sets at 7:00 p.m. the prayer time begins a little after 12:00 noon and continues until a little after 3:30 p.m. Soon after that the time of the next prayer begins. However, there are accurate calendars telling the time of each prayer. But if there is none available, one must resort to one's best judgement.

3. The Mid-Afternoon Prayer (Salatu-l-'Asr), which begins right after the expiration of the Noon Prayer time and extends to sunset.

4. The Sunset Prayer (Salatu-l-Maghrib). The time of this prayer begins immediately after sunset and extends till the red glow in the western horizon disappears. Normally it extends over a period of one hour and twenty to thirty minutes.

5. The Evening Prayer (Salatu-l-'Isha'), which begins after the red glow in the western horizon disappears (nearly one hour and thirty minutes after sunset) and continues till a little before the dawn.

---

[1]Muslims of the Daylight Saving time zones seem to run into some difficulties and confusion over the proper time for the Friday Congregational Prayer (Jum'ah). The problem can be solved easily by setting the prayer time between 1.15 and 2.30 p.m. throughout the year. In this way, there will be no need to change the time from winter to summer. We strongly recommend this to our brethren so that they may work it into their weekly schedules as a permanent arrangement. The same adjustment may be made with regard to the Sunday noon congregations.

It is noticeable that Islam has set the times of prayers in such a way that our spiritual recreation remarkably coincides with our physical nourishment, and combines the peace of mind with the relaxation of body. The Early Morning Prayer is due in the regular period of breakfast; the Noon Prayer coincides with the lunch period; the Mid-Afternoon Prayer falls about the breaktime for tea or coffee; the Sunset Prayer is about the supper time; and the Evening Prayer corresponds with the late snack. It is also noticeable that the Muslim, by observing these prayers, marks the whole day with a spiritual stamp in the beginning, at the end and throughout. So he combines religion and life, feels the presence of God within him throughout the day, concludes his daily transactions with a spiritual feeling and builds up his moral prestige on strong foundations. Moreover, in this way the Muslim introduces spiritual vitality into all aspects of his life, and religion presents itself to all fields of activity. It becomes effective in shops and offices, homes and farms, factories and plants. It extends its light to every circle of business and work. Indeed, this timetable of prayer is remarkable becuase it is the work of God and the product of Islam.

It is always preferable to offer the prayer as soon as the time sets in, lest some things cause unexpected delay or postponement. These prayers are Divine contests. The reward for those who pass the contests is immeasurable, and their delight is beyond imagination. The happiness they attain, the rejoicing they feel, and the honor they receive cannot be expressed in words. On the other hand, failure to participate in these contests is a punishable sin. It causes severe penalties, spiritual deprivation, mental agony, and social isolation.

The Noon (Zuhr) and the Afternoon ('Asr) Prayers may be offered together, if a person is travelling or sick. The same permission is granted with regard to the Sunset (Maghrib) and the Evening ('Isha) Prayers.[2]

The Partial Ablution (Wudu')

Before offering the prayer one must be in good shape and pure condition. It is necessary to wash the parts of the body which are

---

[2]In the first case, joining the prayers is of the advanced type. The Mid-Afternoon is actually offered before its due time and immediately follows the Noon prayer. In the second case, the combination is of the belated type. The Sunset prayer is actually offered after its due time but immediately before the Evening prayer. Such joining of prayers may alleviate the apprehension of the Muslims who cannot, for legitimate reasons (e.g. travel, work shifts, etc.), observe all their prayers in time.

generally exposed to dirt or dust or smog. This performance is called ABLUTION (Wudu') and is preferably carried out as follows:

1. Declare the intention that the act is for the purpose of worship and purity.

2. Wash the hands up to the wrists, three times.

3. Rinse out the mouth with water, three times, preferably with a brush whenever it is possible.

4. Cleanse the nostrils of the nose by sniffing water into them, three times.

5. Wash the whole face three times with both hands, if possible, from the top of the forehead to the bottom of the chin and from ear to ear.

6. Wash the right arm three times up to the far end of the elbow, and then do the same with the left arm.

7. Wipe the whole head or any part of it with a wet hand, once.

8. Wipe the inner sides of the ears with the forefingers and their outer sides with the thumbs. This should be done with wet fingers.

9. Wipe around the neck with wet hands.

10. Wash the two feet up to the ankles, three times, beginning with the right foot.

At this stage the ablution is completed, and the person who has performed it is ready to start his prayer. When the ablution is valid a person may keep it as long as he can, and may use it for as many prayers as he wishes. But it is preferable to renew it as often as possible. It is also preferable to do it in the said order, although it will be accepted from those who fail to keep this order. Ablution in the said way is sufficient for prayer unless it is nullified by any reason.

Nullification of the Ablution

The ablution becomes nullified by any of the following:

1. Natural discharges, i.e., urine, stools, gas, etc.;

2. The flow of blood or pus and the like from any part of the body;

3. Vomiting;

4. Falling asleep;

5. Losing one's reason by taking drugs or any intoxicating stuff.

After the occurrence of any of these things the ablution must be renewed for prayer. Also, after natural discharges, water should be applied because the use of toilet tissues may not be sufficient for the purpose of purity and worship.

Complete Substitute for the Ablution (Tayammum)

Tayammum or resort to pure earth may substitute for the ablution and even the bath. This is allowed in any of the following cases:

1. When a person is sick and cannot use water;

2. When he has no access to water in sufficient quantity;

3. When the use of water is likely to do him harm or cause any disease;

4. When the performance of ablution makes the person miss a funeral or 'Eed prayer, which has no substitute.

In any of these instances it is permissible to make 'Tayammum' which is performed as follows:

1. Strike both hands slightly on pure earth or sand or stone.

2. Shake the hands off and wipe the face with them once in the same way as done in the ablution.

3. Strike the hands again and wipe the right arm to the elbow with the left hand and the left arm with the right hand.

This 'Tayammum' is a symbolic demonstration of the importance of the ablution, which is so vital for both worship and health. When Islam introduced this repeatable ablution, it brought along with it the best hygienic formula which no other spiritual doctrine or medical prescription had anticipated.

Special Facilities in Ablution

With regard to the ablution Islam has offered certain facilities. If socks or stockings are on and have been put on after performing an ablution, it is not necessary to take them off when renewing the ablution. Instead of taking them off, the wet hand may be passed over them. They should be removed, however, and the feet washed at least once in every twenty-four hours. The same practice may be resorted to if the boots are on and their soles and appearances are clean. Similarly if there is a wound in any of the parts which must be washed in the ablution, and if washing that particular part is likely to cause harm, it is permissible to wipe the dressing bandage of the wound with a wet hand.

The Complete Ablution (Ghusl/Bath)

The whole body with the nostrils, mouth and head must be washed by a complete bath before entering prayer in any of the following cases:

1. After intimate intercourse;
2. After wet dreams;
3. Upon expiration of the menstruation period of women;
4. At the end of the confinement period of nursing women, which, is estimated at a maximum of forty days. If it ends before, complete ablution should be done.

It should be pointed out that at the start of the bath or ablution the intention must be clear that it is for the purpose of purity and worship. Also, a person who is performing an ablution, partial or complete, should combine his performance with some utterances glorifying God and praying Him for true guidance. The forms of such utterances are described in detail in the elaborate sources of the religion. One, however, can say one's own best utterances if one does not know the exact wording. That is sufficient as long as it is in the praise of God and is said with sincerity.

The Prayer Call (Adhan)

Now the worshipper has performed his ablution as explained above and is ready for prayer. When the time of prayer comes, it is good practice, after the Traditions of Prophet Muhammad, to say the Prayer Call (Adhan). The caller stands facing the Qiblah (the direction of the Ka'bah at Mecca), raising both hands to his ears and says, in a loud voice, the following:

1. Allahu Akbar (God is the greatest), (repeated four times);

الله أكبر • الله اكــبر •

الله أكبر • الله اكــبر •

2. Ashhadu An La Illa-L-Lah (I bear witness that there is no god but the One God), (repeated twice);

أشهــد ألا اله الا الله

أشهــد ألا اله الا الله •

3. Ashhadu Anna Muhammadan Rasulu-l-lah (I bear witness that Muhammad is the Messenger of God), (repeated twice);

أشهــد أن محمدا رسول الله •

أشهــد أن محمدا رسول الله •

4. Hayya 'Ala-s-salah (Come fast to prayer), (repeated twice, turning the face to the right);

حي على الصلاة حي على الصلاة •

5. Hayya 'Ala-l-falah (Come fast to success), (repeated twice, turning the face to the left;

حي على الفلاح • حي على الفلاح •

6. Allahu Akbar (God is the Greatest of all), (repeated twice);

الله أكبر • الله أكـــــبر •

7. La Ilaha Illa-l-lah (There is no god but the One and True God), (once).

لا اله الا الله •

When the Call is made for the early morning prayer, the caller adds one sentence right after part (5) above. The sentence required is this:

As-salatu Khayrun Minan-nawm

الصلاة خير من النوم •

(Prayer is better than sleep), (repeated twice). Then the caller continues with parts (6) and (7). This exception is made in the morning only because it is the time when people are asleep and in need for a reminder of prayer.

Entrance Into Prayer (Iqamah)

When this call is uttered, the worshippers get ready for prayer and inaugurate it with an announcement called 'Iqamah'. The sentences here are the same as those of the Adhan above with two differences:
(a) the Iqamah is said in a faster and less audible voice and (b) right after part (5) this sentence should be said twice:

'Qad Qamati-s-salah'

قد قامت الصلاة •

(prayer is ready). Then parts (6) and (7) should follow to the end as usual.

The Performance of Prayer

After the worshipper has done the ablution and after the 'Adhan' and 'Iqamah' are said, the prayer starts as follows:

1. The Early Morning Prayer (salatu-l-Fajr)

In this prayer two units (Rak'ahs) are offered first as supererogatory (Sunnah). These are followed by two other units as obligatory (Fard). Both supererogatory and obligatory units are offered in the same manner except that, when declaring the intention, one has to distinguish between the two kinds. This is the description of performance:

Act 1. One stands in reverence and humility, facing the Qiblah, raising his hands up to the ears, and says: "Nawaytu Osalli Sunnata Salati-l-Fajr or Farda Salati-l-Fajr (As the case may be); Allahu Akbar."

This means: "I declare my intention to offer the supererogatory or obligatory (as the case may be) prayer of the morning; God is the Greatest of all." Then he lowers his arms and places the right hand over the left one right below the navel.[3]

Waquf Position

Act 2. He then says in a low voice the following: "Subhanaka-l-lahumma wa bihamdik, wa tabaraka-smuk, wa ta'ala Jadduk, wa La Ilaha Ghayruk. A'udhu bi-l-lahi mina-sh-shaytani-r-rajeem. Bismi-l-lahi-r-rah-mani-r-raheem".

---

[3]This position of the hands is in accordance with one school of law. Other positions are preferred by other schools. However, these are minor differences and do not affect the validity of the prayer. In fact, all such differences are considered as conveniences and facilities rather than hindrances and restrictions.

سبحانك اللهم وبحمدك ، وتبارك اسمك ، وتعالى جـــدك ،
ولا اله غـــيرك · أعوذ بالله من الشـــيطان الرجـــيم ·
بســـم اللـــه الرحمـــن الرحـــــــيم ·

This means: "Glory be to You, O God, and Yours is the praise, and blessed is Your name, and exalted is Your majesty, and there is no god besides You. I seek the refuge of God from the condemned devil. In the name of God, Most Gracious, Most Merciful."[4]

Act 3. Then in a low or audible voice he recites the Opening Chapter of the Qur'an (al-Fatihah), followed by any passage from the Holy Book. (The Opening and examples of these short chapters and verses will be found later in this section.)

Act 4. Then he says: "Allahu Akbar," (God is the Greatest of all), lowering his head down at a right angle, placing the palms of his hands on the knees and saying in a low voice:

"Subhana Rabbiya-l-'Azeem"   سبحان ربي العظيم ·

Ruku' Position

("Glory to my Lord the Great", repeated three times). This is called Ruku'. After that the standing position is resumed with these words: "Sami' a-l-ahu Liman Hamidah; Rabbana Laka-l-Hamd

سمع الله لمن حمده ، ربنا لك الحمد

---

[4]This part is recommended. It is not absolutely essential for the completion of the prayer.

(God accepts any who are thankful to Him; Our Lord, praise be to You). When saying this the hands remain on the sides.

Act 5. The worshipper then says: Allahu Akbar, prostrating himself with the toes of both feet, both knees, both hands and the forehead touching the ground. This is the position of Sujud and is accompanied with these words:

Subhana Rabbiya-l-A'La

سبحان ربي الأعلى

Sujud Position

(Glory to my Lord the Most High, repeated three times).

Act 6. Then with the utterance of Allahu Akbar comes the Julus, a short rest in a sitting posture: the outer side of the left foot and the toes of the right one, which are in an erect position, touching the ground and the two hands are placed on the knees.

Jalsa position

After this a second prostration (Sujud) is repeated in the same way with the same utterances as in the first one. This completes one unit (Rak'ah) of the prayer.

Act 7. After the first unit the worshipper rises, saying Allahu Akbar, to assume a standing position for the second unit and recites the

Opening (the Fatihah) followed by a Qur'anic passage as in the first unit.

Act 8. When he has finished the second bowing and the two prostrations in the same way as the first, he takes a sitting position as in Julus and recites the Tashahhud with its two parts. (This will be found later in this section.)

Act 9. Finally he turns his face to the right side saying these words: "Assalamu 'Alaykum wa rahmatu-l-Lah (Peace be on you and the mercy of God). Then he turns his face to the left side uttering the same greetings.

This is how any prayer of two units (Rak'ahs), whether obligatory or supererogatory, is performed. When knowing how to perform this prayer in the right way, all other prayers will be found very easy. It should be pointed out that every move or every word in the Islamic prayer has a great significance attached to it and is symbolic of a very deep meaning.

2. The Noon Prayer (Salatu-z-Zuhr)

This consists of four units as Sunnah, followed by four units as Fard, and then two others as Sunnah. The performance of the Fard of this prayer is as follows:

(a) The first two units are performed in the same way as in the morning prayer. The Fatihah and a portion of the Qur'an are recited in a low voice. Bowing and prostration postures are observed in the same way.

(b) When reciting the Tashahhud after the second unit, the worshipper stops at the end of the first part of it to resume the posture of standing.

(c) Then he recites the Fatihah only in the third unit without any added portion of the Qur'an.

(d) When he concludes the third unit, he stands for the fourth and recites the Fatihah only as in the third.

(e) After bowing and prostration he takes the sitting posture of Julus and recites the whole Tashahhud with its two parts.

(f) Then he utters the peace greetings right and left.

(g) Offering the two Sunnah units is like the morning prayer but in a low voice.

3. The Mid-Afternoon Prayer (Salatu-I-'Asr)

It consists of four units as Sunnah followed by four others as Fard. These are performed in the same way as the noon prayer and in a low voice.

4. The Sunset Prayer (Salatu-I-Maghrib)

It consists of three units as Fard followed by two as Sunnah. It may be said in the first two units with a low or audible voice; the third unit is in a low voice. It is performed in the same way as the noon or mid-afternoon prayer except that the fourth unit is excluded and the final sitting here, following recital of the Fatihah, bowing, and prostrations, comes after the third unit, which ends with the utterances of peace greetings. The two Sunnah units are offered in the same way as the Early Morning Prayer.

5. The Evening Prayer (Salatu-I-'Isha')

It consists of four units as Fard, two as Sunnah and three as Witr[5] (higher than Sunnah and lower than Fard). The first two units of the four Fard may be said in a low or audible voice. Other than that, it is performed the same way as the noon or mid-afternoon prayer. The two Sunnah units are performed exactly like the early morning prayer.

As for the three Witr units, they are performed just like the sunset prayer with two exceptions: (a) in the third unit the Fatihah is followed by a portion of the Qur'an, and (b) while standing after bowing and before prostration the worshipper says these words:

اللهم انا نستعينك ونستهديك ، ونستغفرك ونتوب اليك ، ونؤمن
بك ونتوكل عليك ، ونثني عليك الخير كله · نشــكرك ولا نكفرك ،
ونخلع ونترك من يفجرك · اللهم اياك نعبد ، ولك نصلـــــي
ونسجد ، واليك نسعى ونحفد · نرجو رحمتك ، ونخشى عذابك ·
ان عذابك بالكفار ملحق · وصل اللهم على سيدنا محمد وعلى آله
وصحبه وسلم

---

[5]There are minor differences of interpretation between the various schools of law. Some require no witr; others require it in the Early Morning prayer with slight variations. However, following any of the authentic schools is acceptable.

"Allahumma inna nasta'eenuk, wa nastahdeek, wa nastaghifiruk, wa natubu ilayk, wa nu'minu bik, wa natawakkalu 'alayk, wa nuthni 'alayka-l-Khayra kullah. Nashkurk, wa la nakfruk, wa nakhla'u wa natruku man yafjuruk. Allahumma iyyaka na'bud, wa laka nusalli wa nasjud, wa ilayka nas'a wa nahfid. Narju rahmatak, wa nakhsha 'adhabak; inna 'adhabaka bi-l-Kuffari mulhaq wa salli-l-llahumma 'ala sayyidina Muhammad wa 'ala alihi wa sahbihi wa sallim."

This is called Qunut and may be interpreted as follows:

"O God! We beseech You for help and guidance, and seek Your protection and believe in You and rely on You, and extol You and are thankful to You and are not ingrate to You, and we declare ourselves clear of, and forsake, him who disobeys You.

"O God! To You do we pray and prostrate ourselves, and to You do we betake ourselves, and to obey You we are quick, and Your mercy do we hope for and Your punishment do we fear, for Your punishment overtakes the unbelievers.

"O God! Exalt our Master Muhammad and his people and his true followers."

If this Qunut cannot be commanded by memory, it is sufficient to say any recitation similar to it till it is mastered. All the Sunnah (supererogatory) prayers are to be said individually, that is, not in congregation except the 'Eed prayers, and the Witr in the month of Ramadan.

The Sunnah Prayers are not required from a person who has missed some Fard Prayers. Instead, he must make up for what he has missed and offer the obligatory services. Also the Sunnah Prayers are not required, if the due time of the accompanying Fard Prayers has expired. So, if a person misses any prayer and wants to make up for it, he has to offer the Fard only.

If a worshipper does not know how to say his whole prayers in the Arabic version, he may use any other language he knows if it can express the same meaning of the Arabic. To make the Arabic version easy we are giving the words in transliteration.

The Fard Prayer is much more preferable when offered in a congregation (Jama'ah) led by an Imam. The congregation is best when it is held in a mosque, but it may be held in other places.

The Congregation (Jama'ah) Prayers

1. The congregation is led by an Imam from among the present worshippers. He must be chosen on his merits of religious knowledge and piety.

2. The Imam of the congregation stands in the front by himself while the followers stand behind him in straight lines, all facing the Qiblah. A congregation can be made up of even two persons: the Imam and one follower.

3. After declaring the intention of prayer the Imam recites the Fatihah and the complementary passage of the Qur'an in an audible voice in the Early Morning Prayer and in the first two units of the Sunset Prayers. When the Imam is reciting the Qur'an aloud, the followers listen to him in meditation and humility. They do not recite the Fatihah nor the other passage after the Imam.

4. When the Imam concludes the Fatihah the followers say 'Ameen'. After the Imam stands from the bowing posture he says: "Sami'a-l-lahu liman Hamidah" (God accepts any who are thankful to Him), and the followers respond in these words: "Rabbana laka-l-Hamd" (our Lord praise be to You).

5. The followers should follow the Imam in his movements without anticipating him in any act. Should any follower supercede the Imam in any movement, this person's prayer will become void.

6. The congregational prayer is not valid unless the Imam declares his intention that he is acting in the service in the capacity of Imam. The followers also must declare their intention that they are following that particular Imam in the same particular prayer he is offering.

7. If a person comes after the start of prayer and joins the congregation, he must, even if he has missed one unit or more, follow the Imam. When the Imam completes the service by uttering the final peace greetings, this late comer does not join in that, but takes a standing position to make up for the early units he has missed. When a person joins the congregation in the bowing position, before rising, he is considered as having joined from the start of this particular unit. But if he joins in any position after bowing, he has missed the unit and must make up for it individually right after the Imam concludes the prayer.

8. Whenever there is an opportunity for praying in a congregation, a Muslim should not miss it. Prayer in congregation is a handsome demonstration of unity in purpose and action, of plural piety and humility before God, of effective solidarity among Muslims, of public order and mutual response.

The Islamic congregation is a positive answer to the acutest probiems of humanity rising from racial discrimination, social castes and human prejudices. In the congregational service of Islam there is no king or subject, rich or poor, white or colored, first or second class, back or front benches, reserved or public pews. All worshippers stand and act shoulder to shoulder in the most disciplinary manner regardless of any worldly considerations.

6. The Friday Prayer (Salatu-l-Jumu'ah)

So far we have been dealing with the daily prayers. Now we come to the weekly convention of Friday Congregation. This service is compulsory upon every Muslim who is required to observe the other prayers and has no reasonable excuses to abstain. It falls on Friday of every week and is especially important because:—

1.   It is the occasion earmarked by God for the Muslims to express their collective devotion.

2.   It is an appointment to review our spiritual accounts of the week gone by and get ready for the following week just as people do in any other business.

3.   It is a convention for the Muslims to reassure themselves and confirm their religious bonds and social solidarity on moral and spiritual foundations.

4.   It shows how the Muslims give preference to the call of God over and above any other concern.

The Highlights of the Prayer

This prayer of Friday is marked by these features:—

1.   Its time falls in the same time as that of the noon prayer (Salatu-z-Zuhr), and it replaces the very same prayer.

2.   It must be said in a congregation led by an Imam. No single person can offer it by himself.

3.   If any person misses it, he cannot make up for it. Instead, he has to offer the noon prayer, the original prayer which this service normally replaces.

4.   All kinds of normal work are allowed on Friday as on any other week day. For Muslims there is no Sabbath. They can carry on with their usual duties and activities provided they come to the congregational service in time. After the service is over, they may resume their mundane activities.

5.   This Friday prayer must be performed in a mosque, if there is one available. Otherwise, it may be said at any gathering place, e.g. homes, farms, parks, etc.

6.   When the time for prayer comes, the Adhan is said. Then, four units of prayer are offered as Sunnah, individually. in a low voice as

in the noon prayer. When this part is completed, the Imam stands up facing the audience and delivers his sermon (khutbah) which is an essential part of the service. While the Imam is talking nobody should talk or pray; everyone present should take a sitting position and listen to the sermon quietly to the end.

7. The sermon (khutbah) consists of two parts each beginning with words of praise of God and prayers of blessing for Prophet Muhammad. In the first part some Qur'anic passage must be recited and explained for the purpose of exhortation and admonition. At the end of the first part the Imam takes a short rest in the sitting posture, then stands up to deliver the second part of his sermon. General affairs of the Muslims may be discussed in either or both parts of the sermon. In the second part, especially, the Imam prays for the general welfare of all Muslims.

8. After that the Iqamah is made and the two obligatory units are offered under the leadership of the Imam who recites the Fatihah and the other Qur'anic passage in an audible voice. When this is done, the prayer is completed. After that two other Sunnah units are offered individually in a low voice.

The earlier four and the late two Sunnah units may be offered at home. Also they may be replaced with some obligatory prayers that one has missed in the past and for which one has to make up.

Any participant in the weekly congregation or the 'Eed Prayers should do his best to be neat and tidy. Though there is no compulsory reason for a complete ablution, a bath is strongly recommended as it makes one fresher and more pleasant.

The Significance of 'Eed Prayers

'Eed means recurring happiness or festivity. The 'Eed Prayer is very important for all Muslims. It has the merits of the daily prayers as explained above, the effects of the weekly convention (Jumu'ah) and the characteristics of annual reunions between Muslims. There are two such 'Eeds. The first is called 'Eedu-l-Fitr (the Festival of Fast-Breaking). It falls on the first day of Shawwal, the tenth month of the Muslim year, following the month of Ramadan in which the Qur'an was revealed and which is the month of Fasting. The second is called 'Eedu-l-Adha (the Festival of Sacrifice). It falls on the tenth day of Dhu-l-Hijjah, the last month of the Muslim year, following completion of the course of Hajj (pilgrimage to Mecca), an extremely devotional course.

The Islamic 'Eeds are unique in every way. To them there can be no similar in any other religion or any other sociopolitical system.

Besides their highly spiritual and moral characteristics, they have matchless qualities:

1. Each 'Eed is a wholesome celebration of a remarkable achievement of the individual Muslim in the service of God. The First 'Eed comes after an entire month of "absolute" fasting during the days of the month. The second 'Eed marks the completion of Hajj to Mecca, a course in which the Muslim handsomely demonstrates his renouncement of the mundane concerns and hearkens only to the Eternal voice of God.

2. Each 'Eed is a Thanksgiving Day where the Muslims assemble in a brotherly and joyful atmosphere to offer their gratitude to God for helping them to fulfill their spiritual obligations prior to the 'Eed. This form of thanksgiving is not confined to spiritual devotion and verbal expressions. It goes far beyond that to manifest itself in a handsome shape of social and humanitarian spirit. The Muslims who have completed the fasting of Ramadan express their thanks to God by means of distributing alms among the poor and needy on the First 'Eed. Similarly, the Muslims who have completed the course of Hajj at Mecca, as well as those who are at home, offer their sacrifices by slaughtering oblations to be distributed among the poor and needy. The distribution of alms and oblations constitutes a major part of the 'Eed's highlights. This Islamic form of thanksgiving is a wholesome combination of spiritual devotion and humanitarian benevolence, a combination which cannot be found except in Islam.

3. Each 'Eed is a Day of Remembrance. Even in their most joyful times the Muslims make a fresh start of the Day by a plural session of worship to God. They pray to Him and glorify His name to demonstrate their remembrance of His favors. Along with that course, they remember the deceased by prayer for their souls, the needy by extending a hand of help, the grieved by showing them sympathy and consolation, the sick by cheerful visits and utterances of good wishes, the absentees by cordial greetings and sincere considerateness, etc. Thus the meaning of Remembrance on the Day transcends all limits and expands over far-reaching dimensions of human life.

4. Each 'Eed is a Day of Victory. The individual who succeeds in securing his spiritual rights and growth receives the 'Eed with a victorious spirit. The individual who faithfully observes the duties, which are associated with the 'Eed, is a triumphant one. He proves that he holds a strong command over his desires, exercises a sound self-control and enjoys the taste of disciplinary life. And once a person acquires these qualities he has achieved his greatest victory; because the person who knows how to control himself and discipline

his desires is free from sin and wrong, from fear and cowardice, from vice and indecency, from jealousy and greed, from humiliation and all other causes of enslavement. So, when he receives the 'Eed, which marks the achievement of this freedom, he is in fact celebrating his victory, and the 'Eed thus becomes a Day of Victory.

5. Each 'Eed is a Harvest Day. All the good workers in the service of God, all the faithful believers reap the fruits of their good deeds on the Day, as God grants His mercy and blessings abundantly. The Islamic society, on the other hand, collects the due subscriptions to religious brotherhood and social responsibility, in which subscriptions are paid in the form of mutual love, sympathy and concern. Every member of the Islamic society will be reaping some fruits or collecting some revenue in one way or another. God gives infinitely, especially to those who are sincerely concerned with the general welfare of their fellow believers. Those beneficiaries who cannot give will receive, along with God's enormous grants, the contributions of their fellow benefactors. The haves and have-nots will all enjoy the providence of God in a most plural fashion, and the Day will indeed be a Good Harvest Day.

6. Each 'Eed is a Day of Forgiveness. When the Muslims assemble in the congregation of the Day, they all whole-heartedly pray for forgiveness and strength of Faith. And God has assured those who approach Him with sincerity of His mercy and forgiveness. In that pure assembly and highly spiritual congregation any true Muslim would feel ashamed of himself before God to hold any enmity or ill feelings toward his brethren. A true Muslim would be deeply impressed by this brotherly and spiritual assembly, and would overcome his ill feelings if he has been exposed to any. Consequently, he would find himself moving along with others responding to the spirit of the Day to purify his heart and soul. In this case, he would forgive those who might have wronged him; because he himself would be praying for God's forgiveness, and would do his best to acquire it. The spirit of this highly devotional assembly would teach him that if he forgives he will be forgiven. And when he forgives, the virtue of forgiveness will be mercifully exercised by God, and widely exchanged between the Muslims. And that marks the Day as a Day of Forgiveness.

7. Each 'Eed is a Day of Peace. When the Muslim establishes peace within his heart by obeying the Law of God and leading a disciplinary life, he has certainly concluded a most inviolable treaty of peace with God. Once a person is at peace with God, he is at peace with himself and, consequently, with the rest of the universe. So when he celebrates the 'Eed in the right manner, he is actually cele-

brating the conclusion of a Peace Treaty between himself and God, and this marks the 'Eed as a Day of Peace.

That is the proper meaning of an Islamic 'Eed: a Day of Peace and Thanksgiving, a Day of Forgiveness and moral victory, a Day of Good Harvest and remarkable Achievements, and a Day of Festive Remembrance. An Islamic 'Eed is all this and is much more; because it is a Day of ISLAM, a Day of God.

The Performance of 'Eed Prayers (Salatu-l-'Eed)

1. As on Friday, every worshipper should go to the 'Eed Congregation in his best, neat, tidy and high-spirited. In the mosque or the place of assembly a certain verbal prayer is said before the actual prayer begins. This is known as Takbeer and will be found at the end of this section.

2. The time of the 'Eed prayers is any time after sunrise and before noon. No Adhan or Iqamah is required. The prayer consists of two units with the Imam reciting in each the Fatihah and another passage from the Qur'an audibly.

3. The Imam declares his intention to lead the prayer saying Allahu Akbar (God is the Greatest of all). Then he repeats the same utterance three times, raising his hands up to the ears and dropping them by his sides at the end of each utterance. On completion of the third Takbeer (utterance) he places the right hand over the left one under the navel as in other prayers. The worshippers follow the Imam in these movements step by step, doing and saying exactly the same.

4. At the end of the first unit, the Imam rises up for the second, saying Allahu Akbar. Then he adds three such utterances doing the same thing as he did in the first unit, and followed by the congregation in a like manner.

5. After the prayer is completed in two units, the Imam delivers a sermon of two parts with a short recess in between. The first part is begun by saying Allahu Akbar, nine times, and the second by making the same utterance seven times. The rest of the sermon goes along the lines of exhortation and advice like those of the Friday sermon.

6. In the sermon of the First 'Eed of the year, the Imam must draw the attention to the matter of Sadaqatu-l-Fitr (the Charity of Breaking the Fast). This is an obligatory tax, whereby every individual Muslim who can afford it must give at least one full meal, or its value, to the poor. If he has any dependents, he must do the same

thing for each one of his dependents. For example, if he provides for himself and three dependents, he has to distribute as a minimum four full meals or their value to the needy. This charity is far more rewarding and preferable if it is distributed early enough before the prayers so that the poor may be able to receive the Day in a festive and cheerful spirit.

7.   In the sermon of the Second 'Eed, the Imam should draw the attention to the duty of Sacrifice.   On the day of 'Eedu-l-Adha (Festival of Sacrifice) every Muslim with means is to offer an oblation.   A goat or sheep suffices for one household.   A cow or steer suffices for seven different households.   It is preferable to slaughter the animal of Sacrifice on the 'Eed Day after prayers. But if it is slaughtered on the second or the third day, it will be accepted.   With regard to the meats of the slaughtered animals the Holy Qur'an stipulates these instructions: Eat of them and feed the poor man who is contented and the beggar...(22:36).

In the same reference, the Holy Qur'an declares that God is neither interested in nor does He get the meats of the oblations or their blood; but it is the piety of His worshippers that He gets and is interested in.

It should be repeated that the 'Eed prayers do not substitute for the obligatory Early Morning (Fajr) Prayers, and cannot themselves be substituted for by any other prayers.

The Takbeer, which is said before the Prayers of both 'Eeds and after the ordinary congregations offered during the three days following the Second 'Eed, is called Takbeeru-t-Tashreeq. It goes as follows:

Allahu Akbar, (thrice). La ilaha illa-L-Lah.	الله أكبر ، الله أكبر ، الله أكبر .
Allahu Akbar (twice) wa lil-Lahi-l-hamd.	لا اله الا الله . الله أكبر .
Allahu Akbaru Kabeera.	الله أكبر ولله الحمد .
Wa-l-hamdu li-l-Lahi Katheera. Wa subhana-l-Lahi bukratan wa aseela.	الله أكبر كبيرا . والحمد لله كثيرا . وسبحان الله بكرة وأصيلا .
La ilaha illa-l-Lahu wahdah. Sadaqa wa 'adah, wa nasara 'abdah.	لا اله الا الله وحده ، صدق ، وعده .
Wa a'azza jundahu wa hazama-l-ahzaba wahdah.	ونصر عبده ، وأعز جنده . وهزم الأحزاب وحده .
La-ilaha illa-l-Lahu wa la na'bdu illa Iyyah, mukhliseena laHud-deena wa law kariha-l-kafirun.	لا اله الا الله ولا نعبد الا اياه . مخلصين له الدين ولوكره الكافرون .

76

Allahumma salli 'ala Sayyidina Muhammad, اللهم صل على سيدنا محمد ،

Wa 'ala ali Sayyidina Muhammad, وعلى آل سيدنا محمد ،

Wa 'ala Ashabi Sayyidina Muhammad, وعلى أصحاب سيدنا محمد ،

Wa 'ala ansari Sayyidina Muhammad, وعلى أنصار سيدنا محمد ،

Wa 'ala azwaji Sayyidina Muhammad, وعلى أزواج سيدنا محمد ،

Wa 'ala dhurriyyati Sayyidina Muhammad, وعلى ذرية سيدنا محمد ،

Wa sallim tasleeman katheera. وسلم تسليما كثيرا ،

This Takbeer means:

God is the Greatest (three times).
There is no god but the One True God.
God is the Greatest (twice) and His is the praise.
Surely God is the Greatest.
His is the abundant praise.
Glory to Him, day and night.
There is no god but God, the One True God.
He fulfilled His promise, supported His servant (Muhammad),
granted His soldiers a manifest victory, and inflicted de-
cisive defeat on the allied enemies. There is no god but God,
and we worship none but Him, with sincere devotion, even
though the disbelievers may resent it.
O God! Exalt and have blessings on our Master Muhammad,
And on the people of our Master Muhammad,
And on the companions of our Master Muhammad,
And on the supporters of our Master Muhammad,
And on the wives of our Master Muhammad,
And on the descendants of our Master Muhammad,
And salute all of them with much peace.

Shortening of the Prayer

1. When a person is travelling with the intention of proceeding
forty-eight miles or over from his home, he should shorten the obligatory prayers of four units to two each. The curtailment is applicable to the Noon (Zuhr) Prayer, the Mid-Afternoon (Asr) Prayer,
and the Evening ('Isha') Prayer. The Early Morning (Fajr) and the
Sunset (Maghrib) Prayers remain unchanged.

2.   This advantage remains effective even after the traveller arrives at his destination, if he does not intend to prolong his stay there for fifteen days or more.   Otherwise, he should offer the reducible prayers in their original and complete number of units.

3.   While traveling under these circumstances, he is exempt from all supererogatory prayers (Sunnah) except the two Sunnah units of the Early Morning (Fijr) and the Witr which follows the Evening ('Isha') prayers.

Times When Prayer is Forbidden

The Muslim is forbidden to offer either obligatory or super-erogatory prayers at:

1.   The time when the sun is rising;
2.   The time when the sun is at its Zenith;
3.   The time when the sun is setting;
4.   The period of menstruation or confinement due to childbirth and nursing;
5.   The time of impurity, partial or complete.

Making Up For Delayed Prayers

1.   As a rule, every Muslim, male or female, should offer the prayer in its due time. Failing to do so is a punishable sin unless there is a reasonable excuse for delay.

2.   With the exception of women in confinement or menstruation and any who remain insane or unconscious for some time, every Muslim must make up for his or her delayed obligatory prayers.

3.   When making up for the delayed prayers one must offer them in their original form, e.g., if they were due shortened they should be offered so and vice-versa.

4.   Order between the delayed prayers and between these and the present ones should be maintained, i.e., the first in dueness is offered first unless the missed prayers are too many to remember their exact dates, or the time available is not sufficient for both missed and present prayers. In this case, the present prayer comes first and the missed ones may be offered later. At any rate, the Muslim must make certain that his record is clear to the best of his knowledge, and that there are no missed prayers.

The Taraweeh Prayers

These prayers are a special characteristic of the month of Ramadan. They follow the Evening ('Isha') Prayers. They consist of eight to twenty units (Rak'ahs) offered two by two with a short break between each two units. It is much more preferable to say them in a congregational form and before the Witr, which is the last part of the Evening Prayer.

Invalidation of Prayers

Any prayer becomes invalid and nullified by any act of the following:

1. To anticipate the Imam in any act or movement of prayer;
2. To eat or drink during the prayer;
3. To talk or say something out of the prescribed course of prayers;
4. To shift the position from the direction of Mecca;
5. To do any noticeable act or move outside the acts and movements of prayer;
6. To do anything that nullifies the ablution, e.g., discharge of urine, stool, gas, blood, etc.;
7. To fail in observing any of the essential acts of prayer, like standing, reciting the Qur'an, Ruku', Sujud, etc.;
8. To uncover the body between the navel and the knees during the prayer in the case of males, or any part of the body, except the hands, face and feet, in the case of females.

Any prayer which becomes invalidated must be repeated properly.

The Funeral Prayers (Salatu-l-Janazah)

1. The prayer to God for the deceased Muslim is a common collective duty (Fard Kifayah). This means that some Muslims should offer this prayer, and when it is offered by some of the Muslims present at the time it is sufficient, and the other Muslims become exempt from responsibility.

2. When a Muslim dies, the whole body—beginning with the exposed parts of ablution (wudu')—must be washed a few times with soap or some other detergent or disinfectant, and cleansed of all visible impurities. When the body is thoroughly clean, it is wrapped in one or more white cotton sheets covering all the parts of the body.

3. The dead body is then placed on a bier or in a coffin and carried

to the place of prayer, a mosque or any other clean premises. The body is put in a position with the face toward the direction of Mecca.

4.   All participants in the prayer must perform an ablution unless they are keeping an earlier one. The Imam stands beside the body facing the Qiblah at Mecca with the followers behind him in lines.

5.   The Imam raises his hands to the ears declaring the intention in a low voice to pray to God for that particular deceased one, and saying Allahu Akbar (God is the Greatest). The worshippers follow the Imam's lead and after him place their right hands over the left ones under the navel as in other prayers.

6.   Then the Imam recites in a low voice what is usually recited in other prayers, i.e., the 'Thana' and the Fatihah only.

7.   At this stage he says Allahu Akbar without raising his hands and recites the second part of the Tashahhud (from " 'Allahumma salli 'ala Sayyidina Muhammad" to the end).

8.   Then he makes the third Takbeer saying Allahu Akbar without raising the hands and offers his supplication (Du 'a') in any suitable words he knows, preferably these:

اللهم اغفر لحينا وميتنا ، وشاهدنا وغائبنا ، وذكرنا وانثانا ، وصغيرنا وكبيرنا · اللهم من أحييته منا فأحيه على الاسلام ، ومن توفيته منا فتوفه على الاسلام · اللهم لا تحرمنا أجره ، ولا تفتنا بعده ·

Allahumma-ghfir li hayyina wa mayyitina, wa shahidina wa gha'ibina' wa sagheerina wa kabeerina wa dhakarina wa unthana. Allahumma man ahyaytahu minna fa ahyihi 'ala-l-Islam. Wa man tawaffaythu minna fa tawafahu 'ala-l-Islam. Allahumma la tahrimna ajrah, wa la taftinna ba'dah.

"O God! grant forgiveness to our living and to our dead, and to those who are present and to those who are absent, and to our young and our old folk, and to our males and our females.

"O God, whomsoever You grant to live, from among us, help him to live in Islam, and whomsoever of us You cause to die, help him to die in Faith."

"O God! do not deprive us of the reward for patience on his loss, and do not make us subject to trial after him."

9. Then the fourth Takbeer (saying Allahu Akbar) without raising the hands is made followed by the concluding peace greetings right and left as in other prayers. It should be remembered that the worshippers behind in lines follow the lead of the Imam step by step and recite privately the same utterances in a Low Voice.

10. After completing the prayer, the body is lowered for burial with the face resting in the direction of Mecca. When lowering the body down, these words are said:

بسم الله ، وبالله ، وعلى ملة رسول الله صلى الله عليه وسلم

"Bismi-l-Lahi wa bi-l-Lahi wa 'ala Millati Rasuli-l-Lahi Salla-l-Lahu 'Alayhi wa Sallam."

"In the name of God and with God, and according to the Sunnah (Traditions) of the Messenger of God upon whom be the blessings and peace of God."

Besides these, any other fit prayers may be offered.

If the deceased is a child under the age of puberty, the prayer is the same except that after the third Takbeer and instead of that long supplication the worshippers recite these words:

اللهم اجعله لنا فرطا ، واجعله لنا ذخرا ، واجعله لنا شافعا ومشفعا

"Allahumma-j'alhu lana faratan wa j'alhu lana dhukhra, wa j'alhu lana shafi'an wa mushaffa'a."

"O God! make him (or her) our fore-runner, and make him for us a reward and a treasure, and make him for us a pleader, and accept his pleading."

The whole funeral prayer is offered in the standing position.
Whenever a funeral procession passes by, be it of a Muslim or otherwise, every Muslim should stand out of respect for the dead.
A man washes a man and a woman washes a woman. A woman may wash her husband, and a man or woman may wash young children. During the washing the washer's hands should be covered by gloves or cloth, and the private parts of the dead body should be washed without being seen.
The grave should be built and marked in a simple way. The dead body should be covered with white cotton sheets of standard material. Any extravagance in building the grave or dressing up the body in fine suits or the like is non-Islamic. It is false vanity and a waste of assets that can be used in many useful ways.

The custom of some North American Muslims of offering a big and costly banquet upon burial of the deceased is also non-Islamic and an irresponsible waste of money and effort that can be of infinite benefit if used otherwise.

General Remarks on Prayers

As already pointed out, the Muslim's mind should always be occupied with the rememberance of God and his tongue be busied with utterances of praise and glory of Him. Besides the above-mentioned forms of prayer, there are many other occasions where prayer is strongly recommended by Prophet Muhammad. Such occasions are like these:

1. The time of excessive rain;
2. The time of drought and shortage of rain;
3. The time of the sun's eclipse.

In times like these the Muslim is advised to pray as many units and as long as he wishes.

There are other times where he utters certain expressions without resorting to the prescribed forms of ordinary prayers. In such utterances he expresses gratitude to God and appreciation of His favors, hope in Him and reliance upon His aid, remembrance of Him and prayer for His mercy. Among these times are:

1. The time of childbirth;
2. The time of performing marriage;
3. The time when going to and rising from bed;
4. The time of leaving the house and returning to it;
5. The time of entering and leaving the toilet;
6. The time of starting a journey or entering a city;
7. The time of riding or driving;
8. The time of entering a boat;
9. The time of distress;
10. Before a looking glass or facing a mirror;
11. After bath or ablution;
12. When receiving the first fruits of the harvest;
13. When visiting the graveyard.

On each of these occasions the Muslim is advised to remember God with proper and fitting utterances expressing his feelings and thoughtfulness.

There are given prayers for these occasions, but one can use whatever one knows as long as it is in praise of God and remembrance of Him. Here we give some specific examples to be used as a suitable pattern:

1.   Before meals or drinks one says:

بسم الله ، وعلى بركة الله .

"Bismi-l-Lahi wa'ala barakati-l-Lah."

"In the name of God and with blessings from God."

It is also good practice to recite the Fatihah before meals.

2.   When finishing meals one says:

الحمد لله الذى أطعمنا وسقانا وجعلنا مسلمين

"Al-Hamdu Lil-Lahi-l-Ladhi At'amana, wasaqana, wa Ja'alana Muslimeen."

"All praise is due to God Who has given us to eat and to drink, and Who has made us Muslims."

3.   When visiting the sick, one says:

أذهب البأس رب الناس ، واشف أنت الشافي ،

لا شفاء الا شفاوءك لا يغـــــادر ســـقما .

"Adhhibi-l-ba'sa Rabba-n-nas, wa-shfi Anta-Sh-shafi; la shifa a' lla shifa-'uk-shifa'an la yughadiru saqama."

"Take away the sickness, O Lord of all people! and restore to health, You are the Healer; there is no healing but the healing You give; grant recovery which leaves no ailment behind."

* * * *

Now it is time to deal with the Fatihah, the Tashahhud and some short passages from the Qur'an.

1. The Fatihah (The Opening or Al-Hamd)

Bismi-l-Iahir-Rahmani-r-Raheem.
Al-Hamdu li-l-lahi Rabbi-l-ala-
    meen;
Ar-Rahmani-r-Raheem;
Maliki yawmi-d-Deen.
Iyyaka na'budu wa Iyyak nasta'-
    een.
Ihdina-s-Sirata-l-Mustaqeem;
Sirata-l-ladheena an'amta 'alayhim,
    ghayri-l-maghdubi 'alayhim wa
    la-d-dalleen. (Ameen)

بِسْمِ اللهِ الرَّحْمٰنِ الرَّحِيمِ
الْحَمْدُ لِلّهِ رَبِّ الْعَالَمِينَ ● الرَّحْمٰنِ الرَّحِيمِ ●
مَالِكِ يَوْمِ الدِّينِ ● إِيَّاكَ نَعْبُدُ وَإِيَّاكَ نَسْتَعِينُ ●
اهْدِنَا الصِّرَاطَ الْمُسْتَقِيمَ ● صِرَاطَ الَّذِينَ أَنْعَمْتَ
عَلَيْهِمْ غَيْرِ الْمَغْضُوبِ عَلَيْهِمْ وَلَا الضَّالِّينَ ●

This may be interpreted as follows:
    In the name of God, Most Gracious, Most Merciful.
    Praise be to God, the Cherisher and Sustainer of the worlds,
    Most Gracious, Most Merciful,
    Master of the Day of Judgement.
    Only Thee do we worship; and Thine aid we seek.
    Show us the Straight Way,
    The way of those on whom Thou hast bestowed Thy Grace,
    Those whose portion is not wrath and who go not astray.
        Amen.

2. The Tashahud
(a)   The first part

At-tahiyyato-li-l-lah wa-s-salawato
    wa-t-tayyibat.

As-salamu 'alayka ayyuha-n-nabiy
    wa rahmatu-l-lahi wa barakatuh.

As-salamu 'alayna wa 'ala 'ibadi-
    -l-lahi-s-saliheen.

Ashhadu an la ilaha illa-l-lah wah-
    dahu la shareeka lah wa ashha-
    du anna Muhammadan 'abduhu
    wa rasuloh.

التحيات لله والصلوات والطيبات ●
السلام عليك أيها النبى ورحمة اللـه
وبركاته ● السلام علينا وعلى عبـــاد
الله الصالحين ● أشهد ألا اله الا
الله وحده لا شريك له ٬ وأشهـد أن
محمـدا عبــده ورســوله ●

Interpretation
    All reverence, all worship, all sanctity are due to God.

84

Peace be upon you, O Prophet, and the mercy of God and
His blessings.

Peace be upon us all and on the righteous servants of God.

I bear witness that there is no god but God alone, and I
bear witness that Muhammad is His servant and His
Messenger.

(This part is recited after the second unit in every prayer con-
sisting of three or four units, and then the worshipper stands up for
the third unit.)

(b) The second part

Allahumma salli 'ala sayyidina
Muhammad wa 'ala ali sayyiddina
Muhammad, Kama sallayta 'ala
sayyidina Ibraheem wa 'ala ali
sayyidina Ibraheem.

Wa barik 'ala sayyidina Muhammad wa 'ala ali sayyidina Muhammad, Kama barakta 'ala
sayyidina Ibraheem wa 'ala ali
sayyidina Ibraheem, fil-'ala-
meena innaka hameedun ma-
jeed.

اللهم صل على سيدنا محمد ، وعلى آل
سيدنا محمد ، كما صليت على سيدنـا
ابراهيم وعلى آل سيدنا ابراهيم ٠ وبارك
على سيدنا محمد وعلى آل سيدنا محمد ،
كما باركت على سيدنا ابراهيم ، وعلى آل
سيدنا ابراهيم فى العالمين انك حميـــد
مجـيـد ٠

Interpretation

O God! Exalt our Master Muhammad and the people of
our Master Muhammad, as Thou didst exalt our Master Abraham and the people of our Master Abraham.

And bless our Master Muhammad and the people of our
Master Muhammad, as Thou didst bless our Master Abraham and the people of our Master Abraham, verily Thou
art praiseworthy, and glorious.

(The two parts of the Tashahhud are recited in the last unit
concluding any prayer, With the end of the second part followed by
the peace greetings, the prayer is completed. The second part alone
is recited in the funeral prayer after the third Takbeer.)

3. Short Passages of the Qur'an

(a)
Bismi-l-lahi-r-Rahmani-r-Raheem.
Qul huwa-l-lahu Ahad

بسم الله الرحمن الرحيم
قل هو الله أحد ٠ الله الصمد ٠

Al-lahu-s-Samad.
Lam yalid wa lam yulad.
Wa lam yakun lahu kufwan ahad.

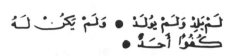

Interpretation

In the name of God, Most Gracious, Most Merciful.

Say: 'He is God, the One and Only
God, the eternally besought of all.
He gives no birth, nor is He born.
And there is none like unto Him' (Qur'an, 112).

(b)

Bismi-l-lahi-r-Rahmani-r-Raheem.
Wa-l-'asr.
Inna-l-insana lafee khusr
Illa-l-ladheena amanu wa 'amilu-s-
salihat wa tawasaw bi-l-haq wa
tawasaw bi-s-sabr.

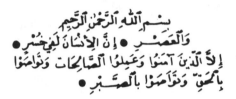

Interpretation

In the name of God, Most Gracious, Most Merciful
By (the token of) time (through ages)
Verily man is in loss
Except those who have Faith, and do righteous deeds, and
join together in the mutual teaching of truth and of
constant patience (Qur'an, 103).

One of such short passages is recited after the Fatihah in each of the first two units. In the third and fourth units no recitation other than the Fatihah is required.

There are many short and easy passages in the Qur'an. Every Muslim must make some efforts to learn by heart as many passages as he can. Also he must read and study the instructions of the Qur'an. Reading the Qur'an is in itself a high form of worship and a fruitful session of devotion.

The Fasting (Sawm)

Another unique moral and spiritual characteristic of Islam is the prescribed institution of Fasting. Literally defined, fasting means to abstain "completely" from foods, drinks, intimate intercourses and smoking, before the break of the dawn till sunset, during the entire month of Ramadan, the ninth month of the Islamic year. But if we restrict the meaning of the Islamic Fasting to this literal sense, we would be sadly mistaken.

When Islam introduced this matchless institution, it planted an evergrowing tree of infinite virtue and invaluable products. Here is an explanation of the spiritual meaning of the Islamic Fasting:

1.   It teaches man the principle of sincere Love; because when he observes the Fasting he does it out of deep love for God. And the man who loves God truly is a man who really knows what love is.

2.   It equips man with a creative sense of Hope and an optimistic outlook on life; because when he fasts he is hoping to please God and is seeking His Grace.

3.   It imbues man with a genuine virtue of effective Devotion, honest Dedication and closeness to God; because when he fasts he does so for God and for His sake alone.

4.   It cultivates in man a vigilant and sound Conscience; because the fasting person keeps his Fast in secret as well as in public. In Fasting, especially, there is no mundane authority to check man's behavior or compel him to observe the Fasting. He keeps it to please God and satisfy his own conscience by being faithful in secret and in public. There is no better way to cultivate a sound conscience in man.

5.   It indoctrinates man in Patience and Unselfishness; because when he fasts he feels the pains of deprivation but endures patiently. Truly this deprivation may be only temporary, yet there is no doubt that the experience makes him realize the severe effects of such pains on others, who might be deprived of essential commodities for days or weeks or probably months together. The meaning of this experience in a social and humanitarian sense is that such a person is much quicker than anybody else in sympathizing with his fellow men and responding to their needs. And that is an eloquent expression of unselfishness and genuine sympathy.

6.   It is an effective lesson in applied Moderation and Willpower. The person who observes his Fasting properly is certainly a man who can discipline his passionate desires and place his self above physical

temptations. Such is the man of personality and character, the man of willpower and determination.

7.   It provides man with a Transparent Soul to transcend, a Clear Mind to think and a Light Body to move and act. All this is the never-failing result of carrying a light stomach. Medical instructions, biological rules and intellectual experience attest to this fact.

8.   It shows man a new way of Wise Savings and Sound Budgeting; because normally when he eats less quantities or less meals he spends less money and effort. And this is a spiritual semester of home economics and budgeting.

9.   It enables man to master the art of Mature Adaptability. We can easily understand the point once we realize that Fasting makes man change the entire course of his daily life. When he makes the change, he naturally adapts himself to a new system and moves along to satisfy the new rules. This, in the long run, develops in him a wise sense of adaptability and a self-created power to overcome the unpredictable hardships of life. A man who values constructive adaptability and courage will readily appreciate the effects of Fasting in this respect.

10.   It grounds man in Discipline and Healthy Survival. When a person observes the regular course of Fasting in consecutive days of the Holy Month and in the Holy Months of the consecutive years, he is certainly applying himself to a high form of discipline and a superb sense of order. Similarly, when he relieves his stomach and relaxes his digestive system, he is indeed insuring his body, not to mention the soul, against all harm that results from stomach over-charge. In this manner of relaxation he may be sure that his body will survive free from the usual disorder and break, and that his soul will continue to shine purely and peacefully.

11.   It originates in man the real Spirit of Social Belonging, of Unity and Brotherhood, of Equality before God as well as before the Law. This spirit is the natural product of the fact that when man fasts, he feels that he is joining the whole Muslim society in observing the same duty in the same manner at the same time for the same motives to the same end. No sociologist can say that there has been at any period of history anything comparable to this fine institution of Islam. People have been crying throughout the ages for acceptable belonging, for unity, for brotherhood, for equality, but how echoless their voice has been, and how very little success they have met! Where can they find their goals without the guiding light of Islam?

12.   It is a Godly prescription for self-reassurance and self-control, for maintenance of human dignity and freedom, for victory and

peace. These results never fail to manifest themselves as a lively reality in the heart of the person who knows how to keep the Fasting. When he fasts in the proper manner, he is in control of himself, exercises full command over his passions, disciplines his desires and resists all evil temptations. By this course, he is in a position to reassure himself, to restore his dignity and integrity and to attain freedom from the captivity of evil. Once he obtains all this, he has established inner peace, which is the source of permanent peace with God and, consequently, with the entire universe.

Now, someone may be tempted to raise the objection: If this is the case with the Islamic institution of Fasting, and if this is the picture of Islam in this aspect, why are the Muslims not living in a utopia? To such an objection we can only say that the Muslims have lived in and enjoyed a utopia in a certain epoch of their history. The realization of that utopia was a phenomenon of a unique achievement in the history of man. We say unique, because no religion or social system other than Islam has ever been able to realize its ideals in reality. The utopia of other religions and social systems has always remained in the category of theories or wishful thinking and dreams—sometimes clear, sometimes vague, sometimes near, most of the time far. But the utopia of Islam was realized and put into practice and production at full capacity. In a human and practical sense this means that the utopia of Islam can be re-established once again right here on this earth, and that it is raised on solid foundations and practicable principles.

The reason why the Islamic utopia is not being established nowadays is manifold and easily explicable. But to restrict our discussion to the institution of Fasting we may say that many Muslims, unfortunately for them, do not observe the fast or, at best, adopt the attitude of indifference. On the other hand, most of those who observe it do not realize its true meaning and, as a result, derive very little benefit out of it or, in fact, no benefit at all. That is why the Muslims of today, on the whole, do not enjoy the real privileges of Fasting.

Again, someone else may say that what is claimed about the Islamic Fasting is also true of other types of fasting like the Jewish Passover, the Christian Lent, the Ghandian Type, etc. Why, then, do the Muslims make these arbitrary claims about their type of Fasting?

To such a person and to all others like him we direct our appeal. It is against our religious principles and our morals as Muslims to defame any prophet of God. or reject any truth, or falsify any Divine religion. Other people do feel free to commit these irresponsible offenses, but we Muslims do not; because we know that once we plunge into this low level of morality or rather immorality, we are virtually out of the ranks of Islam. We do also know that the institution of Fasting is as old as history itself, and that it was prescribed by God for the people before Islam as it has been prescribed by Him for the Muslims. But we do not know—and we do not believe that many people know—the exact form or the proper manners in which God prescribed those other types of Fasting. However, we may, for the sake of the truth and enlightened curiosity, substantiate our contentions by comparing this institution of Islam with the other types of fasting:

Fasting in Comparative Perspective

1. In other religions and dogmas, in other philosophies and doctrines, the observer of fast abstains from certain kinds of food or drinks or material substances, but he is free to substitute for that and fill his stomach to the top with the substituting stuff, which is also of material nature. In Islam one abstains from the things of material nature—food, drink, smoking, etcetera, in order to have spiritual joys and moral nourishment. The Muslim empties his stomach of all the material things: to fill his soul with peace and blessings, to fill his heart with love and sympathy, to fill his spirit with piety and Faith, to fill his mind with wisdom and resolution.

2. The purpose of Fasting in other religions and philosophies is invariably partial. It is either for spiritual aims, OR for physical needs, OR for intellectual cultivations; never for all combined. But in Islam it is for all these gains and many other purposes, social and economic, moral and humanitarian, private and public, personal and common, inner and outer, local and national—all combined together as mentioned above.

3. The non-Islamic Fasting does not demand more than partial abstinence from certain material things. But the Islamic type is accompanied by extra devotion and worship, extra charity and study of the Qur'ān, extra sociability and liveliness, extra self-discipline and conscience-awakening. Thus the fasting Muslim feels a different person altogether. He is so pure and clean inside as well as outside, and his soul is so transparent that he feels close to perfection because he is so near to God.

4. To the best of our knowledge and on the authority of daily experience, other moral philosophies and religions teach man that he cannot attain his moral aims or enter the Kingdom of God unless and until he uproots himself from the stem of worldly affairs. Accordingly, it becomes necessary for such a man to divorce his mundane

interests, neglect his human responsibilities and resort to some kind of self-torture or severe asceticism of which fasting is an essential element. Fasting of this kind with people of this type may be used— and it has been used—as a pretext to cover the humiliating retreat from the normal course of life. But Fasting in Islam is not a divorce from life but a happy marriage with it, not a retreat but a penetration with spiritual armaments, not a negligence but a moral enrichment. The Islamic Fasting does not divorce religion from daily life or separate the soul from the body. It does not break but harmonizes. It does not dissolve but transfuses. It does not disintegrate but bridges and redeems.

5.   Even the timetable of the Islamic Fasting is a striking phenomenon. In other cases the time of Fasting is fixed at a certain time of the year in a most inflexible way. But in Islam the time comes with the month of Ramadan, the ninth month of the year. The Islamic Calendar is a lunar one, and months go according to the various positions of the moon. This means that over a period of a limited number of years the Islamic Fasting covers the four major seasons of the year and circulates back and forth between the summer and the winter through the fall and the spring in a rotating manner. The nature of the lunar calendar is such that the month of Ramadan falls in January, for example, in one year and in December in another year, and at any time in between during the succeeding years. In a spiritual sense this means that the Muslim enjoys the moral experience of Fasting on various levels, and tastes its spiritual flavors at variant seasons of variant climates, sometimes in the winter of short and cold days, sometimes in the summer of long and hot days, sometimes in between. But this variety of experience remains at all times an impressive feature of the liveliness of the Islamic institution. It also stands as an unfailing expression of readiness, dynamism and adaptability on the part of the Muslim believer. This is certainly a healthy, remarkable component of the teachings of Islam.

The Period of Fasting

It has already been indicated that the period of obligatory Fasting is the month of Ramadan. The daily period of observance starts before the break of the dawn and ends immediately after sunset. Normally there are accurate calendars to tell the exact time, but in the absence of such facilities one should consult one's watch and the sun's positions, together with the local newspapers, weather bureau, etc.

The Fasting of Ramadan is obligatory on every responsible and fit Muslim (Mukallaf). But there are other times when it is strongly recommended, after the Traditions of Prophet Muhammad. Among these times are Mondays and Thursdays of every week, a few days of each month in the two months heralding the coming of Ramadan, i.e., Rajab and Sha'ban, six days after Ramadan following the 'Eedu-l-Fitr Day. Besides, it is always compensating to fast any day of any month of the year, except the 'Eed Days and Fridays when no Muslim should fast. However, we may repeat that the only obligatory Fasting is that of Ramadan—which may be 29 or 30 days, depending on the moon's positions. This is a pillar of Islam, and any failure to observe it without reasonable excuses is a severely punishable sin.

Knowing what Fasting can do for man, God has enjoined, as an alternative, the fast of three days on anyone who breaks an oath. Similarly, if someone declares his wife as forbidden for him as his mother,—an old pre-Islamic custom, he must pay for his carelessness and irresponsibility. To expiate for this sin he has, as an alternative, to observe the fast of two consecutive months (Qur'ān, 2:183-185; 5:92; 58:1-4)[7].

Who Must Fast?

The Fasting of Ramadan is compulsory upon every Muslim, male or female, who has these qualifications:

1. To be mentally and physically fit, which means to be sane and able;

2. To be of full age, the age of puberty and discretion, which is normally about fourteen. Children under this age should be encouraged to start this good practice on easy levels, so when they reach the age of puberty they will be mentally and physically prepared to observe the Fasting;

3. To be present at your permanent settlement, your home town,

---

[7]It is interesting to note that expiation for breaking an earnest oath is the feeding, or clothing of ten indigent persons. If that is not possible the offender must emancipate a slave or ransom his freedom. If that also is not possible then the fasting of three days is the last resort (Qur'an, 5:92). In the case of that thoughtless use of words, that distasteful pre-Islamic custom, the offender's first obligation is to emancipate a slave or ransom his freedom. If he cannot afford that, then he must observe the fast of two consecutive months before he resumes intimacy with his wife. If he cannot fast, then he must feed sixty needy persons or distribute sixty average meals among the poor. There are other occasions where fasting is either required or recommended to substitute for unmanageable tasks (Qur'an, 58:1-4, cf- 2:196).

your farm, your business premises, etc. This means not to be travelling on a journey of about fifty miles or more;

4. To be fairly certain that the Fasting is unlikely to cause you any harm, physical or mental, other than the normal reactions to hunger, thirst, etc.

Exemption From Fasting

These said qualifications exclude the following categories:

1. Children under the age of puberty and discretion;

2. The insane people who are unaccountable for their deeds. People of these two categories are exempted from the duty of fast, and no compensation or any other substitute is enjoined on them;

3. Men and women who are too old and feeble to undertake the obligation of fast and bear its hardships. Such people are exempted from this duty, but they must offer, at least, one needy poor Muslim an average full meal or its value per person per day. This compensation indicates that whenever they can fast even for one day of the month, they should do so, and compensate for the rest. Otherwise they are accountable for their negligence;

4. Sick people whose health is likely to be severely affected by the observance of fast. They may postpone the fast, as long as they are sick, to a later date and make up for it, a day for a day;

5. People in the course of travelling of distances about fifty miles or more. In this case such people may break the fast temporarily during their travel only and make up for it in later days, a day for a day. But it is better for them, the Qur'ān tells, to keep the fast if they can without causing extraordinary hardships;

6. Expectant women and women nursing their children may also break the fast, if its observance is likely to endanger their own health or that of their infants. But they must make up for the fast at a delayed time, a day for a day;

7. Women in the period of menstruation (of a maximum of ten days) or of confinement (of a maximum of forty days). These are not allowed to fast even if they can and want to. They must postpone the fast till recovery and then make up for it, a day for a day.

It should be understood that here, like in all other Islamic undertakings, the intention must be made clear that this action is undertaken in obedience to God, in response to His command and out of love for Him.

The fast of any day of Ramadan becomes void by intentional eating or drinking or smoking or indulgence in any intimate intercourses, and by allowing anything to enter through the mouth into the interior parts of the body. And if this is done deliberately without any lawful reason, the penalty is to observe the fast of sixty consecutive days or, as a second alternative, feed sixty poor persons sufficiently, besides observing the fast of one day against the day whose fast was made void.

When the fast of days other than those of Ramadan is broken for a lawful reason like those classified under the heading "Exemption" above, the person involved must make up for that fast later, a day for a day.

If anyone, by mistake, does something that would ordinarily break the fast, his observance is not nullified, and his fast stands valid, provided he stops doing that thing the moment he realizes what he is doing.

On completion of the fast of Ramadan, the special charity known as Sadqatu-l-Fitr (Charity of Fast-breaking) must be distributed.

General Recommendations

It is strongly recommended by Prophet Muhammad to observe these practices especially during Ramadan:

1. To have a light meal before the break of the dawn, known as Suhoor;

2. To eat three dates and have a drink of water right after sunset, saying this prayer: Al-lahumma laka sumna, wa 'ala rizqika aftarna. (O God! for Your sake we have fasted and now we break the fast with the food You have given us);

3. To make your meals as light as possible because, as the Prophet put it, the worst thing man can fill is his stomach;

4. To observe the supererogatory prayer known as Taraweeh;

5. To exchange social visits and intensify humanitarian services;

6. To increase study and recitation of the Qur'ān;

7. To exert the utmost in patience and humbleness;

8. To be extraordinarily cautious in using the senses, the mind and, especially, the tongue; to abstain from careless and gossipy chats and avoid all suspicious motions.

The Alms (Zakah)

Another exceptionally remarkable institution and major pillar of Islam is the Zakah. To the Qur'anic word Zakah and the meaning it conveys, there is no equivalent in any other language as far as we know. It is not just a form of charity or alms-giving or tax or tithe. Nor is it simply an expression of kindness; it is all of these combined and much more. It is not merely a deduction of a certain percentage from one's property, but an abundant enrichment and spiritual investment. It is not simply a voluntary contribution to someone or some cause, nor a government tax that a shrewd clever person can get away with. Rather, it is a duty enjoined by God and undertaken by Muslims in the interest of society as a whole. The Qur'anic word Zakah not only includes charity, alms, tithe, kindness, official tax, voluntary contributions, etc., but it also combines with all these God-mindedness and spiritual as well as moral motives. That is why there can be no equivalent to the word Zakah because of the supreme originality of the Qur'ān, the Divine Book of God.

The literal and simple meaning of Zakah is purity. The technical meaning of the word designates the annual amount in kind or coin which a Muslim with means must distribute among the rightful beneficiaries. But the religious and spiritual significance of Zakah is much deeper and more lively. So is its humanitarian and sociopolitical value. Here is an explanation of the far-reaching effects of Zakah:

1. Zakah purifies the property of the people with means and clears it from the shares which do not belong to it anymore, the shares which must be distributed among the due beneficiaries. When Zakah is payable, a certain percentage of the wealth should be distributed immediately in the right manner, because the owner no longer has moral or legal possession of that percentage. If he fails to do so, he is obviously retaining something which does not belong to him. This is corruption and plain usurpation from every point of view, moral and spiritual, legal and commercial. It means that the unlawfully retained percentage makes the whole lot impure and endangered. But, on the other hand, if the poor's dividends are assorted and distributed among due beneficiaries, the remaining portions of the lot will be pure and decent. Pure capital and decent possessions are the first requisites of permanent prosperity and honest transactions.

2. Zakah does not only purify the property of the contributor but also purifies his heart from selfishness and greed for wealth. In return, it purifies the heart of the recipient from envy and jealousy, from hatred and uneasiness; and it fosters in his heart, instead, good will

and warm wishes for the contributor. As a result, the society at large will purify and free itself from class warfare and suspicion, from ill feelings and distrust, from corruption and disintegration, and from all such evils.

3.   Zakah mitigates to a minimum the sufferings of the needy and poor members of society. It is a most comforting consolation to the less fortunate people, yet it is a loud appeal to everybody to roll up his sleeves and improve his lot. To the needy it means that it is by nature an emergency measure and that he should not depend on it completely but must do something for himself as well as for others. To the contributor it is a warm invitation to earn more so that he can benefit more. To all parties concerned, it is, directly as well as indirectly, an open treasure for spiritual investment that compensates abundantly.

4.   Zakah is a healthy form of internal security against selfish greed and social dissension, against the intrusion and penetration of subversive ideologies. It is an effective instrument in cultivating the spirit of social responsibility on the part of the contributor, and the feeling of security and belonging on the part of the recipient.

5.   Zakah is a vivid manifestation of the spiritual and humanitarian spirit of responsive interactions between the individual and society. It is a sound illustration of the fact that though Islam does not hinder private enterprise or condemn private possessions, yet it does not tolerate selfish and greedy capitalism. It is an expression of the general philosophy of Islam which adopts a moderate and middle but positive and effective course between the Individual and the Society, between the Citizen and the State, between Capitalism and Socialism, between Materialism and Spirituality.

The Rate of Zakah

Every Muslim, male or female, who, at the end of the year, is in possession of approximately fifteen dollars or more, in cash or articles of trade, must give Zakah at the minimum rate of two and one-half percent. In the case of having the amount in cash the matter is easy. But when a person has wealth in business stocks or trade articles, he must evaluate his wealth at the end of every year according to the current value and give Zakah at the same rate of two and one-half percent of the total value of the wealth. If his investment is in immovable property like revenue buildings and industries, the rate of Zakah should go by the total net of the income, and not of the total value of the whole property. But if he puts up buildings and houses for trade or selling, Zakah rate should go by the total value of the entire property. Also if someone is a creditor and the indebted person is reliable one should pay Zakah for the amount he has lent because it is still a portion of his guaranteed wealth.

In all cases it should be remembered that one pays only for his net balance. His personal expenses, his family allowances, his necessary expenditures, his due credits—all are paid first, and Zakah is for the net balance.

It should also be remembered that the rate of 2.5% is only a minimum. In times of emergency or arising needs there is no rate limit; the more one gives, the better it is for all concerned. The distribution of Zakah serves all purposes for which numerous fund-raising campaigns are launched. The Zakah fund substitutes for all the other funds. It is authentically reported that there were times in the history of the Islamic administration when there was no person eligible to receive Zakah; every subject—Muslim, Christian, and Jew—of the vast Islamic empire had enough to satisfy his needs, and the rulers had to deposit the Zakah collections in the Public Treasury. This shows that when the Zakah law is enacted properly it minimizes the needs of the citizens and enriches the Public Treasury to such an extent that there may be no needy or poor, and that enormous amounts of surplus are available.

The unfailing power of this effective measure of public interest stems from the fact that it is a Divine injunction, an ordinance from God Himself. It is not a personal matter or a voluntary contribution; rather, it is an obligation for the fulfillment of which one will be responsible to God directly. Because Zakah is the legislation of God Himself to be enforced in the common interest, no Muslim is allowed to neglect it. When it is not observed properly, the rightful authorities of the State must interfere on behalf of the public to establish the institution and see to it that it is enforced.

The Due Recipients of Zakah

The Holy Qur'ān classifies the due recipients of Zakah as follows:

1. The poor Muslims, to relieve their distress;
2. The needy Muslims, to supply them with means whereby they can earn their livelihood;
3. The new Muslim converts, to enable them to settle down and meet their unusual needs;
4. The Muslim prisoners of war, to liberate them by payment of ransom money;

5. The Muslims in debt, to free them from their liabilities incurred under pressing necessities;

6. The Muslim employees appointed by a Muslim governor for the collection of Zakah to pay their wages;

7. The Muslims in service of the cause of God by means of research or study or propagation of Islam. This share is to cover their expenses and help them to continue their services;

8. The Muslim wayfarers who are stranded in a foreign land and in need of help.

The due recipient of Zakah is one who has nothing to meet his necessities or has little (less than $15.00) at the end of the year. If one has approximately $15.00 or more he must be a contributor, not a recipient of Zakah. If a recipient receives his share and finds that it is sufficient for his immediate needs with a balance of about $15.00, he should not accept any more. He should return whatever he may receive to other eligible recipients.

Zakah may be distributed directly to individuals of one or more of the said classes, or to welfare organizations which look after them. It may also be distributed in the form of scholarships to bright and promising MUSLIM students and researchers, or in the form of grants to welfare organizations and public service institutions which patronize such causes.

A disabled or invalid poor Muslim is preferable to one who is able and capable of making some earnings. The contributor should use his best judgement in finding the most deserving beneficiaries.

The taxes we pay to governments nowadays do not substitute for this religious duty; it must be earmarked as a special obligation and paid separately, aside from the government taxes. However, the Muslims of North America may take advantage of the tax laws that allow certain deductions for charity. They should pay their Zakah to the deserving beneficiaries and then claim the sums paid as proper legal deductions.

The contributor should not seek pride or fame by carrying out this duty. He should make it as covert as possible so that he may not be victimized by hypocrisy or passion for vanity which nullifies all good deeds. However, if the disclosure of his name or the announcement of his contribution is likely to encourage others and stimulate them, it is all right to do so.

Zakah is also obligatory on cattle and agricultural products. The shares payable in this regard vary from case to case, and need a detailed discussion. So the reader may be advised to consult the elaborate sources of Law and religion.

The Pilgrimage (Hajj)

The final pillar and one of the finest institutions of Islam is the Hajj or pilgrimage to Mecca. The performance of the Hajj is obligatory, at least once in a lifetime, upon every Muslim, male or female, who is mentally, financially and physically fit. The Muslim who is of responsible age, in fairly good health, and is financially capable and secure must make the Hajj at least once in his or her lifetime. The financial security here means that he should have enough to cover his own expenses and those of his dependents, and to pay his debts, if he is in debt, until he completes the course of Hajj.

The course of Hajj is another unique characteristic of Islam. It is enjoined by God to serve many purposes among which are the following:

1. It is the largest annual convention of Faith where Muslims meet to know one another, study their common affairs and promote their general welfare. It is also the greatest regular conference of peace known in the history of mankind. In the course of Hajj peace is the dominant theme; peace with God and one's soul, peace with one another and with animals, peace with birds and even with insects. To disturb the peace of anyone or any creatures in any shape or form is strictly prohibited.

2. It is a wholesome demonstration of the universality of Islam and the brotherhood and equality of the Muslims. From all walks of life, from all trades and classes, and from every corner of the globe the Muslims assemble at Mecca in response to the call of God. They dress in the same simple way, observe the same regulations, utter the same supplications at the same time in the same way, for the same end. There is no royalty, but loyalty of all to God. There is no aristocracy, but humility and devotion.

3. It is to confirm the commitment of the Muslims to God and their readiness to forsake the material interests in His service.

4. It is to acquaint the pilgrims with the spiritual and historical environment of Prophet Muhammad, so that they may derive warm inspirations and strengthen their Faith.

5. It is to commemorate the Divine rituals observed by Abraham and Ishmael (Ibraheem and Isma'eel), who are known to have been the first pilgrims to the first house of God on earth, i.e., the Ka'bah at Mecca (Makkah).

6. It is a reminder of the Grand Assembly on the Day of Judgement when people will stand equal before God, waiting for their

Final Destiny, and where no superiority of race or stock can be claimed. It is also a reminder of the fact that Mecca alone, in the whole existing world, was honored by God in being the center of monotheism since the time of Abraham, and that it will continue to be the center of Islam, the religion of pure monotheism, till the end of time.

In the performance of Hajj it can easily be observed that it is a course of spiritual enrichment and moral rearmament, a course of intensified devotion and disciplinary experience, a course of humanitarian interests and inspiring knowledge—all put together in one single institution of Islam.

The description of the rules and steps followed during the Hajj are rather lengthy. They will not be discussed here. For further details the reader may consult the elaborate works on the subject. However, it should be pointed out that during the whole course of Hajj there are informed guides always available to help the pilgrims with right instructions.

It should also be pointed out that the entire course of devotion is to God alone. The Muslims go to Mecca in glory of God, not to kiss a stone or worship a man or a semi-divinity. Kissing or touching the Black Stone at the Ka'bah is an optional action, not an obligation or a prescription. Those who kiss the Black Stone or touch it do not do it because they have faith in the Stone or attribute any superstitious qualities to it. Their Faith is in God only. They kiss or touch or point to the Stone only as a token of respect or a symbol of love for Prophet Muhammad, who laid the Stone at the foundation of the Ka'bah when it was reconstructed. That event has a special significance. It depicts Muhammad as a man designated for peace. When the Ka'bah was under reconstruction, some years before the advent of Islam, the Black Stone was to be laid at its foundation. The tribal chieftains had a quarrelsome dispute over him who was to have the honor of restoring the Stone. This was a very serious matter and the shadows of civil war hung over the holy place. The Stone was held in especially high reverence by the chieftains, although it was nothing more than a piece of stone. This reverence may be attributed to the fact that the Stone was connected with Prophet Abraham, the Great Grandfather of the Arabs, and that it was, perhaps, the only solid stone remaining from the antique structure of the Sacred Edifice. Be that as it may, the Stone as such has no significance whatsoever as far as Islam and the Muslims are concerned.

When the chieftains failed to settle the dispute among themselves, they agreed to let the first incomer decide the issue. Muhammad was the first incomer. He then decided to wrap up the Stone in a piece of cloth and asked the disputants to hold it together and restore it in such a way that each chieftain would have had a part in the operation. They were happy with his wise decision and put it into effect immediately. Thus the issue died out and peace was maintained. This is the moral of the story of the Black Stone. So when the pilgrims kiss the Stone or point at it with reverence, they do so in remembrance of Muhammad, the wise peace-maker. The point may become clearer by comparison. It is a natural thing for a good patriot returning from exile, or a fighting soldier coming back from the battlefield to do certain things upon reaching the borders of his beloved homeland. For example, he may kiss the ground at the borders, or embrace with deep emotions the first few compatriots he meets, or show admiration for some landmarks. This is considered normal and appreciable, but no one would think that the patriot or the soldier worships the ground or deifies his fellow compatriots or attributes some Divine qualities to the landmarks. The behavior of the pilgrims should be interpreted in a similar way. The Ka'bah at Mecca is the spiritual center of Islam and the spiritual homeland of every Muslim. When the pilgrim reaches Mecca his feelings would be like those of a patriot coming home from exile or a triumphant soldier returning from a decisive battle. This is not a figurative interpretation. It corresponds with the facts of history. The early Muslims were expelled out of their home and forced to live in exile for years They were denied the right to worship in the Ka'bah, the most sacred house of God in existence. When they returned from exile, the Ka'bah was their main destination. They joyfully entered the Sacred Shrine, destroyed all the idols and images that were there, and completed the rites of pilgrimage.

This interpretation is enlightened by some unusual experiences of extraordinary people. For example, a famous Hungarian writer fled his invaded country and took with him a handful of earth. Literary annals tell that the writer found his greatest comfort and deepest joy in that handful of earth. It was his source of inspiration and symbol of hope that he would return to a free homeland at last[8].

Similarly, a documentary called "The Palestinians" was prepared by CBS and televized on Saturday June 15, 1974. In it, a wealthy businessman, who fled the Zionist terror in Palestine, was interviewed at his extermely fashionable home in Beirut. When he was reminded of his good fortune in exile he smiled, pointing to a small bottle half-full of earth. To make his point, he added that he brought it with him from Jerusalem when he fled; that it is more valuable to him than anything he possesses; and that he would give

---

[8]I read this account during the fifties and, very much to my regret, cannot locate the exact source or remember the writer's name.

up all his possessions to return to Palestine, his homeland. What is more significant about this interview is that the man's family was more emphatic and expressed stronger feelings. It will not be at all surprising if it turns out that this man represents many others like him and if that small "earth treasure" becomes a very special, even a sacred, thing in the years to come.

In a more tangible sense, the Associated Press reported on October 14, 1973, that "The last Israeli strongpoints on the eastern bank of the Suez Canal surrendered . . . and 37 tired and bedraggled Israeli troops were paddled in dinghies across the waterway to captivity. ...Some of the Egyptian troops, carried away with the emotion of finally liberating this last stronghold (the Bar-Lev line), grabbed handfuls of sand and put it in their mouths. Others kissed the ground." (*Dispatch Observer,* p. 2A)

More recently, the same news agency, reporting on the returning Syrian prisoners of war, said that the first man off the plane "sat upright on a stretcher on the stumps of his amputated legs . . . 'Legs are nothing. We are ready to give our soul . . .' he shouted. He then insisted on being lifted from his stretcher and placed on the ground so that he could bend down to kiss the soil." (*Dispatch Observer,* June 2, 1974, p. 3A)

It is in this human perspective that the Black Stone story should be viewed. And it is in the light of such human experiences under extraordinary circumstances that it is best understood.

Concluding Remarks

The visit to the tomb of Prophet Muhammad at Medina (Madeenah) is not an essential obligation in making the Hajj valid and complete. But it is always advisable and strongly recommended that whoever can reach Medina should visit the Prophet's tomb to pay his respect to the greatest teacher that humanity has ever known.

It should be remembered that the climax of Hajj is marked by offering a sacrifice, an oblation in the way of God, to celebrate the completion of this devotional course and feed the poor so that they may feel the universal joy of the 'Eed Day. This duty is not undertaken by pilgrims only but by all Muslims with means in every corner of the globe.

Some Muslims have raised the serious question that during the hajj season so many animals are slaughtered in sacrifice that enormous quantities of meat are wasted. The heat, lack of refrigeration facilities, inadequate transportation, and oversupply of meat over a few days leave most of that meat unused or unusable. This is a new situation with new problems. The conscientious Muslim wants to know what he should do in this case.

It is not necessary to engage in legalistic debates over the learned opinions of respectable religious scholars, both classical and contemporary. But we must remember that Islam tolerates no waste of any kind or degree; that it responds first to the greater need and allows resort to the "lesser evil"; that it works with a system of priorities from the most important to the least important and from the least to the most undesirable; and that it is both resourceful and adaptive. Based on these principles, the problem can be solved easily. The solution derives from the spirit of Islam even though it may appear to depart slightly from some literal interpretations. The solution can be implemented in stages and on various levels.

First, the Muslims should do everything possible to provide adequate facilities for refrigeration so that the surplus meat may be conserved and used by the poor in and around the holy places throughout the year. Secondly, efforts should also be made to transport the surplus meat to the needy Muslims wherever they may be. The sacrifice animals can be slaughtered in Mecca and the meat may be canned or frozen and then transported to any part of the world where there are needy Muslims. Thirdly, the surplus meat can be sold and the money used for charitable purposes on a local, regional, national, or international scale. These are practicable measures which the Muslims should enact jointly. In the meantime and until such steps are taken, any Muslim who feels that the surplus meat will go to waste may delay or advance the date of his sacrifice. He may choose the proper time and place to avoid any waste. Or he could pay in charity to a legitimate cause the money value of the animal that was to have been sacrificed at Mecca during the days of Hajj[9].

One last remark relates to the question of sacrifice and what it

---

[9]There is a highly learned discussion by the late great Imam Mahmud Shaltoot in his *Al-Fatawa* (Cairo: al-Azhar University Press, 1959), pp. 152-160. We respectfully disagree with certain points in that statement. Yet we cannot say that our view is the only true Islamic position; such an attitude would be presumptuous and even irresponsible. But we can say this: to the extent that the institution of hajj bears on social life it belongs to that branch of *shareeah* (Islamic law) which is called *Mu'amalat* (human transactions). This branch of law complements the branch of *'ibadat* (matters of "worship" and rituals), to which the hajj institution is commonly believed to belong. However, the two branches are inseparable and it can be said that the hajj, in a very significant sense, is part of the *mu'amalat*. Recognizing that social dimension of hajj and the practical problem of wasting so much needed food, money and effort, we should reinterpret the rules of sacrifice in such a way as to remain in harmony with the spirit of Islam and retain a reasonable level of sanity, rationality, and realism. We therefore, offer the said interpretation with a prayer that it will be acceptable to God and helpful to our fellow Muslims.

actually symbolizes. As already stated in the discussion of the 'Eeds, it is not the meat or blood that pleases God. It is the expression of thankfulness to Him, the affirmation of faith in Him, that historic event when Prophet Abraham (Ibraheem) was ordered to offer his son in sacrifice, an order which the father and son were ready to obey unquestioningly. But the son's life was spared and ransomed by a ram. The offering of the sacrifice has become an annual celebration to commemorate the occasion and thank God for His favors. There have been two versions of which one of Abraham's sons was to have been sacrificed, Ishmael (Ismaeel) or Isaac (Ishaq).

The Muslims believe that it was Ishmael (Ismaeel), not Isaac (Ishaq), who was to have been sacrificed in response to God's command. But he was ransomed after he and his father were ready to obey God's ordinance. There are at least twenty arguments in support of this belief. However, none of these is meant to belittle the historical role of the Children of Israel or the light and wisdom delivered to them by Prophet Moses. On the contrary, the Qur'an points that out in numerous statements (e.g. 2:40, 47; 7:137; 17:2; 40:53; 45:16).

Among these arguments are the following:

1.   The whole context of the event as recorded in the Qur'an (37:101-113) leaves no doubt that Ismaeel was the son to have been sacrificed by his father in response to God's command.

2.   The present Old Testament (Gen. 21:5) says that Isaac was born when his father Abraham was 100 years old, while Ismaeel was born when his father was 86 years old (Gen. 21:16). For a span of fourteen years then Ismaeel was the only son of his father. At no time was Isaac in the same position. Yet the Old Testament (Gen. 22:2) states that the order was issued to Abraham to "Take now thy son, thine only son Isaac ... and get thee into the land of Moriah and offer him there for a burnt offering." The appearance of Isaac's name in this context seems an obvious insertion. And it is not clear just where that land of Moriah was unless it was the mount of Marwah at Mecca, which supports the Islamic version.

3.   The whole event took place around Mecca. And we know that it was Ismaeel and his mother who accompanied Abraham to Mecca, settled there, and helped him raise the Kabah as a sacred sanctuary (Qur'an, 2:124-130; 14:35-40).

4.   Perhaps the most important argument in favor of the Islamic belief is this: the Jewish-Christian version leads to seriously objectionable conclusions: (a) discrimination between brothers just be-

cause the mother of one was a slave and that of the other was a free woman, (b) discrimination between people because of race, creed, or color, (c) claiming spiritual superiority in the name of one's ancestors, and (d) denial of legitimacy to a child whose mother is a slave. All such inferences and conclusions are contrary to the spirit of Islam. Anything that may lead to them must be rejected by the Muslim. The status of one's ancestors, the nobility or humbleness of the mother, and the social origin or color shades have no bearings on the spiritual and human quality of man, at least not in the sight of God[10].

---

[10]In addition to these remarks, see A. Yusuf Ali, *The Holy Qur'an, Text, Translation and Commentary* (1946), pp. 1204-1206; Ibn Qayyim al-Jawazayh, *Zad al-Ma'ad* ... (Beirut edition, n.d.), vol. I, pp. 15-17.

CHAPTER IV

APPLICATION OF ISLAM TO DAILY LIFE

The Muslims rightfully maintain that Islam is not simply an abstract ideal conceived just for nominal adoration or a stagnant idol to be frequented by admirers every now and then. Islam is a code of life, a living force manifest in every aspect of human Life. The Muslims also maintain that the individual is the center of gravity and is the launching instrument which can put Islam, or any other system for that matter, into full action on a full scale. And this is why Islam always begins with the individual and invariably prefers quality to quantity.

Let us begin, where Islam begins, with the individual. Let us examine the nature of the individual and find out how Islam views this nature. To clarify things as much as possible, without getting entangled in philosophical disputes or abstract controversy, we can define man as having two complementary natures, very intimately interrelated and continually interacting upon each other. These are the inner nature and the outer nature. Or one might say that man has one nature only with two bridged sections hardly separable from each other. One is internal and another external. The internal nature of man refers to the Ruh (soul or self or heart) and 'Aql (mind or power of reasoning or intelligence).

In our illustration of the internal nature of man we shall have to deal with two aspects: (1) the spiritual or moral aspect and (2) the intellectual aspect. The rest of man's activities and transactions will have to be classified as the external or outer nature of man. After all, it is a universally admitted fact that man does not live by bread alone.

106

THE INTERNAL NATURE

The Spiritual Life

Islam organizes the spiritual or moral life of man in such a way as to provide him with all the spiritual nourishment needed for piety and righteousness, for safety and peace. The Islamic prescription for the spiritual life of man grants, when faithfully applied, maximum positive results as far as man's spiritual growth and maturity are concerned. The main items in this Islamic prescription are:

1. Prayers (Salah);

2. Zakah or Alms–giving;

3. Fasting (Sawm);

4. Pilgrimage (Hajj);

5. Love for God and His Messenger, love for truth and humanity for the sake of God;

6. Hope and trust in God at all times; and

7. Sacrifice for the sake of God by virtue of actual unselfishness.

Various aspects of these items have already been discussed in some detail, and here we have only to add that without these fundamental elements there can be no true Faith as far as Islam is concerned. The reader is advised to refer to the previous sections of this work.

The Intellectual Life

The intellectual nature of man is made up, as already mentioned, of mind or intelligence or reasoning power. To this aspect Islam pays extraordinary attention and builds the intellectual structure of man on most sound foundations which may be classified as follows:

1. True knowledge based on clear proofs and indisputable evidence acquired by "experience" or experiment or by both. In this connection it is safe to say, beyond doubt, that the Qur'ān is the first authority to enjoin zealous quest for knowledge through "experience" as well as experiment, meditation and observation. In fact, it is a Divine injunction incumbent upon every Muslim, male and female, to seek knowledge in the broadest sense of the word and search for truth. Nature and the whole universe are open and ever-revealing treasures of knowledge and truth, and the Qur'ān was the first book to point to these rich sources of knowledge. It does not accept inherited "truths" or claimed facts which have no proof or evidence to substantiate them. As far as we have been able to know,

the Qur'ān was the first Scripture to say intelligently: "Why" and to demand proof in support of any conviction or contention (Qur'ān, 2:111 and 21:24).

The Qur'ān itself is an outstanding intellectual challenge; it challenges the human intellect to dispute any Qur'anic truth or produce anything similar to the Qur'ān. Open any chapter of the Qur'ān and you will find the warmest appeal to search for knowledge through the infinite sources of nature. Devotion to true knowledge is regarded by Islam a devotion to God in the most compensating sense.

2. The second part of this point is faith in God, an ever-revealing source of knowledge and a spiritual insight into countless fields of thought. In Islam Faith in God is the cornerstone of the whole religious structure. But in order to make Faith in God valid, Islam requires that it should be founded on unshakable certainty and convictions. These, in turn, cannot be acquired without the proper investment of the intellect. Any stagnant or indifferent mind and any limited vision cannot possibly reach the height of the Most Supreme Truth, God, nor can it attain the real depth of Faith.

Islam does not recognize faith when it is attained through blind imitation, when it is accepted blindly or unquestioningly. This fact is very important as far as the intellectual life of man is concerned. Islam requires Faith in God; and the Qur'ān makes numerous statements calling for Faith in God. But the significance of such statements is not in shelving them in the studyroom or even in the mind. The significance of such statements is that they constitute a warm invitation and an urgent appeal to the intellect to wake and think. to ponder and meditate. It is true that the Qur'ān reveals the essential truth and facts about God, yet it is equally true that it does not want man to behave like a lazy heir who makes no effort of his own. It wants man to enrich his intellectual wealth through serious endeavor and honest earning, so that he may become intellectually secure. "Easy come, easy go," and Islam disapproves of easy coming faith which is bound to be easy going. Islam wants Faith in God to be effective and permanent, to light every corner in man's heart and prevail in every aspect of his life. Easy coming faith cannot possibly do that, and Islam would not accept anything less.

When Islam demands Faith in God on the basis of knowledge and research, it leaves wide open all fields of thought before the intellect to penetrate as far as it can reach. It lays down no restrictions against the free thinker who is seeking knowledge to widen his vision and broaden his mind. It urges him to resort to all methods of knowledge, be they purely rational or experimental. By calling on the intellect in this way, Islam shows its high regard for and confidence in the intellectual abilities of man and wishes to free his mind from the tight shackles and limits of tangibility. It wants to elevate the individual and empower him with self-confidence and Heavenly authority to expand the domain of his mind into all fields of thought: physical and metaphysical, scientific and philosophical, intuitive and experimental, organic and otherwise. That is how Faith in God nourishes the intellect and makes the intellectual life prosperous and productive. When the spiritual and intellectual activities of man are organized according to the teachings of Islam as mentioned above, the internal nature of man becomes sound and healthy. And when man is internally secure and sound, his external life will be of the same nature.

THE EXTERNAL NATURE

The external nature of man is as complex, subtle and wide as his internal nature. We need to re-emphasize the fact that the soundness of the former is greatly dependent upon that of the latter and viceversa, because man's complete nature is made up of both aspects. For the sake of clarification, once more, we have to classify the external nature of man into divisions and subdivisions. But we should always bear in mind that any imbalance in the system of human nature may become destructive and fatal. The fact of the matter is that both the internal and external natures of man act and interact responsively, and that Islam has extended its Divine touch to the internal as well as the external aspects of life.

The Personal Life

Islam deals with the very personal life of man in such a way as to insure his purity and cleanliness; as to give him a healthy diet and show him the proper manners of clothing, behavior, adornment, sports and so on.

1.   Purity and Cleanliness

It is an Islamic injunction that before offering the prayer the Muslim must perform an ablution, unless he has done one earlier and kept it valid. This obligatory ablution is sometimes partial, sometimes complete, depending on his or her condition. Now, if we remember that a Muslim has to offer at least five obligatory prayers every day in pure heart and mind, in clean body and clothes, on pure ground and intention—we can very well realize the vital effect and beneficial results of this single act for man (cf. Qur'ān, 4:43, 5:7).

109

2. Diet

To maintain a pure heart and a sound mind, to nourish an aspiring soul and a clean healthy body, special attention should be given to the diet on which man lives. And this is exactly what Islam does. Some superficial or self-deceived persons may imagine that food and drinking stuff has no direct or important effect on the general condition of the person who fills his stomach regularly. But this is certainly not the viewpoint of Islam which takes the matter in a most serious way. The general principle of Islam in this respect is this: All the things which are pure in themselves and good for man are lawful for diet as long as they are taken in moderate quantities. And all the things which are impure and bad or harmful are unlawful under all ordinary circumstances. There is always room and flexibility for exceptions to meet cases of absolute necessity (Qur'ān, 7:157; see the section on Islamic Morals above).

Beyond this general principle, there are certain foods and drinks specified by God as forbidden. Among these are: meat of dead animals and birds, the flesh of swine and that of anything slaughtered with the invocation of any name other than that of God (2:173; 5:4). The drinks which Islam considers harmful and destructive to the human spirit and morality as well as to the physique and morale of man are included in the Qur'anic verse which forbids all intoxicants and all forms of gambling or games of chance (5:93-94).

The prohibition of these foods and drinks is not by any means an arbitrary action or a dictatorial decree of God. It is first and foremost a Divine intervention in the best interest of man and for his own sake. When the Qur'ān describes these forbidden things as bad, impure and harmful, it has a vigilant eye on man's morality and wisdom, on his health and wealth, on his piety and common behavior—all of which are invaluable assets in the estimation of Islam. The reasons behind this Divine intervention are numerous. They are of a nature intellectual and spiritual, moral and mental, physical and economical. And the sole purpose is to show man how to develop himself according to an upright course of life in order to be a healthy unit in the structure of the family, then of society, and eventually of humanity at large. Reliable medical doctors and social scientists should be able now to verify the benefits of these Islamic legislations.

Islam is as orthodox and uncompromising on the quality of the organic nourishment of man as it is on his spiritual soundness and intellectual growth. This point is brought to light by the fact that some dietary items are forbidden in kind, as mentioned above, and some in degree. The things which are lawful for the Muslim should be taken in moderate quantities without indulgence or excess

(Qur'ān, 7:31). After shunning all the forbidden items in kind and degree, the Muslim is invited by God to enjoy His gracious provisions and to experience gratitude to the Merciful Provider (2:168, 172; 5:90-91).[1]

3. Clothing and Adornment

In man's clothing and adornment Islam takes into serious consideration the principles of decency, modesty, chastity and manliness. Anything in clothing or adornment incompatible with the attainment, maintenance and development of these qualities is inhibited by Islam. The clothing material and the dressing manners which may stimulate arrogance or false pride and vanity are strictly prohibited. So are the adornments which may weaken the morality of man or undermine his manliness. Man should remain loyal to his manly nature, which God has chosen for him, and keep away from all the things that are likely to weaken or endanger his character. This is the reason why Islam warns man not to use certain clothing materials, e.g., pure silk, and certain precious stones, e.g., gold, for the purpose of adornment. These are things which suit the feminine nature alone. The handsomeness of man is not in wearing precious stones or flaunting in pure and natural silken clothes but in high morality, sweet nature and sound conduct.

When Islam allows woman to use the things which are forbidden for man and which are suitable for the feminine nature alone, Islam does not let woman go loose or wander unrestricted. It allows her the things which suit her nature and, at the same time, cautions her against anything that might abuse or upset that nature. The manner in which women should dress up, beautify, walk and even look is a very delicate question, and Islam pays special attention to the matter. The vision of Islam in this respect is focused on the general welfare of women. Islam has served advice to both man and woman to help women in particular to retain and develop their dignity and chastity, safe from being the subject of idle gossip or vicious rumors and suspicious thoughts. The advice is imparted in these Qur'anic verses:

Say to the believing men that they should lower their gaze and guard their modesty; that will make for greater purity for them. And God is well-acquainted with all that they do. And say to the believing women that they should lower their gaze and guard their modesty;

---

[1]This partial repetion is meant to re-emphasize the point and may therefore be forgiven. In connection with the whole discussion, see the Concept of Morality above and also Ebrahim Kazim, M.D. "Medical Aspects of Forbidden Foods in Islam," *AL-ITTIHAD* (The Muslim Students Association of the Unites States and Canada), 1391/1971, vol. 8, no. 1, pp. 4-6. This article concludes with an excellent bibliography of medical and religious sources.

that they should not display their beauty and ornaments except what (must ordinarily) appear thereof; that they should draw their veils over their bosoms and not display their beauty except before their husbands, their fathers . . . (and certain other members of the household); and that they should not strike their feet in order to draw attention to their hidden ornaments (24:30-31).

Islam is very sensitive to the manners of clothing and ornaments. It makes it crystal clear that both man and woman should be confined to their respective natures to safeguard their natural instincts and endow them with modesty and high morality. Prophet Muhammad is reported as having said that God condemns those men who behave or act in a womanlike fashion, and those women who behave or act in a manlike fashion. Nevertheless, it should be borne in mind that Islam lays no restrictions on the harmless or proper items of clothing and ornaments. In fact, the Qur'ān calls such things the beautiful gifts of God and reproaches those who look upon them as forbidden (7:32-33).

4. Sports and Amusements

It is gratifying to notice that most of the Islamic forms of worship, e.g., Prayers, Fasting, Pilgrimage, display some sportive characteristics, although they are basically and by nature meant for spiritual purposes. But who would deny the constant interaction between the physique and morale of man? Yet that is not all that Islam has to say on the subject of sports and amusements. Anything that provokes sound thinking or refreshes the mind and revitalizes the body to keep man in healthy shape is encouraged and invited to by Islam so long as it does not anticipate or involve any sin, or cause any harm or delay and hamper the fulfillment of other obligations. The general precept in this matter is the statement in which the Prophet said that all believers in God have good qualities but the strong one is better than the weak. It is also reported that he approved of the sports and amusements which build up the enduring physique and strengthen the morale.

It is a regrettable mistake to associate with sports and amusements things which are not really sportive or amusing. Some people consider gambling and drinking as sports and amusements, but this is not the viewpoint of Islam. Life is worth living and is granted to us for a definite purpose. No one is supposed to abuse it by letting it go loose or become dependent entirely on luck and chance. So it is no intrusion on or violation of the personal rights of man when Islam extends its Divine touch to organize life even in its very personal aspects. Because life is man's most valuable asset and is designed for noble purposes, Islam has shown man the way to live it properly and enjoyably. Among the measures taken in this respect is inhibition of gambling which is really more tension-accelerating than tension-reducing. It is a grave abuse of life to make it subject to luck and mere chance. It is a deviation from the normal course of life, if one entrusts his lot to the mad wheel of games, and invests his abilities in the most unpredictable moves on a gambling table. To protect man from all these unnecessary mental strains and shattering of nerves, and to enable him to lead a natural life in means as well as in ends, Islam has forbidden gambling of all forms and kinds.

Similarly, it is a shameful retreat from reality and an irresponsible insult to the best quality in man, i.e., mind, to get entangled in the tight strands of intoxication or cornered in the vicious whirl of alcohol. The menaces and tragedies of intoxication are too obvious to be elaborated. Many lives are being lost every day on this account. Many families break up because of this menace. Many billions of dollars are swallowed in the drinking channel every year. Countless doors are closed on misery and unhappiness arising from the drinking habits. Besides the destruction of health, the depression of mind, the dullness of soul, the absorption of wealth, the disintegration of families, the abuse of human dignity, the sabotage of morality, the humiliating retreat from realty; everyone of the so-called social drinkers is a highly potential alcoholic. Islam cannot tolerate these menaces or let man abuse the very sense of life in this tragic way. That is the reason why Islam does not associate gambling and drinking with good sports and refreshing amusements and, instead, has banned them once and for all. To appreciate the viewpoint of Islam in this respect one has only to check any news medium, read any medical report, visit any social service agency, or watch any court proceedings. Of all the agonizing social problems, alcoholism is by far the most serious. More than one-half million Americans become alcoholics every year. One in every ten to twelve people who take their first drink in any given year is destined to become alcoholic. All these painful tragedies and real losses speak much louder than any theological or trade arguments.

The Family Life[2]

There have been many definitions and descriptions of the family. For our purpose, we shall adopt the following simplified definition. The family is a human social group whose members are

---

[2]This discussion is merely an outline of the author's extensive study of *The Family Structure in Islam* which will be published soon by American Trust Publications.

bound together by the bond of blood ties and/or marital relationship.

The family bond entails mutual expectations of rights and obligations that are prescribed by religion, enforced by law, and observed by the group members. Accordingly, the family members share certain mutual commitments. These pertain to identity and provision, inheritance and counsel, affection for the young and security for the aged, and maximization of effort to ensure the family continuity in peace.

As can be clearly seen from this, the foundations of the family in Islam are blood ties and/or marital commitments. Adoption, mutual alliance, clientage, private consent to sexual intimacy, and "common law" or "trial" marriages do not institute a family in the Islamic sense. Islam builds the family on solid grounds that are capable of providing reasonable continuity, true security, and mature intimacy. The foundations of the family have to be so firm and natural as to nurture sincere reciprocity and moral gratification. Islam recognizes that there is no more natural relationship than that of blood, and no more wholesome pattern of sexual intimacy than one in which morality and gratification are joined.

Islam recognizes the religious virtue, the social necessity, and the moral advantages of marriage. The normal course of behavior for the Muslim individual is to be family oriented and to seek a family of his own. Marriage and the family are central in the Islamic system. There are many passages in the Qur'ān and statements by the Prophet which go as far as to say that when a Muslim marries, he has thereby perfected half his religion; so let him be God-minded and careful with the other half.

Muslim scholars have interpreted the Qur'ān to mean that marriage is a religious duty, a moral safeguard, and a social commitment. As a religious duty, it must be fulfilled; but like all other duties in Islam, it is enjoined only upon those who are capable of meeting the responsibilities involved.

1. The Meaning of Marriage

Whatever meanings people assign to marriage, Islam views it as a strong bond (*mithaqun ghaleez*), a challenging commitment in the fullest sense of the word. It is a commitment to life itself, to society, and to the dignified, meaningful survival of the human race. It is a commitment that married partners make to one another as well as to God. It is the kind of commitment in which they find mutual fulfillment and self-realization, love and peace, compassion and serenity, comfort and hope. All this is because marriage in Islam is regarded first and foremost as a righteous act, an act of responsible devotion.

114

Sexual control may be a moral triumph, reproduction a social necessity or service, and sound health a gratifying state of mind. Yet, these values and purposes of marriage would take on a special meaning and be reinforced if they are intertwined with the idea of God, conceived also as religious commitments, and internalized as divine blessings. And this seems to be the focal point of marriage in Islam. To paraphrase some Qur'anic verses, the call is addressed to mankind to be dutiful to God, Who created them from a single soul, and from it or of it created its mate, and from the two of them scattered abroad many men and women (4:1). It was God Who created mankind out of one living soul, and created of that soul a spouse so that he might find comfort and rest in her (7:107). And it is a sign of God that He has created for men, of themselves, mates to seek in their company peace and tranquillity, and has set between them mutual love and mercy. Surely, in that are signs for those who contemplate (30:21). Even at the most trying times of married life, and in the midst of legal disputes and litigation, the Qur'ān reminds the parties of God's law; it commands them to be kind to one another, truly charitable toward one another, and above all dutiful to God.

It is noteworthy that the Islamic provisions of marriage apply to men and women equally. For example, if celibacy is not recommended for men, it is equally so for women. This is in recognition of the fact that women's needs are equally legitimate and are seriously taken into consideration. In fact, Islam regards marriage to be the normal, natural course for women just as it is for men. It may even be more so for women because it assures them, among other things, of relative economic security. This significant additional advantage for women does not, however, characterize marriage as a purely economic transaction. In fact, the least focal aspect of marriage in Islam is the economic factor, no matter how powerful this may be. The Prophet is reported to have said that a woman is ordinarily sought as wife for her wealth, for her beauty, for the nobility of her stock, or for her religious qualities; but blessed and fortunate is he who chooses his mate for piety in preference to everything else. The Qur'ān commands marriage to the spouseless and the pious even though they may be poor and slaves (24:32). On the other hand, whatever dowry (marriage gifts) a man gives his prospective wife belongs to her; and whatever she may have acquired prior to or after marriage is hers alone. There is no *necessary* community of property of husbands and wives. Furthermore, it is the husband who is responsible for the maintenance and economic security of the family. He must even provide the wife with the kind of help and service to which she was used before marriage, and, according to some scholars, she is under no *legal* obligation to do the routine housework, although she may do so, and usually does, for some reason or other, e.g. cooperation, economy, etc.

2.   The Permanence of Marriage

Because Islam considers marriage a very serious commitment, it has prescribed certain measures to make the marital bond as permanent as humanly possible. The parties must strive to meet the conditions of proper age, general compatibility, reasonable dowry, good will, free consent, unselfish guardianship, honorable intentions, and judicious discretion. When the parties enter into a marital contract, the intention must be clear to make the bond permanent, free from the casual and temporary designations. For this reason, trial marriages, term marriages, and all marriages that appear experimental, casual, or temporary are forbidden in Islam.[3] In one of his most unequivocal statements, the Prophet (صَلَّى ٱللّٰهُ عَلَيْهِ وَسَلَّم) declared that condemned are the men and women who relish the frequent change of marital partners, that is, the "tasters" who enjoy one partner for a while, then shift to another, then to a third, and so on.

However, to insist on the permanent character of marriage does not mean that the marital contract is absolutely indissoluble. Muslims are designated by the Qur'ān as a Middle Nation أُمَّةً وَسَطاً and Islam is truly a religion of the "Golden Mean", the well-balanced and well-integrated system. This is particularly clear in the case of marriage which Islam regards as neither a sacrament nor a simple civil contract. Rather, marriage in Islam is something unique with very special features of both sacramental and contractural nature. It is equally true that the alternative to this casual or temporary extremity is not the other extreme of absolute indissolubility of the marital contract. The Islamic course is one of equitable and realistic moderation. The marriage contract should be taken as a serious, permanent bond. But if it does not work well for any valid reason, it may be terminated in kindness and honor, with equity and peace.

---

[3]We are aware of the complex and intricate arguments used by some Sheea Muslims as regards the so-called *mut'ah* marriage. We appreciate the scholarly dimension of the problem but see no purpose in pursuing it here. Interested readers are referred to the detailed discussion of the whole matter in our forthcoming book *The Family Structure in Islam*.

3. The Husband-Wife Relationship

With piety as the basis of mate selection, and with the earnest satisfaction of the conditions of marriage, the parties should be well on the way to a happy and fulfilling married life. However, Islam goes much further than this in setting the course of behavior for husbands and wives. Many are the statements of the Qur'ān and the Sunnah that prescribe kindness and equity, compassion and love, sympathy and consideration, patience and good will. The Prophet goes as far as to declare that the best Muslim is the one who is best to his family, and the greatest, most blessed joy in life is a good, righteous wife.

The consummation of marriage creates new roles for the parties concerned. Each role is a set of equitable, proportionate rights and obligations. The role of the husband evolves around the moral principle that it is his solemn duty to God to treat his wife with kindness, honor, and patience; to keep her honorably or free her from the marital bond honorably; and to cause her no harm or grief (Qur'ān, 2:229-232; 4:19). The role of the wife is summarized in the verse that women have rights even as they have duties, according to what is equitable; but men have a degree over them (2:228). This degree is usually interpreted by Muslim scholars in conjunction with another passage which states, among other things, that men are trustees, guardians, and protectors of women because God has made some of them excel others and because men expend of their means (Qur'ān, 4:34). This degree may be likened to what sociologists call "instrumental leadership" or external authority in the household due to the division of labor and role differentiation. It does not, however, mean any categorical discrimination or superiority of one sex to the other[4].

A. The Wife's Rights: The Husband's Obligations. Translated into rules of behavior, these ethical principles allocate to the wife certain rights and corresponding obligations. Because the Qur'ān and the Sunnah of the Prophet have commanded kindness to women, it is the husband's duty to consort with his wife in an equitable and kind manner. One specific consequence of this Divine command is his responsibility for the full maintenance of the wife, a duty which he must discharge cheerfully, without reproach, injury, or condescendence.

---

[4]This degree question has been misunderstood by Muslims and non-Muslims alike. We dealt with the whole matter in great detail in *The Family Structure in Islam*. Our conclusion is that the verse does not say men are better or worse than women. Nor does it say what excellence really refers to, let alone identify it with manhood or womanhood.

Components of Maintenance. Maintenance entails the wife's incontestable right to lodging, clothing, nourishing, and general care and well-being. The wife's residence must be adequate so as to provide her with the reasonable level of privacy, comfort, and independence. Foremost is the welfare of the wife and the stability of the marriage. What is true of the residence is true of clothing, food, and general care. The wife has the right to be clothed, fed, and cared for by the husband, in accordance with his means and her style of life. These rights are to be exercised without extravagance or miserliness.

Non-Material Rights. The wife's material rights are not her only assurances and securities. She has other rights of a moral nature; and they are equally binding and specific. A husband is commanded by the law of God to treat his wife with equity, to respect her feelings, and to show her kindness and consideration. She is not to be shown any aversion by the husband or subjected to suspense and uncertainty. A corollary of this rule is that no man is allowed to keep his wife with the intention of inflicting harm on her or hindering her freedom. If he has no love or sympathy for her, she has the right to demand freedom from the marital bond, and no one may stand in her way to a new life.

B. The Wife's Obligations: The Husband's Rights. The main obligation of the wife as a partner in a marital relationship is to contribute to the success and blissfulness of the marriage as much as possible. She must be attentive to the comfort and well-being of her mate. She may neither offend him nor hurt his feelings. Perhaps nothing can illustrate the point better than the Qur'anic statement which describes the righteous people as those who pray:

رينا هب لنا من أزواجنا وذرياتنا قرة أعين ، واجعلنا للمتقين اماما .

Our Lord! Grant unto us wives and offspring who will be
the joy and the comfort of our eyes, and guide us to be
models of righteousness (Qur'ān, 25:74).

This is the basis on which all the wife's obligations rest and from which they flow. To fulfill this basic obligation, the wife must be faithful, trustworthy, and honest. More specifically, she must not deceive her mate by deliberately avoiding conception lest it deprive him of legitimate progeny. Nor must she allow any other person to have access to that which is exclusively the husband's right, i.e. sexual intimacy. A corollary of this is that she must not receive or

118

entertain strange males in her home without his knowledge and consent. Nor may she accept their gifts without his approval. This is probably meant to avoid jealousy, suspicion, gossip, etc., and also to maintain the integrity of all parties concerned. The husband's possessions are her trust. If she has access to any portion thereof, or if she is entrusted with any fund, she must discharge her duty wisely and thriftily. She may not lend or dispose of any of his belongings without his permission.

With respect to intimacy, the wife is to make herself desirable; to be attractive, responsive, and cooperative. A wife may not deny herself to her husband, for the Qur'ān speaks of them as a comfort to each other. Due consideration is, of course, given to health and decency. Moreover, the wife is not permitted to do anything that may render her companionship less desirable or less gratifying. If she does any such thing or neglects herself, the husband has the right to interfere with her freedom to rectify the situation. To insure maximum self-fulfillment for both partners, he is not permitted to do anything on his part that may impede her gratification.

4. The Parent-Child Relationship

A. The Child's Rights: The Parent's Duties. Islam's general approach to children may be summarized in a few principles. First, it is a divine injunction that no child may become the cause of harm to the parents (Qur'ān, 2:233). Secondly, by implication the parents should reciprocate and cause the child no harm either. The Qur'ān recognizes very clearly that parents are not always immune from overprotectiveness or negligence. On the basis of this recognition, it has, thirdly, established certain guidelines and pointed out certain facts with respect to children. It points out that children are joys of life as well as sources of pride, seeds of vanity and false security, fountains of distress and temptation. But it hastens to stress the greater joys of the spirit and caution parents against overconfidence, false pride, or misdeeds that might be caused by children. The religious moral principle of this position is that every individual, parent or child, relates to God directly and is independently responsible for his deeds. No child can absolve the parent on the Day of Judgement. Nor can a parent intercede on behalf of his child. Finally, Islam is strongly sensitive to the crucial dependence of the child on the parents. Their decisive role in forming the child's personality is clearly recognized in Islam. In a very suggestive statement, the Prophet declared that every child is born into the true malleable nature of *fitrah* (i.e., the pure natural state of *Islam*), its parents later on make it into a Jew, Christian or pagan.

119

According to these guidelines, and more specifically, one of the most inalienable rights of the child in Islam is the right to life and equal life chances. Preservation of the child's life is the third commandment in Islam. (6:151, cf. 17:23 ff).

Another equally inalienable right is the right of legitimacy, which holds that every child shall have a father, and one father only. A third set of rights comes under socialization, upbringing, and general care. To take good care of children is one of the most commendable deeds in Islam. The Prophet was fond of children and he expressed his conviction that his Muslim community would be noted among other communities for its kindness to children. It is charity of a higher order to attend to their spiritual welfare, educational needs, and general well-being. Interest in and responsibility for the child's welfare are questions of first priority. According to the Prophet's instructions, by the seventh day the child should be given a good, pleasant name and its head should be shaved, along with all the other hygienic measures required for healthy growing. This should be made a festive occasion marked with joy and charity.

Responsibility for and compassion toward the child is a matter of religious importance as well as social concern. Whether the parents are alive or deceased, present or absent, known or unknown, the child is to be provided with optimum care. Whenever there are executers or relatives close enough to be held responsible for the child's welfare, they shall be directed to discharge this duty. But if there is no next of kin, care for the child becomes a joint responsibility of the entire Muslim community, designated officials and commoners alike.

B.   The Child's Duties: The Parent's Rights. The parent-child relationship is complementary. Parent and child in Islam are bound together by mutual obligations and reciprocal commitments. But the age differential is sometimes so wide as to cause parents to grow physically weak and mentally feeble. This is often accompanied by impatience, degeneration of energy, heightened sensitivity, and perhaps misjudgement. It may also result in abuses of parental authority or intergenerational estrangement and uneasiness, something similar to what is now called the "generation gap". It was probably in view of these considerations that Islam has taken cognizance of certain facts and made basic provisions to govern the individual's relationship to his parents.

The fact that parents are advanced in age and are generally believed to be more experienced does not by itself validate their views or certify their standards. Similarly, youth *per se* is not the sole fountain of energy, idealism, or wisdom. In various contexts, the Qur'ān cites instances where the parents were proven wrong in their encounter with their children and also where children misjudged the positions of their parents (see Qur'ān, 6:74; 11:42-46; 19:42-48).

More significant, perhaps, is the fact that customs, folkways, traditions, or the parents' value system and standards do not in themselves constitute truth and rightness. In several passages the Qur'ān strongly reproaches those who may stray away from the truth just because it is new to them, or contrary to the familiar, or incompatible with the parents' values. Furthermore, it focalizes the fact that if loyalty or obedience to the parents is likely to alienate the individual from God, he must side with God, as it were. It is true, the parents merit consideration, love, compassion, and mercy. But if they step out of their proper line to intrude upon the rights of God, a demarcation line must be drawn and maintained.

The Qur'ān sums up the whole question in the master concept of *ihsan*, which denotes what is right, good, and beautiful. The practical implications of the concept of *ihsān* to the parents entail active empathy and patience, gratitude and compassion, respect for them and prayers for their souls, honoring their legitimate commitments and providing them with sincere counsel.

One basic dimension of *ihsān* is deference. Parents have the right to expect obedience from their children if only in partial return for what the parents have done for them. But if parents demand the wrong or ask for the improper, disobedience becomes not only justifiable, but also imperative. Obey or disobey, the children's attitude toward parents may not be categorical submissiveness or irresponsible defiance.

The last integral part of *ihsān* to be mentioned here is that children are responsible for the support and maintenance of parents. It is an absolute religious duty to provide for the parents in case of need and help them to make their lives as comfortable as possible.

5. Other Aspects of the Family Life

Closely connected with the family life is the treatment of "servants", other family members, relations, and neighbors. To those who keep permanent maids Prophet Muhammad has given advice and good tidings. "Masters" are enjoined to treat their servants like brothers, and not like slaves, because whoever treats his servant well, said the Prophet, God will make his death easy and pleasant, a moment which is ordinarily painful and difficult. Servants are entitled to justice, kindness, mercy, food, clothing, accommodation and other personal expenses. The Prophet goes as far as to say that they should be fed and dressed of the same stuff as used by their masters, and this is to be provided by the masters themselves as a part of their obligations to the servants. These are not to be persecuted or disdained or overcharged with work. This stipulation is designed to show how Islam dignifies humanity and honors labor without inviting the class warfare or the despotic authority of the proletariat. Being a servant or laborer does not deprive any person of his rights or affect his dignity as a human being. Nor does it make him addicted to the opium of the utopian proletariat. All citizens of a real Muslim society stand on equal footing, because Islam does not recognize the caste system or the second class citizenship. The only superiority acknowledged by Islam is that of piety and good deeds in the service of God (Qur'ān, 9:105; 49:13).

Man is ordained by God to extend his utmost help and kindness to other family members and relations, to show them true feelings of love and care. It might be interesting to note that the word 'kinship' in Arabic is derived from a root word which means mercy (Rahim and Rahmah). Kindness to one's kinsfolk is a short cut to Paradise, which is otherwise forbidden for those who neglect their duties in this respect. The extension of kind treatment to relatives is described by the Prophet as a Divine blessing of one's life and provisions. It is a sacred duty to be good to the kin even though they may not respond in a similar way. The duty is enjoined by God and should be observed for the sake of God regardless of the kin's response (Qur'ān, 2:177; 4:36; 16:90; 17:23-26).

The status of neighbors is very high in the viewpoint of Islam. Neighbors of all kinds enjoy a great number of privileges conferred on them by Islam. In his elaboration on the Qur'anic teachings relevant to this point, Prophet Muhammad is reported as saying that nobody can be a true Believer unless his neighbors feel secure and safe from his side. Also, nobody can be a true Believer, if his neighbors pass the night hungry while he has his belly full. He who is best to his neighbors, stated the Prophet, will enjoy the neighborhood of God on the Day of Resurrection. Presents, gifts and sharing of joys and sorrows should be exchanged between neighbors. In another declaration the Prophet said: "Do you know what the rights of a neighbor are? Help him if he asks your help; give him relief if he seeks your relief; lend him if he needs loan; show him concern if he is distressed; nurse him when he is ill; attend his funeral if he dies; congratulate him if he meets any good; sympathize with him if any calamity befalls him; do not block his air by raising your building high without his permission; harass him not; give him a share when you buy fruits, and if you do not give him, bring your buys right to your house quietly and let not your children take them out to excite the anger of his children". Moreover, the Prophet is reported as having said that the rights of the neighbors were so much emphasized by the angel Gabriel that he thought neighbors would perhaps be entitled to partake of one's inheritance. (See also the verses numbered in the previous paragraph).

The Social Life

The social life of the true Muslim is based upon supreme principles and designed to secure happiness with prosperity for the individual as well as for the society. Class warfare, social castes and domination of the individual over society or viceversa are alien to the social life of Islam. Nowhere in the Qur'ān or the Traditions of Prophet Muhammad can one find any mention of superiority on account of class or origin or wealth. On the contrary, there are many verses of the Qur'ān and sayings of Muhammad to remind mankind of the vital facts of life, facts which serve at the same time as principles of the social structure of the Islamic life. Among these is the fact that humanity represents one family springing from one and the same father and mother, and aspiring to the same ultimate goals.

The unity of mankind is conceived in the light of the common parentage of Adam and Eve. Every human being is a member of the universal family established by the First Father and the First Mother, and is entitled therefore to enjoy the common benefits as he is enjoined to share the common responsibilities. When people realize that they all belong to Adam and Eve and that these were the creation of God, there will be no room for racial prejudice or social injustice or second class citizenship. People will be united in their social behavior as they are united in nature by the bond of common parentage. In the Qur'ān and the Traditions of Muhammad there is a constant reminder of this important fact, the unity of humanity by nature and origin. This is to eliminate racial pride and claims to national or ethnic superiority, and pave the way for genuine brotherhood (Qur'ān, 4:1; 7:189; 49:10-13).

The unity of humanity is not only in its origin but also in its ultimate aims. According to Islam, the final goal of humanity is God. From Him we come, for Him we live and to Him we shall all return. In fact, the sole purpose of creation as described by the Qur'ān is to worship God and serve His cause, the cause of truth and justice, of love and mercy, of brotherhood and morality (Qur'ān, 51:56-58).

On this unity of origin and ultimate goal as the background of the social life in Islam, the relations between the individual and society are based. The role of the individual is complementary to that of society. Between the two there are social solidarity and mutual responsibility. The individual is responsible for the common welfare and prosperity of his society. This responsibility is not only to the society but also to God. In this way the individual works with a sound social-mindedness and a genuine feeling of inescapable responsibility. It is his role to do the utmost for his society and contribute to its common welfare. On the other hand, the society is also responsible to God for the welfare of the individual. When the individual is able he is the contributor and society is the beneficiary. In return he is entitled to security and care, should he become disabled. In this case he is the beneficiary and society is the contributor. So duties and rights correspond harmoniously. Responsibility and concern are mutual. There is no state to dominate the individual and abrogate his personal entity. Likewise, there is no individual or class of individuals to exploit the society and corrupt the State. There is harmony with peace and mutual security. There is a constructive interaction between the individual and society.

Besides the unity of humanity in origin and ultimate goal, and besides this mutual responsibility and concern, the social life of Islam is characterized by cooperation in goodness and piety. It is marked with full recognition of the individual and his sacred rights to life, property and honor. It is also marked with an effective role played by the individual in the domain of social morals and ethics. In an Islamic society the individual cannot be indifferent. He is enjoined to play an active part in the establishment of sound social morals by way of inviting to the good and combating the evil in any form with all lawful means at his disposal. In so doing, not only does he shun evil and do good but also helps others to do the same. The individual who feels indifferent to his society is a selfish sinner; his morals are in trouble, his conscience is in disorder, and his faith is undernourished.

The structure of social life in Islam is very lofty, sound and comprehensive. Among the substantial elements of this structure are sincere love for one's fellow human beings, mercy for the young, respect for the elders, comfort and consolation for the distressed, visiting the sick, relieving the grieved, genuine feelings of brotherhood and social solidarity; respect for the rights of other people to life, property, and honor; mutual responsibility between the individual and society. It is a common thing to come across Prophetic statements like these:

Whoever relieves a human being from a grief of this world, God will relieve him from a grief on the Day of Judgement.

Anyone who has no mercy on the juniors and respect for the seniors is not one of us Muslims.

None of you is a true believer in Islam until and unless he loves for his fellow man what he loves for his own self.

Whoever invites others to good is like the doer of good and will be rewarded accordingly, and whoever instigates evil is like the doer of evil and will be punished accordingly.

In the Qur'ān, on the other hand, one finds numerous Divine instructions like these:

O you who believe! Mind God as He should be minded, and die not except in a state of Islam. And hold fast, all together, by the Rope of God, and be not divided among yourselves. And remember with gratitude God's favor on you; for you were enemies and He joined your hearts in love, so that by His Grace you have become brethren; and you were on the brink of the Pit of Fire and He saved you from it. Thus does God make His Signs clear to you that you may be guided. Let there arise out of you a band of people inviting to all that is good, enjoining what is right, and forbidding what is wrong. They are the ones to attain felicity (3:102-104).

O you who believe! Fulfill all obligations . . . and help you one another in righteousness and piety, but help you not one another in sin and rancor. Mind God; for God is strict in punishment (5:1-3).

In addition to what has already been said, the social patterns of Islam could be seen, once more, in the last sermon of Prophet Muhammad during the course of pilgrimage. Addressing the tens of thousands of pilgrims, he said, among other things:

O people! listen to my words, for I know not whether another year will be vouchsafe to me after this to find myself amongst you at this place.

Your lives and properties are sacred and inviolable amongst one another until you appear before the Lord, as this day of this month is sacred for all. And remember that you shall have to appear before your Lord Who shall demand from you an account of all your actions.

O people! you have rights over your wives and your wives have rights over you. Treat your wives with love and kindness. Verily you have taken them as the trust of God, and have made their persons lawful unto you by the words of God. Keep always faithful to the trust reposed in you, and avoid sins.

Henceforth, the vengeance of blood practiced in the days of ignorance and paganism is prohibited and all blood feud abolished.

And your slaves! See that you feed them with such food as you eat yourselves. and clothe them with the stuff you wear; and if they commit a fault which you are not inclined to forgive, then part from them, for they are the servants of the Lord, and are not to be harshly treated.

O people! Listen to my words and understand the same. Know that all Muslims are brothers unto one another. You are One Brotherhood. Nothing which belongs to another is lawful unto his brother unless freely given out of good will. Guard yourselves from committing injustice.

Like this day of this month in this territory sacred and inviolable, God has made the life and property and honor of each of you unto the other, until you meet your Lord.

Let him that is present tell it to him that is absent. Haply he that shall be told may remember better than he who has heard it.

Verily, I have fulfilled my mission. I have left that amongst you, a plain command, the Book of God, and manifest Ordinances which if you hold fast, you shall never go astray.

The Economic Life

The economic life of Islam is also based upon solid foundations and Divine instructions. Earning one's living through decent labor is not only a duty but a great virtue as well. Dependence of any able effortless person on somebody else for a livelihood is a religious sin, a social stigma and disgraceful humility.

A Muslim is enjoined by God to be self-supporting and to stay away from being a liability on anybody. Islam respects all kinds of work for earning one's livelihood so long as there is no indecency or wrong involved. With a clear conscience and due respect from society the Muslim can roll up his sleeves and undertake any kind of work available to provide for himself and his dependents. Prophet Muhammad is reported as having said that it is far better for one even to take his rope, cut wood, pile it up and sell it in order to eat and give charity than to beg others whether they give him or not. According to Islam, the status of honest working men cannot be lowered on account of the kind of work they are doing for a living. Yet the laboring workers have no limited scope for improving their lots and raising their standards as high as possible. They have equal opportunities at their disposal and enjoy freedom of enterprise.

Whatever the individual makes or earns through lawful means is his private possession, which neither the State nor anybody else can justifiably claim. In return for this right of private possession he has only to fulfill certain obligations to the society and pay certain taxes to the State. When this is done, he has full rights to protection by the State, and his freedom ot enterprise is secure and guaranteed. Under the Islamic system the menace of greedy capitalism and destructive communism never arises. The enterprising individual is responsible for the prosperity of the State, and the State in turn is responsible for the security of the individual. Class conflicts are replaced by co-operation and harmony; fear and suspicion are remedied by mutual security and confidence.

The economic system of Islam is not drawn in the light of arithmetical calculations and capacities of production alone. Rather, it is drawn and conceived in the light of a comprehensive system of morals and principles. The person who is working for another person or for a firm or an institution is ordained by God to do his work with efficiency and honesty. The Prophet said that if any of you under-takes to do any work, God loves to see him do it well and with efficiency. Once the work is done, the worker is entitled to a fair wage for his services. Failure by the employer to pay the just wage, or attempts to cut it down and waver on it is a punishable act, according to the Law of God.

Business transactions enjoy a great deal of attention from Islam. Honest trade is permitted and blessed by God. This may be carried out through individuals, companies, agencies and the like. But all business deals should be concluded with frankness and honesty. Cheating, hiding defects of merchandise from the dealers, exploiting the needs of customers, monopoly of stocks to force one's own prices are all sinful acts and punishable by the Islamic Law. If one is to make a decent living, it has to be made through honest ways and hard endeavor. Otherwise, easy come, easy go, and it is not only that, but anybody that is bred with unlawful provisions will be, according to the Prophet, a burning fuel to the Hell Fire on the Day of Judgement. To combat cheating and exploitation, Islam demands honesty in business, warns the cheaters, encourages decent work and forbids usury or the taking of interest just in return for lending money to the needy. This is to show man that he rightfully owns only what he works for, and that exploitation of other people's pressing needs is irreligious, inhuman and immoral. In the Qur'ān God says:

Those who devour usury will not stand except as stands one whom the Evil One by his touch has driven to madness. That is because they say: 'trade is like usury'. But God has permitted trade and forbidden usury. Those who, after receiving direction from their Lord, desist, shall be pardoned for the past; their case is for God (to judge). But those who repeat (the offence) are Companions of the Fire; they will abide therein (for ever). God will deprive usury of all blessing, but will give increase for deeds of charity; for He loves not creatures ungrateful and wicked (2:274-276).

And the Firmament has He raised high, and He has set up the Balance (of Justice) in order that you may not transgress (due) balance. So establish weight with justice and fall not short in the balance (55:7-9). This is to guide man to resort to justice and straight-forwardness in all his dealings and transactions. The future of cheaters is grim and their doom is awful. Here is how the Qur'ān looks into the matter:

Woe to those who deal in fraud, those who, when they have to receive by measure from men, exact full measure, but when they have to give by measure or weight to men give less than due. Do they not think that they will be called to account on a Mighty Day, a Day when (all) mankind will stand before the Lord of the Worlds (83:1-6)?

Besides that, there are numerous Traditions of Prophet Muhammad excluding the cheaters, exploiters, monopolizers and dishonest business people from the band of the true Muslims. Any business deal that involves injustice or cheating or exploitation is strictly inhibited and cancellable by the Law even after it is concluded. The main purpose of the Islamic legislations on economics and commerce is to secure the rights of the individual and maintain the solidarity of society, to introduce high morality to the world of business and enforce the Law of God in that sphere of enterprise. It is logical and consistent that Islam should be concerned with such aspects as these, because it is not merely a spiritual formula but a complete system of life in all its walks.

Proprietors are constantly reminded of the fact that they are in reality mere agents appointed by God to administer their holdings. There is nothing in Islam to stop the Muslim from attaining wealth and endeavoring for material improvements through lawful means and decent channels. Yet the fact remains that man comes to this world empty-handed and departs from it likewise. The actual and real owner of things is God alone of Whom any proprietor is simply an appointed agent, a mere trustee. This is not only a fact of life but also has a significant bearing on human behavior. It makes the proprietor always ready to spend in the way of God and to contribute to worthy causes. It makes him responsive to the needs of his society and gives him an important role to play, a sacred mission to fulfill. It saves him from the pit of selfishness, greed and injustice. This is the true conception of property in Islam, and that is the actual status of proprietors. The Qur'ān considers possession of wealth a trying test, and not a token of virtuous excellence or privileged nobility or a means of exploitation. God says: It is He Who has made you (His) agents, inheritors of the earth: He has raised you in ranks, some above others; that He may try you in the gifts He has given you. Verily, your Lord is quick in punishment, yet He is indeed Oft-Forgiving, Most Merciful (6:165).

Moreover, the Qur'ān reports to mankind an interesting discourse between Moses and his people. It runs as follows:

Said Moses to his people, 'pray for help from God, and wait in patience and constancy; for the earth is God's. He gives it as a heritage to such of His servants as He pleases; and the end is best for the righteous.'
They said, 'We have had nothing but trouble, both before and after you came to us.' He said: 'It may be that your Lord will destroy your enemies and make you inheritors in the earth; that so He may try you by your deeds' (7:128-129).

This discourse between Moses and his people does not imply in any sense a recognition of any privileged genus of mankind on account of racial origin or ethnic identity. Nor does it mean that the Qur'ān approves completely of the conduct and conceptions of the followers of Moses in later centuries. The tone of the text is rather reproachful and critical of the doubters; and reassuring of the fact that everything in the earth belongs to God, Who distributes it among His servants in the form of inherited trusts and objects of trial. The point is brought home time and again throughout the Qur'an. For example, it says:

To Him belongs the dominion of the heavens and the earth, and all affairs are referred back to God . . . Believe in God and His Messenger, and spend (in charity) out of the (substance) whereof He has made you heirs. For, those of you who believe and spend (in charity)—for them there is a great reward. And what cause have you why you should not spend in the cause of God? For to God belongs the heritage of the heavens and the earth (57:5, 7, 10).

Unlike Communism, Islam replaces the totalitarian artificial supremacy of the Communist State by the beneficial supremacy of God; and the Communist theory of class warfare by sound morals, mutual responsibilities and cooperation. On the other hand, it gives utmost assurances against greedy capitalism and ruthless exploitation by proprietors. The economic system of Islam grants full recognition of the "independent" entity of the individual and his natural aspirations to work and possessions. Yet it does not conceive of him as absolutely independent of God or the universe. It does not deify man or his capital, nor does it deify the proletariat and abolish free enterprise. It accepts man the way he is created and deals with him accordingly, making allowances for his instinctive aspirations and limited power. Man is a man, and he should be accepted and dealt with as such. He is not a god or a semi-god to arrogate to himself absolute powers and unquestionable infallibility. Nor is he a countless or insignificant entity.

He is someone to be recognized but in his real status and non-exaggerated or belittled nature. He is not above or out of the rest of the universe but a part of a whole system, an element in the total foundation of the universe.

Although man is encouraged to work, is free to enterprise, is entitled to earn and possess, the fact that he is a mere trustee provides the necessary measure to insure proper handling of his possessions, his trusts. He has authority to earn, to invest and to spend. Yet in so doing he is guided by high principles to save him from going astray. An example may be sufficient to illustrate the point. Proprietors are not unreservedly free to spend their money or handle their properties the way they please. There are certain rules of expenditure to be followed. In the words of the Qur'ān, God enjoins upon the proprietor to fulfill his financial obligations towards his fellow men, and to be moderate in his private spending. He is always reminded of the fact that God is the Real Provider and Actual Possessor. Here is the declaration of the Qur'ān:

And render to the kindred their due rights, as (also) to those in want, and to the wayfarer. But squander not (your wealth) in the manner of a spendthrift. Verily, spendthrifts are brothers of the Evil Ones, and the Evil One is to his Lord (Himself) ungrateful.

Make not your hand tied (like a niggard's) to your neck, nor stretch it iorth to its utmost reach (like a foolish spendthrift); lest you become rebuked and destitute. Verily your Lord does provide sustenance in abundance for whom He pleases, and He provides in a just measure. For He does know and regard all His servants (17:26-27, 29-30).

The Political Life

Like the social and economic life, the political life of Islam is based on sound spiritual and moral foundations, and is guided by Divine instructions. The political system of Islam is unique in its structure, its function, and its purpose. It is not pragmatic or instrumentalistic. It is not theocracy whereby a certain class of people assumes divine rights, hereditary or otherwise, and poses, above other citizens, beyond accountability. Nor is it a proletariat whereby some revengeful laborers capture power. It is not even democracy in its popular sense. It is something different from all that. To appreciate the political outlook of Islam one has only to know that it is based on the following principles:

1. Every deed of the Muslim individual or group of individuals must be inspired and guided by the Law of God, the Qur'ān, which is the constitution chosen by God for His true servants. And if any do

fail to judge (or rule) according to what God has revealed, they are the unbelievers . . . they are the wrong-doers . . . they are the rebels (5:47-50). Verily this Qur'ān does guide to that which is most right and best (17:9).

2. The sovereignty in the Islamic State does not belong to tne ruler nor even to the people themselves. It belongs to God, and the people as a whole exercise it by trust from Him to enforce His law and enact His will. The ruler, any ruler, is only an acting executive chosen by the people to serve them according to the Law of God. This is the foundation of the Islamic State and is only consistent with the general outlook of Islam on the universe of which God is the Creator and in which He is the Sole Sovereign. In the Qur'ān, one comes across statements like these: Authority, power and sovereignty belong to none but God, or Blessed be He in Whose hands is dominion, and He over all things has power (Qur'ān, 67:1), or Verily God does command you to render back your trusts to those to whom they are due; and when you judge (or rule) between people that you judge with justice. Verily how excellent is the teaching which He gives you! (4:58), or And to God belongs the dominion of the heavens and the earth, and all that is between; and unto Him is the final goal (of all) (5:20).

3. The aim of the Islamic State is to administer justice and provide security and protection for all citizens, regardless of color or race or creed, in conformity with the stipulations of God in His constitution, the Qur'ān. The question of religious or racial minorities does not arise so long as they are law-abiding and peaceful citizens. The Qur'ān says:

O you who believe! Stand out firmly for justice, as witnesses to fair dealing, and let not the hatred of others to you make you swerve to wrong and depart from justice. Be just: that is most close to piety, and mind God for God is well-acquainted with all that you do (5:9; cf. 4:135).

Verily God will defend those who believe, - - - -, those who, if We establish them in the Land, establish regular prayers and give regular charity, enjoin the right and forbid the wrong. With God rests the end (and decision) of all affairs (22:38-41).

4. Formed for the above-mentioned purposes and established to enforce the Law of God, the Islamic State cannot be controlled by any political party of a non-Islamic platform or subjected to foreign powers. It has to be independent to exercise its due authority on behalf of God and in His cause. This originates from the principle that a Muslim is one who submits to God alone and pledges loyalty to His Law, offering utmost cooperation and support to those who

administer the Law and observe its stipulations. It is incompatible with Islam, therefore, for a Muslim nation to pledge support to any political party of a non-Islamic platform or to yield to a non-Islamic government of alien origins and aims. And never will God grant to the Unbelievers a way (to triumph or rule) over the Believers (4:141). The answer of the Believers, when summoned to God and His Messenger, in order that He may judge (or rule) between them, is no other than this: they say 'We hear and we obey' - - - - God has promised, to those among you who believe and work righteous deeds, that He will, of a surety, make them His vicegerents in the land, as He made those before them; that He will establish in authority their religion—the one which He has chosen for them; and that He will change (their state), after the fear in which they (lived), to one of security and peace: 'They will worship Me (alone) and not associate any partner with Me.' (24:51, 55). God has decreed: It is I and My apostles who must prevail. Verily God is One full of strength, able to enforce His will. You will not find any people who believe in God and the Last Day, loving those who resist God and His apostles, even though they were their fathers or their sons, or their brothers or their kindred. For such believers He has written Faith in their hearts and strengthened them with a spirit for Himself (58:21-22).

5.   The ruler, any ruler, is not a sovereign over the people. He is a representative employee chosen by the people and derives his authority from his obedience to the Law of God, the Law which binds the rulers and the ruled alike by a solemn contract over which God is the Supervisor. The political contract of Islam is not concluded between the administration and the public alone. It is between these combined on one side and God on the other, and it is morally valid and binding only as long as the human sides fulfill their obligations to the Divine. The rulers who are chosen by their people to administer the words of God are entitled to support and cooperation from the public inasmuch as they observe the very words of God. Should the public or any member of society fail to render support to and co-operation with such administrators, their act would be considered an irresponsible offense against the administration as well as against God Himself. Likewise, if the administration swerves from the Path of God or fails to observe His Law, it is not only committing a like offense but also has no right to the support and loyalty of the public. The Qur'ān says:

O you who believe! Obey God, and obey the Messenger (of God) and those charged with authority among you. If you differ in anything among yourselves, refer it to God and His Messenger, if you do believe in God and the Last Day. That is best, and most suitable for final determination (4:59).

Obedience to those charged with authority is conditioned by their own obedience to the Law of God and the Traditions of His Messenger. In one of his conclusive statements Muhammad said that there is no obedience or loyalty to any human being, ruler or otherwise, who is not himself obedient to God and bound by His Law. The early successors of Muhammad understood this principle very clearly and declared in their first statements of policy that they were to be obeyed and helped by the public as long as they themselves obeyed God, and that they had no claims to obedience from the people if they were to depart from the way of God.

6. The rulers and administrators must be chosen from among the best qualified citizens on the basis of their own merits of virtue, fitness and competence. Racial origin or family prestige and financial status do not in themselves make any potential candidates more or less qualified for high public offices. They neither promote nor hinder the merits of the individual. Every candidate must be judged on his own merits, of which family prestige, wealth, race and age as such constitute no significant part. The candidates may be chosen by public consent through general elections, or they may be selected and authorized by public leaders, who are, in turn, entrusted to leadership by the free accord of the various sections of society. Thus, an Islamic State can have as many representative councils or municipal governments as desired. The right of election or selection and the conduct of administration are governed by the Law of God and must be aimed at the best interest of society as a whole. Prophet Muhammad said: "Whoever entrusts a man to a public office where in his society there is a better man than this trustee, he has betrayed the trust of God and His Messenger and the Muslims". In a political sense this means that the electorate cannot, morally speaking, be indifferent to public events and that they, whenever they cast ballots, vote after careful investigations and premeditated choice. In this way the State could have the best possible safeguard of security and responsible citizenship, something which many democratic states of modernity lack.

7. After the people make their choice through election or selection of their ruler, every citizen is enjoined to supervise, with his means, the conduct of the administration and question its handling of public affairs, whenever he sees anything wrong with it. If the administration betrays the trust of God and the public, it has no right to continue in office. It must be ousted and replaced by another, and it is the responsibility of every citizen to see to it that this is done in the public interest. The question of hereditary power or lifetime government is therefore inapplicable to an Islamic State.

8.   Although the ruler is chosen and appointed by the people, his first responsibility is to God and, then, to the people. His office is not just symbolic nor is his role simply abstract. He is not a helpless puppet whose function is to sign papers or execute the public will invariably, i.e., whether it is right or wrong. He must exercise actual powers on behalf of the people for their best interest in accordance with the Law of God, because he has a dual responsibility. On the one hand, he is accountable to God for his conduct and, on the other, he is responsible to the people who have put their trust in him. He will have to give full account before God of how he treated his people themselves or their representatives. But both the ruler and his people will also have to give full account before God of how they treated the Qur'ān, how they regarded the Law of God which He has given as a binding force. It is by his responsibility to the people that he should handle their affairs in the best common interest, and it is by his accountability to God that he should do so according to the Law of God. Thus, the political system of Islam is fundamentally different from all other political systems and doctrines known to mankind, and the ruler is not to govern the people according to their own desires. He is to serve them by making justice a common law, by making their genuine obedience to the Sovereign Lord of the universe a regular function of the state, and by making sound morality a noble undertaking of the administration.

9.   Although the Qur'ān is the Constitution of the Islamic State, Muslims are ordained by God to handle their common affairs through consultative methods. This makes room for legislative councils and consultative bodies on the local as well as on the national and international levels. Every citizen in the Islamic State is enjoined to offer his best advice on common matters and must be entitled to do so. To insure fulfillment of this obligation in a practicable and useful way, the rulers must seek the advice of the learned and experienced people in the state. But this does not in any sense deny the right of average citizens who must speak out whenever the occasion arises.

In this way every citizen of the Islamic State has an obligation, in one capacity or another, to fulfill and is deeply concerned, directly or otherwise, about the conduct of public affairs. Islamic history provides authentic records of how the chief rulers and Caliphs were questioned, advised and corrected by common people, men and women alike. The principle of mutual consultation is so fundamental in Islam that not only has one to speak up his mind, but also to do so in the sincerest and most effective manner, for the best interest of society. Consultative methods in politics, or in any other field for that matter, are not only a democratic formula of government, but a religious injunction and a moral duty enjoined upon the rulers as well as the ruled. Besides his constant practice of this principle, the Prophet said that it is an essential part of religion to give good counsel. The purpose of such counsel is to insure that the Law of God is observed, and that the rights of citizens are honored and their obligations fulfilled. To prevent the rise of professional politics and counteract the underground politicians of opportunist platforms, the Prophet, speaking on the authority of God, said that whoever speaks—be it in a form of counsel or any other form—must say the right and good things; or else he had better keep silent. This is to warn counselors and advisers against selfish inclinations or egoistic temptations. It is to guarantee that counsel is given with the sincerest intentions and in the best interest of the public, because it is authorized by God, carried on His behalf and aimed at the common welfare. The seeking of counsel on the part of the ruler and rendering it on the part of the public is not a matter of choice or a voluntary measure. It is an article of Faith, a religious ordinance. Muhammad himself, although wise, "infallible" and unselfish, was not above the maxim or an exception to the rule. God instructs him in this way:

It is by the mercy of God that you dealt gently with them (your people). Were you severe or harsh-hearted, they would have broken away from about you. So pass over their faults, and ask for (God's) forgiveness for them; and consult them in affairs (of moment). Then, when you have taken a decision, put your trust (in Him) (3:159).

Enumerating the characteristics of the Believers, the Qur'ān makes clear mention of mutual counsel as an article of Faith. The Believers are those who believe in God and put their trust in their Lord, those who avoid the greater crimes and shameful deeds, and, when they are angry even then forgive; those who hearken to their Lord, and establish regular prayer, and conduct their affairs by mutual consultation, and spend out of what We bestow on them for sustenance (by way of charity); and those who, when an oppressive wrong is inflicted on them, (are not cowed but) help and defend themselves (42:36-39).

10. Under the political system of Islam, every citizen is entitled to enjoy freedom of belief and conscience, and freedom of thought and expression. He is free to develop his potentialities and improve his lot, to work and compete, to earn and possess, to approve and disapprove of things, according to his honest judgement. But his freedom is not, and cannot be, absolute; or else it amounts to chaos and anarchy. It is guaranteed by the Law of God and governed by the very same Law. As long as it is in line with this Law it is the rightful privilege of every individual citizen; but if it transgresses the limits of

Law or conflicts with the common interest, it becomes a violation of God's Law and must, therefore, be controlled. The individual is part of the whole universe, so he must adjust himself to the Law and order of God, the Law by which the entire universe is administered. On the other hand, he is a member of his community or nation, and must adapt his own rights and interests to those of others in a mutually beneficial manner. If the individual takes an independent attitude on a certain matter of public concern and finds the majority taking a different attitude, he must in the end side with the majority to maintain solidarity and co-operation, provided the majority's decision is not contrary to the Law of God. Yet in the process of forming a public opinion he is fully entitled to express his own opinion and persuade others of his convictions without disturbance or distoriton. When it becomes clear that the majority have chosen a different course, then he is bound to go along with them, because the matter in question is no longer under individual consideration or deliberation but is undergoing public implementation (3:102-105; 8:46).

11.   The governorship of the Islamic State is a public trust, to which the administrators are entrusted by the word of God as well as by the common consent of the people. With God being the Supreme Sovereign of the State, whoever represents Him in the top office must be faithful to the Entrusting Authority, must be a believer in God. And with the majority of the people being Muslims, whoever assumes the office of Presidency or Caliphate must be a true Muslim. These measures are taken to serve the common interest and fulfill all the obligations of the State to God as well as to the citizens. They are also to secure and honor the rights of the so-called religious or racial minorities.

It is unfortunate for humanity that this ruling of Islam has been poorly understood and badly distorted. The fact of the matter is that this ruling is not discriminating against minorities but is rather protective and assertive of their rights. Whoever wishes to be a law-abiding citizen of the Islamic State is welcome to it, and shares with others the duties and prerogatives of responsible citizenship. His being a non-Muslim does not lower his status or drop him down to second class citizenship, as long as he obeys the common Law of the State and exercises his rights in a responsible manner. If he wishes, for example, to pay the religious tax (Zakah) and other state taxes, like the Muslim citizens, towards the maintenance of the State and in return for his own security and welfare, he may do so. But if he thinks that paying the Islamic Tax (Zakah) is humiliating to his dignity or injurious to his feelings on account of his being a non-Muslim, he may pay his taxes in a different form known as "tributes"

136

or jizyah — so he in fact enjoys a choice which Muslims of the same state do not themselves enjoy. In return for his contributions to the State, he is fully entitled to protection and security by the State officials and the society.

Similarly, if such a citizen wants to administer his personal life of marriage, divorce, foods, inheritance, and so on, according to the Islamic Law, his desire must be recognized, and his rights must be respected. But if he wishes to administer these affairs according to his own religious teachings, he is absolutely free to do so, and no one can hamper the exercise of his rights in that respect. So in personal or sentimental matters, he may resort to his own teachings or to the public regulations. But in matters of public interest and common affairs he must abide by the Law of the State, the Law of God. No matter what he chooses, he is no less entitled to protection and security than any other citizen. All this is not a dream of a heavenly kingdom yet to come. It is the teaching of the Qur'ān, the practice of Muhammad and the record of Islamic history. It is reported, for example, that 'Umar ibn al-Khattab, the second Caliph after Muhammad, was once passing by a place where he found an old Jew in pitiful condition. 'Umar inquired about the man and found out what his state was like. In a regretful tone he said to the man: "We collected tributes (taxes) from you when you were able. Now you are deserted and neglected. How unjust to you 'Umar has been!" After he finished his remark, a regular pension for the old man was ordered and the order was made effective immediately. 'Umar and other rulers received their political orientation at the hands of Muhammad, who in turn had been taught by God. These teachings are recorded in the Qur'ān in verses like these:

God forbids you not, with regard to those who do not fight you for (your) Faith nor drive you out of your homes, from dealing kindly and justly with them. For God loves those who are just. God only forbids you with regard to those who fight you for (your) Faith, and drive you out of your homes, and support others in driving you out, from turning to them for friendship and protection. Those who turn to them for friendship and protection are the wrongdoers (60:8-9).

Finally, it is a categorical error to compare the Islamic State and its need for a Muslim head with the secular state where it is, theoretically, conceivable to have a head of state who may belong to a minority group. The comparison is fallacious and misleading for several reasons. First, it assumes that secularism, however superficial, is sounder than the Islamic ideology. Such an assumption or premise is pretentious. Secondly, the duties and rights of a head of state under Islam are quite different from those of his counterpart in a secular order, as outlined above. Thirdly, the modern secular spirit is for the most part a redemptive, apologetic restitution, a case which does not apply to Islam. Moreover, a head of secular state, if there can be a real one, may belong to a racial, ethnic, or religious minority. But he almost invariably has to join a majority party. What this does in fact is to substitute a political majority for a religious one, which is hardly an improvement of the minority status as such. Furthermore, the whole secular argument presupposes that the state headship is a right or privilege that may be conferred upon or denied to the individual. The Islamic position is radically different. In Islam, the state headship is first and foremost an obligation, a trying commitment, an awesome responsibility. It would be inequitable, therefore, if Islam were to impose such responsibilities upon non-Muslims.

The International Life

The international life in Islam is the course of relationships between an Islamic state or nation and other states or nations. Like the other aspects of the Islamic life, this one stems from Divine guidance and follows the Godly pattern. It is laid down on the following foundations:

1. An unshakable belief in the unity of mankind in origin, in human status, and in aims (Qur'ān, 4:1; 7:189; 49:13);

2. Due respect for other people's interests and rights to life, honor and property, as long as they do not encroach upon the rights of Muslims. This is because usurpation, transgression and wrong of all kinds are strictly forbidden (2:190-193; 42:42);

3. Peace as the normal course of relations, with exchange of goodwill missions and mutually honest endeavors for the sake of humanity in which all people share equally (see above and Qur'ān, 8:61);

4. Intolerance of appeasement and encroachment in international relations. Should someone be tempted to violate the rights of the Islamic State, or disturb its peace, or endanger its security or exploit its peaceful policies, the State must hasten to defend itself and suppress all attempts of such a nature. Only here, under such circumstances, Islam justifies war. But even then there are moral principles to be followed to confine its scope to a minimum and carry its course only as far as it is necessary. The Law of war and peace in Islam is highly moral and unique, comprehensive and sound. It deserves a special study by jurists and moralists alike, something which this work cannot cover. But it should be remarked, however, that Islam neither justifies an aggressive war, nor does it make destruction of

crops, animals, homes, etc., an objective of war. It neither allows the killing of non-fighting women, children and aged people, nor does it tolerate the torture of war prisoners and the imposition of its teachings on the defeated. It is only a defensive measure, justified by the practical principles of Islam, as long as wrong, injustice and aggression exist in the world (2:190-195, 216:218; 22:39-41; see also the discussion on Jihad below);

5.   Fulfilling the obligations undertaken by the Islamic State and honoring the treaties concluded between the Islamic State and other states. This is only binding if the other parties remain faithful to their obligations and honor their treaties. Otherwise, there can be no validity of treaties or binding obligations (5:1; 8:55-56, 58; 9:3-4);

6.   Maintenance of internal peace and security, and genuine contribution to human understanding and universal brotherhood on the international level.

These are the inspiring sources in the making of the international life of an Islamic state.   The Islamic State does not live just for itself and its own subjects. It has a wide scope and an important mission in the international field. By the order of Islam it has to endeavor for the prosperity and advancement of its own citizens in every aspect of life, and by the same order it should make valuable contributions to humanity at large. This provides for friendly relations, in the broadest sense of the word, with friendly people and states. It enjoins the Islamic State to play a vital role in the interest of humanity on the international level in education, economics, industry, politics, and so on. This role was initiated by Muhammad himself and maintained by his followers throughout the succeeding generations.

Before we conclude this chapter, it should be pointed out that whatever is discussed here is based on the sound, genuine and true principles of Islam as stated in the Qur'ān and the Traditions of Muhammad. This is Islam which Muhammad and his faithful followers practiced and exemplified in the most excellent manner. It is not the Islam of any particular theologian or any particular jurist or ruler. Rather, it is Islam, the writer believes, as it really is, and as it is meant to be.

It should also be borne in mind that the Islamic system of life is unique and different from all other systems and ideologies. Whether one looks at it from a spiritual or moral, intellectual or cultural, political or economic or any other point of view, one can readily see that it is marked with distinguished characteristics. To illustrate, one may mention a few examples:

1.   The source of the Islamic ideology is different. It is not man-made. It is not the production of subversive politicians or revengeful economists. Nor is it the work of pragmatic moralists or selfish industrialists. It is the work of God, the art of the Infinite One, created in the best interest of humanity as a whole. And by its nature it is binding and venerated by all the faithful. It is intelligible to every sound mind because it is free from the puzzling mysteries, secret reservations and arrogated prerogatives.

2.   The aims of the Islamic ideology are also different. It is not aimed at world domination or physical expansion. Rather, it is aimed at world submission to the Will of God and world confinement to the limits of God's Law. Its principal objective is to please God and cultivate man in such a way as to help him to obey the Law of the Creator and be a faithful vicegerent of the Lord. To achieve this end, it deals with all aspects of life; its purpose is to develop in man a clear mind, a pure spirit, a live conscience, a healthy body and responsive feelings. A person with these qualities cannot fail to obey God and adopt the most sound course of life. So the objectives of the Islamic ideology are far from being simply human or temporal.

3.   The Islamic ideology has all the elements and forces that make it comprehensive and practicable, moderate and flexible. Its Divine origin reveals only the fundamental and inviolable principles, leaving a due scope for the human intelligence to work out details and make the necessary adaptation. In whatever way one looks at it, one can see that the Islamic ideology is composed of comprehensive, practicable and resourceful principles. They are comprehensive because they deal with all the major aspects of life; practicable because they have been put into practice and translated into reality at one time or another; moderate because they do not favor the individual capitalist or the proletariat; they are not exclusively concerned with the mundane or with the spiritual; they are confined neither to this world nor to the Future life. They mark a middle way between all extremes and are a guide to a moderate and stable life. Apart from these established principles, there is a great deal of flexibility for working out details suitable to various regions and ages. This felxibility is a matter of fact, a necessity, because the ideology is the work of God and in it, as in all of His work, there is a wide scope for the human mind and human trial.

CHAPTER V

DISTORTIONS ABOUT ISLAM

This chapter is designed to deal with certain aspects of Islam which have been forgotten by some Muslims and distorted by practically all others. An effort will be made here to present these aspects in their true light and clear picture. In so doing, there is no attempt to be apologetic, for Islam needs no apology. Nor is there any intention to appease, condemn, or flatter anybody, because Islam does not tolerate such things but commands a straightforward course of thought as well as deed. The purpose, therefore, is to find out the truth about these aspects, present it afresh to the non-Muslim mind, and let everybody see and decide for himself, like intelligent, responsible rational beings.

Muslims living in the Western World or familiar with the Western literature are often confronted with surprising inquiries and shocking remarks made by some Westerners. Questions of the "Holy War", the "Anti-Jesus Islam", "Polygamy", "Divorce", "Status of Women in Islam", and so on, are the most frequent ones. And it is in the service of truth, and for the sake of the honest people among those innocent and misinformed inquirers, that the attempt is made to examine these questions briefly.

1. The Holy War (Jihad)

Was Islam spread at the point of sword? Was the Muslim emblem "The Qur'ān or the sword?" Were the Muslims imperialist and after mundane power or loot? Some people like to think about that in affirmative terms; some others in the negative, and some are undecided, perplexed and reluctant. But where does the Qur'ān stand? What does the history of Muhammad reveal in this connection? It is certainly imperative on every honest person who has respect for

141

truth and human dignity to find out for himself, and to reveal his findings to others.

The Qur'an makes it clear that, whether we want it or not, war is a necessity of existence, a fact of life, so long as there exist in the world injustice, oppression, capricious ambitions, and arbitrary claims. This may sound strange. But is it not a matter of historical record that humanity—from the early dawn of history up till now—has suffered from local, civil and global wars? And is it not also a fact that, more often than not, victorious allies settle their disputes over their gains and the status of their defeated enemies through wars and threats of war? Even today humanity lives under constant fear and buzzes of war over many hot spots in the world. Could God overlook these facts of life? Or could the Qur'ān fail to deal with the matter in a realistic and effective manner? Certainly not! And that is why Islam has recognized war as a lawful and justifiable course for self-defense and restoration of justice, freedom and peace. The Qur'ān says:

Fighting is prescribed for you, and you dislike it. But it is possible that you dislike a thing which is good for you, and that you love a thing which is bad for you. God knows, and you know not (2:216).

And did not God check one set of people by means of another, the earth would indeed be full of mischief: But God is Full of bounty to all the worlds (2:251). And did not God check one set of people by means of another, there would surely have been pulled down monasteries, churches, synagogues, and mosques in which the name of God is commemorated in abundant measure (22:40).

Although realistic in its approach, Islam never tolerates aggression from its own side or from any other side, nor does it entertain aggressive wars or the initiation of aggressive wars. Muslims are commanded by God not to begin hostilities, or embark on any act of aggression, or violate any rights of others. In addition to what has been already said in the previous chapter, some particular verses of the Qur'ān are of significant bearing. God says:

Fight in the cause of God those who fight you, and do not transgress limits (begin not hostility): For God loves not transgressors. And slay them wherever you catch them, and turn them out from where they have turned you out; for tumult and oppression are worse than slaughter; but fight them not at the Sacred Mosque, unless they (first) fight you there; but if they fight you, slay them. Such is the reward of those who suppress faith. But if they cease, God is Forgiving, Most Merciful. And fight them on until there is no more persecution or oppression, and there prevail justice and faith in God; but if they cease, let there be no hostility except to those who practice oppression (2:190-193).

War is not an objective of Islam nor is it the normal course of Muslims. It is only the last resort and is used under the most extraordinary circumstances when all other measures fail. This is the actual status of war in Islam. Islam is the religion of peace: its meaning is peace; one of God's names is peace; the daily greetings of Muslims and angels are peace; paradise is the house of peace, the adjective 'Muslim' means Peaceful. Peace is the nature, the meaning, the emblem and the objective of Islam. Every being is entitled to enjoy the peace of Islam and the kindness of the peaceful Muslims, regardless of religious or geographical or racial considerations, so long as there is no aggression against Islam or the Muslims. If non-Muslims are peaceful with the Muslims or even indifferent to Islam, there can be no ground or justification to declare war on them. There is no such thing as religious war to force Islam on non-Muslims, because if Islam does not emerge from deep convictions, from within, it is not acceptable to God, nor can it help its professor. If there is any religion or constitution to guarantee peaceful freedom of religion and forbid compulsion in religion, it is Islam, and Islam alone. To this point the Qur'ān refers as follows:

Let there be no compulsion in religion: Truth stands out clear from Error; Whoever rejects Evil and believes in God has grasped the most trustworthy handhold, that never breaks. And God hears and knows all things (2:256).

Even in the propagation of Islam a Muslim is not only forbidden to employ force but is also commanded to use the most peaceful methods. To Muhammad God says:

Invite (all) to the Way of your Lord with wisdom and beautiful preaching; and argue with them in ways that are best and most gracious: For your Lord knows best who have strayed from His Path and who receive guidance (16:125).

And dispute you not with the People of the Book (Jews and Christians) except with means better (than mere disputation), unless it be with those of them who inflict wrong (and injury): But say: 'We believe in the Revelation which has come down to us and in that which came down to you; our God and your God is One; and it is to Him we bow (in Islam) (29:46).

Now if Islam is so designated for peace, and if the Muslims are so dedicated to peace, and if the Qur'ān is favorable to peace, why then did Muhammad launch wars and command battles? Why does the Qur'ān say 'slay them' and fight them? To examine this seemingly innocent inquiry, it is indispensable to mention some historical facts that accompanied and anticipated the Muslim wars against the infidels.

143

After receiving the Charge from God, Muhammad called a public meeting and told the assembly of what he had received, appealing to them to give up their idol-worship and believe in the One True God. His first peaceful and logical appeal was met not only with resistance but also with jeers, mockery and laughter. He tried continually to present his people with the blessed Call but had little success. Because he was not left free to propagate Islam in the open, he had to resort to private preaching for some years to save the lives of his few followers and mitigate their hardships. When instructions from God came to him to preach in the open, persecutions and torture increased and were brutally inflicted on the Muslims. But the more the persecutions increased, the higher the number of Muslims arose. The infidels tried all kinds of pressure and temptation to silence the Call of God. But the more they tried, the firmer Muhammad and the Muslims stood. When the infidels failed to shake the Faith of the Believers by threats, pressure, confiscation of property, jeers, etc., they organized a harsh boycott, a fierce campaign of ostracism, against the Muslims. For some years the Muslims were forced to remain within a very tight circle of association, unable to preach or sell or buy or marry or contact any of their fellow Meccans. Even this did not shake the Muslims' Faith. The boycott went on until the infidels themselves were tired of its observance and had to call it off.

Bringing the severe boycott to an end was no indication of peace or anticipation of tranquillity on the part of the infidels. On the contrary, pressure and persecution continued with a rapid increase, but it was all in vain as far as the Muslims were concerned. Finally, the infidels convened a summit conference behind closed doors to discuss what to do next to eliminate Islam and get rid of Muhammad once and for all. A unanimous resolution was adopted to select a strong man from every tribe and murder Muahmmad in his bed. The mission of Muhammad was not destined to end at that level. So, God instructed him to leave Mecca, his dear hometown, and migrate to Medina to reunite with the native Muslims and the earlier emigrants who had fled from Mecca to Medina (see Qur'ān, 8:30; 9:40). This was the Great Event of Hijrah or Emigration with which the history of Islam began and by which the Muslim Calendar goes.

Fleeing from Mecca, the Muslims were forced by a variety of circumstances to leave behind practically all their properties, belongings and even families. As soon as they settled in Medina, Muhammad resumed his peaceful preaching and his gracious invitation to Islam. Some natives responded favorably to the Call of God and immediately became full-fledged members of the Muslim community. Others did not embrace Islam but maintained their traditional beliefs. And because Muhammad was dedicated to dignified peace and reform, he concluded treaties with the non-Muslims assuring them of freedom and security, and creating in their hearts, for the first time, a socio-national conscience instead of the narrow tribal allegiance.

While Muhammad was engaged in these reforms, trying to organize the Muslim community at Medina and lay down the foundations of a stable and peaceful society wherein Muslims and non-Muslims could live side by side, the enemies at Mecca were restless. Their hatred of the Muslims was burning, and their determination to eliminate Islam was getting stronger and stronger every day. They reviewed their tactics and as soon as they completed their new plans, they started to implement them. They decided to make trouble for the Muslims from within and from without. Plundering and fighting raids were organized to attack Medina and get back to Mecca with whatever loot they could lay their hands on. The non-Muslims at Medina were getting increasingly envious of the popularity of Islam and the novel spirit of brotherhood among the Muslims, something which they themselves did not experience or particularly like to see experienced. So, the enemies at Mecca hastened to exploit the situation and stir internal troubles for the Muslims. The response of the envious non-Muslims of Medina to the instigation of the Meccans was quick and manifest, and serious troubles were arising all over Medina.

Now the Muslims were being constantly threatened from within by the disenchanted at Medina as well as by the raids organized from Mecca. They were driven to a point where they could not stand any more persecution and threats. Their families were separated from them by force. Their properties were confiscated. Their blood was shed. They were forced to leave their dear hometown in three waves of migration: two to Abyssinia and one to Medina. They endured for over thirteen years. With the new tactics of the Meccan enemies there was no course for the Muslims except to await their final annihilation in a plural massacre or defend themselves against oppression and persecution.

It must have been a paradox. Islam came to assure them of dignity and strength, freedom and security, and to ally them with God the Supreme Source of goodness and help, power and peace. Yet here they were helpless and anxious, threatened and terrified. Islam commissioned them to establish peace, to enjoin the right and forbid the wrong, to support the oppressed and emancipate the subjugated, and to prove how reliable and helpful to His servants God is. But how could they do that, if they themselves were oppressed, subjugated to terror and projected to helplessness?

What perplexed them most of all was that the Qur'ān had been silent on the matter, and had given them no specific instructions as

145

to what to do. Their perplexity did not last long, and God relieved their grief by a Divine resolution to solve their problems and those of any who might find themselves in a similar situation. Here is how God words His resolution:

Verily God will defend those who believe: Verily God loves not any that is a traitor to faith or shows ingratitude. To those against whom war is made, permission is given (to fight), because they are wronged; and verily, God is Most Powerful for their aid; (they are) those who have been expelled from their homes in defiance of right, (for no cause) except that they say: 'Our Lord is God'. Did not God check one set of people by means of another, there would surely have been pulled down monasteries, churches, synagogues, and mosques, in which the name of God is commemorated in abundant measure. God will certainly aid those who aid His (cause); for verily God is Full of strength, Exalted in Might, (Able to enforce His Will). (They are) those who, if We establish them in the land, establish regular prayer and give regular charity, enjoin the right and forbid the wrong. With God rests the end (and decision) of all affairs (22:38-41).

With this permission from God there was no more persecution or oppression to be inflicted on the Muslims. There was resistance from their side to restore tranquillity, to regain their peace and freedom, to reunite with their families and take back their belongings. There were battles and wars with the malicious infidels who flagrantly denied the Muslims peace and freedom. But never was there any aggression from the Muslim side, or any destruction of homes, crops, supplies, etc., or any killing of non-fighting children, women, elders and disabled people. The Muslims observed these rules and remained within the limits of God. That was something which had never been experienced before nor has been experienced after. It was under these circumstances that the Muslims had to fight, and it was with these principles and instructions of God that they in the end achieved decisive victories.

So much has been said or written about the "ruthless" Muslims, who emerged from the burning and dry deserts of dark Arabia to conquer the Roman and Persian protectorates, and even to venture around the walls of Europe. Many have expressed the opinion that those Muslims were motivated by religious zeal to spread Islam by force as far as they could reach. Many others consider this opinion silly and naive, because Islam—by its nature—cannot be forced; and even if it were supposedly forced on the conquered people, it could not have lasted there for long, and non-Muslims would have been liquidated from the conquered regions. History bears witness to the fact that wherever Islam reached it survived—with the exception of

Spain on account of certain reasons, and that wherever the Muslim conquerors went, they lived side by side with non-Muslim natives. Moreover, they argue, one cannot force a religion like Islam on anyone and find him so sincere and honest about his faith as were those Muslim converts of the new lands. It needs more than compulsion to develop such good Muslims out of a defeated people, and it requires much more than suppression to make them uphold and cherish the "forced" religion.

Another trend of thought is adopted by some who like to call themselves intellectuals or enlightened critics and authorities. They are not satisfied with that silly and naive opinion about the spread of Islam by force. They attribute the expansion of Islam to the aggressive wars launched by Muslims who suffocated in the heat and drought of Arabia, and were simply motivated by economic needs and circumstances. Those wars and adventures were not religious or spiritual but merely the outcome of pressing wants. This may indicate that the Arabs had not arisen to such a high level of sacrifice and devotion, or that after the death of Muhammad his survivors and theirs lost interest in religion altogether and took off to satisfy their immediate wants. It may also indicate that Islam itself is incapable of generating such fervor and zeal in those Muslim Arab warriors. The indication here is manifold, and the "intellectuals" of this opinion are uncertain as to which probability should have preference over others.

There is still one more trend adopted by some people who ascribe the Muslim wars out of Arabia to passionate lust for plunder and raiding. They cannot see any motive or appreciate any appeal in the Muslims except hunger for blood and desire for loot. They refuse to see any virtue in Islam and to associate the Muslims with any high motives.

The dispute between these various sections is quite serious and sometimes takes the shape of academic discussion. But be that as it may. The fact of the matter is that none of these critics has made any serious attempt to understand the whole question and present the truth in any honest manner. None of them has had the needed insight and the moral courage to come out with the true version of the entire case. How heavy their burden will be when they discover some day that they have misled and misinformed millions of people! How serious their responsibility will be when they know that they have committed grave offenses against the truth, against the Muslims and against their own followers!

It will be impossible to present here the viewpoint of Islam in detail concerning each war or battle. However, there are certain main points which will, when mentioned, give a fair idea of the whole matter.

1. It should be remembered that Muhammad, who was commissioned by God as a mercy for all mankind, tried to approach the rulers of the neighboring territories, inviting them to embrace Islam and share in the mercy of God. It should also be remembered that they did not only reject his gracious invitation but also derided him and declared open wars against the Muslims. In his lifetime the Roman and Persian soldiers crossed the Muslim borders in various raids. So by the time of his death the Muslims were involuntarily at war with their neighbors.

That state of affairs continued, and whatever happened later in the following generations has to be seen in the context of those first incidents. This meant at the time that all Christendom, including Spain and France, was at war with the emerging world of Islam. The adventure of the Muslims in Europe has also to be seen in the light of these circumstances. The fact that all Christendom was operating as one power is proven by the unquestionable authority of the Roman papacy over Christians. It is also proven by the general mobilization of Christian powers against Islam during the Crusades of the Middle Ages and even of the first quarter of this twentieth century.

So, when Rome sanctioned war against Islam, the Muslims could not be denied the full right to fight back on any battleground—whether in Palestine or in the Fertile Crescent, Italy or Hungary. This is what took them to Spain and Southern France. They could not afford to be encircled from all around by the mighty power of Rome and Persia. Nor could they just wait to be wiped out from the face of the earth. Orders were issued from Rome to slay Muhammad and present the Royal Court with his cut head, something which the pagan Romans had done to the early Christian pioneers. However, it must be admitted that some wars of later centuries had no relation to Islam, although they were fought by Muslims. They were not for the spread of Islam. Rather, they were motivated by certain local and, perhaps, personal reasons. Aggression is aggression, whether it be from or against the Muslims, and the attitude of Islam toward aggression is known and unchangeable. So, if there was aggression in those later wars, it could not be justified by Islam or acceptable to God.

2. None of the said critics tries to understand the nature and circumstances of those early centuries. The media of mass communication did not exist. There was no press or radio or television or even regular mail service. There was no way of public information or preaching except by personal contacts. There was no respect for life or property or honor or treaties of the individuals and of the weak

nations. There was no security or freedom of expression. Whoever stood for a noble cause or came out with unpopular beliefs was menaced. This is revealed from the history of Socrates the Greek philosopher, of the Christian pioneers, and of the early Muslims. Many emissaries commissioned to deliver special messages to rulers and governors never came back alive. They were cold-bloodedly murdered or captured by their very hosts.

With all these hardships the Muslims of Arabia had to cope, and under all these circumstances they had to work. They had a message to deliver to mankind, a contribution to make to humanity, and a formula of salvation to offer. The Qur'ān says invite to the Way of God by wisdom and beautiful preaching, and argue in the most gracious manner. But who was there prepared to listen to the peaceful Call of God? It is a fact that many disbelievers used to avoid hearing the Prophet lest they might be affected by his peaceful preaching. They even resisted by force the peaceful Call of Islam. The early experience of Arabia taught the Muslims that it is more effective to be peaceful and at the same time stand on guard; that you can move in peace only when you are strong enough to guard your peace; that your voice of peace would echo better when you are able to resist pressure and eliminate oppression.

Now they had, by the order of God, to make Islam known to the outside world, but there was no telecommunication system or press or any other mass medium of communication. There was only one course to take, namely, personal and direct contacts, which meant that they had to cross the borders. But they could not do that in small or unarmed groups. So they had to move in large protected groups which must have appeared like an army, but was not an army in the real sense. They crossed the borders in various directions at different times. What took place then deserves consideration. In some areas they were warmly welcomed by the natives, who had long been oppressed and subjugated by the foreign powers of Rome and Persia. In some other areas they were first to offer Islam to those who were prepared to accept it, and there were many. Those who did not embrace Islam were asked to pay tributes equivalent to the Islamic tax (Zakah). The reasons for demanding this kind of tax were: (i) that they wanted to be sure this taxpayer knew what he was doing, and that Islam was presented to him but he rejected it with his own free will and choice; (ii) that they undertook to protect the taxpayer and guarantee his security and freedom in a way equal to that of the Muslim himself, because any danger to him was a danger to his Muslim compatriot—and, to defend the Muslim, they had to defend the non-Muslim and insure his security; (iii) that the new state of affairs demanded the support and cooperation of all sectors,

Muslims and non-Muslims alike: the former by Zakah, the latter by tributes, which were all spent in the public interest; and (iv) that they wanted to be certain he was not hostile to them and their new brethren, or inclined to make troubles for his Muslim compatriots.

Those who rejected Islam and refused to pay tributes in collaboration with other sectors to support their state made it hard for themselves. They resorted to a hostile course from the beginning, and meant to create trouble, not so much for the new Muslim comers as for the new Muslim converts and their compatriots, the tribute-payers. In a national sense, that attitude was treacherous; in a human sense, mean; in a social sense, careless; and in a military sense, provocative. But in a practical sense it needed suppression, not so much for the comfort of the newcomers as for the sake of the state in which these very traitors were living. This is the only time force was applied to bring such people to their senses and make them realize their responsibilities: either as Muslims by accepting Islam freely, or as loyal citizens by being tributepayers, capable of living with their Muslim compatriots and sharing with them equal rights and duties.

3.   It may be wise for these critics to study the Qur'ān with honest intentions to see what it ordains with regard to war and peace. It may be wiser still for them to investigate the status of the "conquered" people, and the conditions under which they lived before and after their contact with the Muslims. What will they say, if they find out that urgent appeals were made to the Muslims by natives of the Persian and Roman protectorates to come and deliver them from the oppressing foreign rule? What will they think, if they happen to discover that the Muslim "conquerors" were joyfully welcomed by common people as well as by the religious patriarchs, who were longing for Muslim protection and Muslim justice of administration? How would they explain the phenomenon that some of the "conquered" people not only welcomed the "invading" Muslims but also fought on their side against the oppressors? How would they conceive the prosperity, freedom and progress of the "invaded" regions under Islam, in comparison to what had prevailed therein before?

We are not ascertaining any particular point of view on the matter or making any hasty conclusions. We simply believe that the question is worth reconsidering and deserves serious investigation. The findings will certainly be interesting and significant. Perhaps a Western mind can understand better, if the whole matter is considered in the light of the prevailing conditions in today's world. The deep concern of the Western Allies over Berlin, the appeals of the oppressed everywhere, the anxiety of the South Koreans, the fears of the Laotians, the NATO business, the SEATO affairs, the instability of the Communist Satellites—all that may help the Western mind to understand the events of those remote centuries and the actual policies of the Muslims of those days.

4.   The idea that Muslim wars in the outside world were motivated by economic needs of the Arabs is worth considering too. Although seemingly certain of their own assumptions, the upholders of such an idea have not really studied the case seriously. Do they honestly think that the economic needs were the reasons to urge the Muslims to cross their Arabian borders? On what ground do they assume that Arabia—with its ancient centers of business, valleys and oases—was no longer capable of producing enough for the Muslims? Have they made any serious inquiry as to how much the "invading" Muslims made for themselves, how much they distributed among the people under their rule, and how much they sent back to the Central Administration in Medina or Damascus or Baghdad or Cairo? Have they compared the revenues of the "invaded" territories before and after Islam, and found out whether or not the "invaders" were simply self-interested business adventurers? Have they any reasons to believe that those Muslims took more than what they gave, or drew more than what they had deposited, or made more than what they had invested? Have they come across any evidence to prove if the Central Government in Arabia had at any time received tributes or taxes from its "conquered" protectorates which were needed for the development of these very protectorates, and if so how much was received, and was it worth the adventure in the unknown world? Have they collected any reliable information to show that Arabia was privileged or given preference, in expenditures or development programs over the "invaded" areas?   Finally, did Arabia, all of a sudden feel the threat of a "population explosion" which forced the Muslims to carry out adventurous wars and/or economic explorations?

The attempt to interpret the Muslim contacts with non-Muslims in terms of economic needs may sound novel and worthy of sympathy, but it does not seem to have much truth in it or carry much bearing on serious scholarship. The least reservation that can be made as regards this attempt is that it is so far from being satisfactory and complete. There is so much yet to be done in terms of research, investigation, analysis and comparison. Until this is done, no critic has any moral right to pass his own theoretical assumptions as valid or binding. This presents another gracious invitation of Islam to all critics to make more serious attempts to search for the truth.

5.   There is not much need to take as serious the opinions of those who consider the Muslim wars in terms of plunder and loot. What can be more casual or more stereotyped than such an opinion? It is a short cut in the field of scholarship and an easy way out of some

intellectual and moral problems, but it is so far from being the truth. The same questions of points 3 and 4 above can be asked again, just to find out how much loot the Muslim adventurers took or sent back to Arabia, and how many of their men returned home with spoils. This is not to mention the flourishing, the renaissance and prosperity of the "looted" territories under these very "looters". It is not even to mention the harsh persecutions and heavy losses of lives and properties inflicted on Muslims, or the provocation and threats hurled at them. It is simply an appeal to those of such an opinion to make more careful studies of the case and present more responsible conclusions. However, they have to remember that whatever loot collected by the Muslims was very little compared to what they had lost by confiscation, usurpation, persecution and other provocative action inflicted on them from the hostile camps.

Whether or not the critics of these various grades accept the point of view of this survey, the fact remains that Islam is the religion of peace in the fullest sense of the term; that unjust war was never among its teachings; that aggression was never in its tenets or tolerated by it; that force was never employed to impose it on anyone; that the expansion of Islam was never due to compulsion or oppression; that misappropriation was never forgivable by God or acceptable to Islam; and that whoever distorts or misrepresents the Islamic teachings will do more harm to his own self and his associates than to Islam. Because it is the religion of God and the straight path to Him, it survived under the most difficult conditions, and it will survive to be the safe bridge to happy eternity. Should these critics have any doubt about this fact, they would be wise to study Islam, re-read the Qur'ān, and refresh their memory of history.

The fact that economic prosperity and cultural renaissance followed the spread of Islam into the "conquered" regions does not necessarily mean that the Muslims were after economic gains and military spoils. Even if such alleged gains and spoils became incentives in later periods of Islamic history, it still does not follow that Islam prefers war to peace and the Muslims relish war spoils. There are better explanations. One of these should be very clear to those who are familiar with the classical discussion of The Protestant Ethic and the Spirit of Capitalism where Protestantism, along with other factors, led to the rise of modern capitalism. No serious mind would contend that the Protestants developed their ethic to become economically prosperous or that modern capitalism still depends on the Protestant Ethic.

2. Jesus, Son of Mary

One of the most controversial problems in human history is the question of Jesus. Was he completely Divine or only human, or was he semi-Divine and semi-human at the same time? Was he true or just another pretending impostor? Was he born in an ordinary way to a father and a mother like any other child? Was he born in the winter or in the summer? Many questions like these were and are still raised by Christians and non-Christians alike. Disputes and arguments about such matters have been continuous from the time of Jesus until today. Many denominations among the Christians have arisen on account of little differences in the interpretation of some insignificant aspects of these questions. This is all known to Christians as well as to non-Christians. But just where does Islam stand? Can Islam offer any interpretation to settle these perplexing questions?[1]

Before anything can be said, three points must be made clear. First, a Muslim is quite at ease as far as the attitude of Islam towards Jesus is concerned; his mind is settled, his conscience is clear, and his belief is sound. Secondly, a Muslim's concept of God, religion, prophethood, revelation and humanity makes him accept Jesus not only as a historical fact but also as one of the most distinguished apostles of God. It should be remembered here that acceptance of Jesus by Muslims is a fundamental article of Faith in Islam, and that a Muslim can never think of Jesus in any derogatory terms. A Muslim is happily denied the liberty of defaming Jesus or any other prophet of God.

Thirdly, whatever will be mentioned here is what the Qur'ān says and teaches. Although very unpopular among the Christians, the Islamic beliefs about Jesus do not intend in any way to belittle his role or underestimate his character or degrade his great personality. On the contrary, these Islamic beliefs depict Jesus in a most respectable manner and place him as high in status as God Himself has placed him. In fact, the Muslim is more respectful of Jesus than many Christians. But the attitude of Islam should not be misunderstood. It must not be interpreted as appeasing or flattering or compromising. It is to be taken as the truth in which the Muslim

---

[1] There is no agreement on anything significant in Jesus' life: how, when, and where he was born, lived, received his Message, died, and was burried; whether he really performed "miracles" and what kind; whether, when, and how he rose from the dead. Lack of space and the blasphemous defamatory character of the arguments force us to limit our discussion of these provocative questions. For a critical survey and an excellent bibliography, see Qazi Muhammad Barakatullah, *Jesus Son of Mary, Fallacy and Factuality*. (Philadelphia: Dorrance & Company), 1973.

unshakably believes and will continue to believe. It is the truth of yesterday, the truth of today, and the truth of tomorrow.

The environment in which Jesus was born and raised deserves some attention. The people to whom he was sent had peculiar characteristics, among which were: (i) that they interpolated and misinterpreted the Scriptures of God in meaning and word alike; (ii) that they rejected some of their prophets, including Jesus, and killed some; and (iii) that they were outspoken and irresponsible as regards their wealth. The Qur'ān says:

Is it that whenever there comes to you (children of Israel) an apostle with what you desire not, you are puffed up with pride? Some you called impostors, and others you slay! (2:87).

God has heard the taunt of those who say: 'Truly, God is indigent and we are rich!' We shall certainly record their word and (their act) of slaying the prophets in defiance of right, and We shall say: 'Taste you the penalty of the Scorching Fire!' (3:181).

God did aforetime take a Covenant from the Children of Israel. But because of their breach of their Covenant, We cursed them, and made their hearts grow hard: They change the words from their (right) places and forget a good part of the Message that was sent them (5:13-14).

This was the second nature of the people to whom Jesus was sent. As for the date of his birth, Christians have not been able to establish any specific season or year. "Astronomers still have not pinned down any scientific explanation of the Star of Bethlehem . . . 'Neither the year of Christ's birth nor the season of the year when it (the Star) occurred are known with certainty' . . .Historians estimate the earliest year was 11 BC and the latest, 4 BC . . . 'Also,' . . . 'while the time of year when the birth occurred has not been fully establish- ed most probably it occurred in the springtime, rather than in December . . .' " (Mrs. Simone Daro Gossner of the U.S. Naval Observatory, quoted on p. 12 of The Edmonton Journal of December 23, 1960).

Be that as it may, the more important question to the Muslim is how Jesus was born. Up to the time of Jesus three kinds of creation had been experienced, in each of which the power, the knowledge and the wisdom of God the Creator were clearly demonstrated. First, there was a human being created without the physical interference or presence of any known human father or mother, and that was Adam. Secondly, there was a human being created without the physical existence or the precedence of any known mother or female ancestor, and that was Eve. She was anticipated by Adam who might be thought of as the symbolic or figurative father of mankind. Thirdly, there were millions of people created through the normal intimacy of fathers and mothers. Curious and inquiring minds might have pondered on the possibility of the fourth kind of creation, namely, the creation of a human being without the physical interference of any human father. This possibility seems to have been translated into reality by God in the creation of Jesus to, perhaps, complete the four possible kinds of creation, and to illustrate the power of the Creator in every possible shape and form. The birth of Jesus to the pious Mary was a miraculous action, an act of the will of God. The choice of this kind of creation at that particular time may be as much intelligible as it is interesting. It seems that medicine was quite popular in one way or another, in one region or another. The contemporaries of Jesus swerved so far from the Path of God and were also stubborn. God showed them His power in a new form of creation. He showed them that His power is infinite, and that their salvation would come about only by submission to Him and belief in Him. The illustration was presented in the vivid manifestation of the creation of Jesus. This, perhaps, was also an anticipation of the kind of miracles which Jesus was to perform later on with the help of God, the miracles which were more or less of a medical nature.

It should be pointed out that this hypothetical interpretation of the birth of Jesus is not based on the authority of the Qur'ān or the Traditions of Muhammad. These four logically possible forms of creation and the induction that the birth of Jesus constitutes the fourth and final form are the personal views of the writer and his own hypothesis. This personal view has no bearing whatsoever on the authority or genuineness of the Qur'ān and the Traditions of Muhammad. Whether this hypothesis about the four kinds of creation is valid or not, it does not in any way affect the Muslim's belief in the truth of the Qur'ān and its statement about the birth of Jesus being the miraculous will and work of God. At any rate, the whole point is worth pursuing.

Now if anyone wishes to call Jesus the son of God or God because he was created without the precedence of a human father, and because God Himself adopted him or acted as his father, if this holds true the same thing should even be more applicable to and more appropriate for Adam, who had neither a father nor a mother. And if the fatherhood of God is interpreted in a figurative sense, then it should apply to all mankind, particularly those who distinguished themselves in the service of the Supreme Lord. Human beings are the magnificent creation of God and, in a sense, are His children. Whether the Fatherhood of God is interpreted literally or figuratively it would be quite arbitrary to confine it to Jesus alone, discarding Adam in the first interpretation and the rest of mankind in the second. The Qur'ān reveals the birth of Jesus in the following manner:

And relate (O Muhammad) in the Book (the story of) Mary, when she withdrew from her family to a place in the East. She placed a screen (to screen herself) from them; then We sent to her our angel, and he appeared before her as a man in all respects. She said: 'I seek refuge from you to (God) Most Gracious: (come not near) if you do fear God.' He said: 'Nay, I am only a messenger from your Lord, (To announce) to you the gift of a pure growing son.' She said: 'How shall I have a son, seeing that no man has touched me, and I am not unchaste?' He said: 'So (it will be): your Lord said: That is easy for Me, and (We wish) to appoint him as a Sign unto men and a Mercy from Us. It is a matter so decreed.' So she conceived him, and she retired with him to a remote place. And the pains of childbirth drove her to the trunk of a palm-tree: She cried (in her anguish): 'Ah! how I wish I had died before this! how I wish I had been a thing forgotten or out of sight!' But a voice cried to her from beneath the palm-tree: 'Grieve not! for your Lord has provided a rivulet beneath you; and shake towards yourself the trunk of the palm-tree: It will let fall fresh ripe dates upon you. So eat and drink and cool (your) eye (be happy). And if you do see any man, say: 'I have vowed a fast to (God) Most Gracious, and this day will I enter into no talk with any human being.' At length she brought him to her people carrying him (in her arms). They said: 'O Mary! truly an amazing thing you have brought! O sister of Aaron! your father was not a man of evil, nor your mother was a woman unchaste!' But she pointed to him. They said: 'How can we talk to one who is a child in the cradle?' He said: 'I am indeed a servant of God: He has given me revelation and made me a prophet; and He has made me blessed wheresoever I be, and has enjoined on me prayer and charity as long as I live; and (He) has made me kind to my mother, and not over-bearing or miserable; so peace is on me the day I was born, the day that I die, and the day that I shall be raised up to life (again)!' Such (was) Jesus the son of Mary. (It is) a statement of truth, about which they (vainly) dispute. It is not befitting to (the Majesty) of God that He should beget a son. Glory be to Him! When he determines a matter, He only says to it: 'Be; and it is. Verily God is my Lord and your Lord: Him therefore serve you: this is a Way that is straight (19:16-36; cf. 3:42-64; 4:171-172; 5:17, 72-75; 25:2; 43:57-65).

The mission which God entrusted to Jesus was not salvation through total atonement by blood sacrifice, but salvation by virtue of right guidance and self-discipline, by quickening the stagnant minds and softening the hard souls. It was to install the true religion of God and restore His revelations which had been misinterpreted and abused. In approaching those stagnant minds and hard souls,

Jesus not only preached the word of God but also brought tangible Signs and performed "miracles" in support of his mission. Logical and spiritual as well as "supernatural" and extraordinary proofs were provided by God at the hands of Jesus to show those hard-hearted people the true path of God. Relating the mission of Jesus and the "miraculous" nature of his proofs, the Qur'ān says:

Behold! the angels said: 'O Mary! God gives you glad tidings of a Word from Him: his name is the Messiah Jesus, the son of Mary, held in honor in this world and the Hereafter and of (the company of) those nearest to God; he shall speak to the people in childhood and in maturity. And he shall be (of the company) of the righteous.' 'And God will teach him the Book and Wisdom, the Law (Torah) and the Gospel, and (appoint him) an apostle to the children of Israel, (with this message): 'I have come to you, with a Sign from your Lord, in that I make for you out of clay, as it were, the figure of a bird, and breathe into it, and it becomes a bird by God's leave: and I heal those born blind and the lepers, and I quicken the dead by God's leave; and I declare to you what you eat and what you store in your houses. Surely therein is a Sign for you if you did believe; (I have come to you), to attest the Law (Torah) which was before me, and to make lawful to you part of what was (before) forbidden to you. I have come to you with a Sign from your Lord. So fear God's displeasure and obey me. It is God Who is my Lord and your Lord; then worship Him. This is a Way that is straight (3:45-51).

Then will God say: 'O Jesus the son of Mary! recount My favor to you and to your mother. Behold! I strengthened you with the holy spirit, so that you did speak to the people in childhood and in maturity. Behold! I taught you the Book and Wisdom, the Law and the Gospel. And behold: you make out of clay, as it were, the figure of a bird, by My leave, and you breathe into it, and it becomes a bird by My leave, and you heal those born blind, and the lepers by My leave. And behold! you bring forth the dead by My leave. And behold! I did restrain the children of Israel from (violence to you) when you did show them the Clear Signs, and the unbelievers among them said: 'This is nothing but evident magic.' And behold! God will say: 'O Jesus the son of Mary! did you say unto men, 'worship me and my mother as gods in derogation of God?' He will say: 'Glory to You! never could I say what I have no right (to say) . . . Never said I to them aught except what You did command me to say, to wit, 'Worship God my Lord and your Lord;' and I was a witness over them while I dwelt amongst them; when You did take me up You were the Watcher over them, and You are a Witness to all things (5:110-117).

These verses are only representative of numerous similar ones throughout the Qur'ān. They all emphasize the fact that Jesus never claimed to be a god or the son of God, and that he was only the servant and apostle of the Lord in the pattern of those before him. The Qur'ān stresses this fact in the following way:

And in their (the prophets') footsteps we sent Jesus the son of Mary confirming the Law that had come before him: We sent him the Gospel: therein was guidance and light, and confirmation of the Law that had come before him: a guidance and an admonition to those who fear God's displeasure (5:46).

They do blaspheme who say: 'God is Christ the son of Mary.' But said Christ: 'O children of Israel! worship God my Lord and your Lord. Whoever joins other gods with God,—God will forbid him the Garden, and the Fire will be his abode. There will for wrong-doers be no one to help'. They do blaspheme who say: 'God is one of three in a Trinity:' for there is no god except One God. If they desist not from their word (of blasphemy), verily, a grievous penalty will befall the blasphemers among them. Why turn they not to God, and seek His forgiveness? For God is Most Forgiving, Most Merciful, Christ the son of Mary was no more than an apostle; many were the apostles that passed away before him. His mother was a woman of truth. They had both to eat their (daily) food. See how God does make His Signs clear to them; yet see in what ways they are deluded away from the truth! . . . Say: 'O People of the Book! exceed not in your religion the bounds (of what is proper), trespassing beyond the truth. Nor follow the vain desires of people who went wrong in times gone by, who misled many, and strayed (themselves) from the even Way (5:72-75; cf. 4:171-172).

The beginning of Jesus was controversial. So was his end. In between he was persistent in carrying out his mission, strengthened by the Book of God, by wisdom, by the Clear Signs and by the holy spirit. Yet very few were those who accepted him whole-heartedly. Although tolerant and peace-minded, Jesus could not tolerate the hypocrisy of the children of Israel and their devotion to the letter of the Law at the expense of its spirit. He was rejected and opposed by them, and his violent death was actually plotted. It was customary among them to reject some of their prophets and kill some. Jesus was no exception to this rule. They almost killed him on the cross. In fact they believed that they did crucify him. The story was climaxed and dramatized at this stage, and religious mournings became sacred for the Christians as was wailing for the Jews.

A plot was planned to crucify Jesus; an actual execution on the cross took place; someone was really crucified. But it was not Jesus; it was someone else who was crucified in his place.

As for Jesus himself, God came to his rescue and saved him

from the enemies. God crowned his mission on the earth by saving him from violent death and raising him up high to Heaven. Whether he was raised in rank by means of excellence or whether he was raised alive in soul and body or in soul only after he died a natural death has not much bearing on the Islamic beliefs. It is no article of Faith, because what is important and binding to a Muslim is what God reveals; and God revealed that Jesus was not crucified but was raised to Him. The Qur'ān relates the end of Jesus as follows:

The People of the Book ask you (Muhammad) to cause a book to descend to them from Heaven: indeed they asked Moses for an even greater (miracle), for they said: 'Show us God in public'. But they were dazed, for their presumption, with a thunder and lightning. Yet they worshipped the Calf even after Clear Signs had come to them; even so We forgave them; and gave Moses manifest proofs of authority. And for their Covenant We raised over them (the towering height) of Mount (Sinai); and (on another occasion) We said: 'Enter the gate with humility'; and (once again) We commanded them: 'Transgress not in the matter of the Sabbath'. And We took from them a solemn Covenant. (They have incurred divine displeasure); in that they broke their Covenant; that they rejected the Signs of God; that they slew the Messengers in defiance of right; that they said: 'Our hearts are the wrappings (which preserve God's Word; we need no more)'; nay God has set the seal in their hearts for their blasphemy, and little is it they believe; that they rejected Faith; that they uttered against Mary a grave false charge; that they said (in boast and derision): 'We killed Christ Jesus the son of Mary, the apostle of God.' But they killed him not, nor crucified him, but so it was made to appear to them. And those who differ therein are full of doubts, with no (certain) knowledge except only conjecture to follow, for of a surety they killed him not. Nay, God raised him up to Himself; and God is Exalted in Power, Wise (5:153-158; cf. 3:52-59).

Islam rejects the doctrine of the Crucifixion of Jesus by the enemies of God and also the foundations of the doctrine. This rejection is based on the authority of God Himself as revealed in the Qur'ān, and on a deeper rejection of blood sacrifice and vicarious atonement for sins. Islam teaches that the First Sin of Adam was forgiven after he himself had made the atonement; that every sinner, if not forgiven by God, will himself be accountable for his sins; and that no one can make atonement for the sins of another. This makes no room for the entertainment of the doctrine of Blood Sacrifice or atonement on another person's behalf. However, some of the early Christian sects did not believe that Jesus was killed on the Cross. The Bacilidans believed that someone else was crucified in his place. The

Docetae held that Jesus never had a real physical or natural body, but only an apparent body, and that his crucifixion was apparent, not real. The Marcionite Gospel (about 138 A.D.) denied that Jesus was born, and merely said that he appeared in human form. The Gospel of Saint Barnabas—of which there is an English translation in the State Library of Vienna and an Arabic version in the Arab world—supports the theory of substitution on the Cross.

As regards the end of Jesus, the Muslim is quite at ease as he is with regard to his beginning. The Muslim believes that Jesus was neither killed nor crucified, but God raised him up to Himself in honor and grace. The mind of the Muslim is clear as far as the whole matter is concerned. The Qur'ān has settled the disputes for him once and for all. The belief that Jesus was crucified raises a number of unavoidable inquiries. Some of these may be presented here:

1. Does the crucifixion of Jesus as conceived by the Christian churches befit the Justice, the Mercy, the Power, and Wisdom of God?

2. Is it just on God's part, or anybody's part for that matter, to make someone repent for the sins or wrongs of others, the sins to which the repenter is no party?

3. Is it consistent with God's Mercy and Wisdom to believe that Jesus was humiliated and murdered the way he is said to have been?

4. Is it a fulfillment of God's promise (to defend His allies and protect His beloved ones) that Jesus was so deserted that he became an easy prey to God's enemies? Is this to be taken as a way of fulfilling one's obligations or as a precedence in honoring one's word?

5. Is it justifiable and proper to believe that God, the Most Forgiving, was unable to forgive Adam and his children for the Original Sin, and that He held them in suspense or bewilderment until Jesus came to make the atonement with his own blood?

6. Does the belief of crucifixion and blood sacrifice appear in any religion apart from the pagan creeds of the early Greeks, Romans, Indians, Persians, and the like?

7. Is there any parallel to Jesus in human history besides the fictitious figures of Bacchus, Apollo, Adonis, Horus and other virgin-born gods?

8. Does it not give new insight to compare the words attributed to Jesus with those of Bacchus, who said that he was the Alpha and Omega of the world, and had come to redeem humanity by his blood? Could the similarity of these words to those ascribed to Jesus in later years stimulate a new zeal to search for the whole truth of the matter?

160

9. What did the Roman authorities have against Jesus? He was no threat to their control. In fact he did many favors for their leading personalities and their households. He taught his followers to render unto Caesar what belonged to Caesar and unto God what belonged to God. He was a peaceful preacher and a great help to the Roman authorities in keeping law and order in the land. Why then would they crucify him and lose such a good law-abiding citizen and supporter?

10. How much is known about the character of the Roman Governor, Pilate? Was he on good terms with the contemporary Jews who appealed to Rome against him? Was his rule in Judaea not expressive of his hatred and contempt of them? Was he not vulnerable to bribes? Why then would he hasten to do their will or implement their order? Why would he not accept the bribe of a rich admirer of Jesus such as Joseph of Armathaea? This Joseph, according to Luke, was wealthy and very interested in Jesus, and was a counselor who did not consent to the counsel in the decision to refer Jesus for crucifixion. Could he not have tried, even by bribing the corruptible governor, to save Jesus from crucifixion after he had failed to do so in the council chamber?

11. How many disciples did actually witness the alleged crucifixion of Jesus, and what were their reactions? Can it be true what Matthew says (26:56) that all the disciples forsook Him and fled? Is this the criterion of the integrity and character of such great disciples of a great teacher? Only the beloved John is reported to have been present at the scene. But how long was he present and how long did it take the condemned person to die on the cross in those days? According to some reliable historical sources (see the article on the Cross, *The Chambers' Encyclopaedia*, 1950), it usually took a few days for the condemned to die on the cross. But why was it only a few hours, not the usual few days, in the case of Jesus? And why did he "die" on the cross while his two other companions survived him? What about the darkness which overshadowed all the land for three hours of the crucifixion period (Matthew, 27:45; Mark, 15:33; Luke, 23:44); Could a replacement or substitution have taken place on the cross under the purple robe during that period of darkness and confusion?

12. How familiar with Jesus were those Roman soldiers who came to take him to the cross? How certain were they that it was the right person they took to the scene? Did they really recognize him when they went to arrest him? Did they have any particular interest or urge to identify Jesus at that time when public festivities were taking place and fear of public outburst was imminent?

13. Can a believer imagine that Jesus (who was one of the five most determined and persistent messengers of God) would speak to God from the cross in the manner he is said to have spoken, in a tone of reproach or at best of anxiety? Is it proper for a distinguished prophet like Jesus to say to God at a trying time that God has forsaken him? Is that to be taken as a pattern or precedence in addressing God or in reacting to the trying experiences?

14. Was God the Most Merciful, the Most Forgiving and the Most High unable to forgive men's sins except by inflicting this cruel and most humiliating alleged crucifixion on one who was not only innocent but also dedicated to His service and cause in a most remarkable way? Is this the application of God's mercy and forgiveness or the reflection of His justice and love?

A study of the surrounding circumstances of the time, the behavior of the mundane authorities, the public reactions, the concept of God, the status of man, the purpose of religion and life—a study of these can provoke interesting thoughts similar to the ones I have mentioned. Until a satisfactory explanation of such inquiries is found, the believer cannot be at ease, nor can he enjoy any true peace of mind. So it may be advisable for all parties concerned to make a serious study of the matter and embark on a deeper course of investigation.

However, as far as the Muslims are concerned, such inquiries never arise, and such perplexities are irrelevant, for Islam stands firm in maintaining that Jesus was not crucified or killed, but was honored and raised to God Himself. It is reported in Christian Literature that Jesus appeared, after crucifixion, to some disciples. His appearance is quite probable and conflicts in no way with the Islamic beliefs. If it was true that he appeared, the Muslim would believe that this appearance was not after death on the Cross but after the asylum, which he had taken by the order of God as a step in God's plan to save him and counteract the vicious conspiracy of the enemies. Instead of being crucified and humiliated as had been planned by the enemy, he was more exalted in rank and more honored as had been counter-planned by God.

The greatness of Jesus and the distinction of his role do not, according to the Muslims, emanate from the Christian belief that he was cold-bloodedly crucified because of his teachings and to atone for man's sins. If this popular belief is valid, one might be tempted to say that the sacrifice of Jesus for atonement was in vain because sin has not been eliminated. Or one may even say that there are thousands of great heroes, like Jesus, who died in promotion of their causes, worthy and otherwise. These can be found everywhere, among the Germans, the Allies, the Communists, the officials of the

United Nations Organization, the religious warriors, the freedom fighters, etc. So if this violent death is going to deify the dead, humanity must have countless gods and deities, and it would be arbitrary on anybody's part to confine such deity to Jesus alone, disregarding the other heroes who died in similar situations.

Again, the Muslim does not face such a paradox. He believes that the greatness of Jesus arises from the fact that he was chosen by God and honored with His word; that he was entrusted with the revelations of God and commissioned to teach His message; that he was a prophet of character and personality; that he was sincere inwardly and outwardly; that he fought hypocrisy and blasphemy; that he was distinguished in the beginning at the time of his birth and in the end at the time of his ascension; and that he was a Sign to the people and a mercy from God. Peace be on him and his fellow prophets.

The nature of this survey does not permit us to deal thoroughly with the statements of the Qur'ān on Jesus and his mission. What has been given here is only the fundamental part. For further study and investigation the reader may be referred to the Qur'ān itself. To facilitate the references, a table showing the relevant chapters and verses in the Qur'ān is here presented.

CHAPTER NUMBER	VERSE NUMBER
2	87, 136, 253
3	42-59, 84
4	156-159, 171-172
5	17, 46, 72, 75, 78, 110-118
6	85
9	30-31
19	1-40
23	50
33	7
42	13
43	57-65
57	27
61	6, 14

3. Polygamy (Plurality of Wives)

Strictly speaking, polygamy means the plurality of mates. More specifically, if a man has more than one wife at the same time, this is called polygyny. But since the average common reader makes no distinction between the two terms, they will be used here interchangeably. When we say polygamy in this context, it actually means polygyny in the proper sense of the term. On the other hand, if a woman has more than one mate, it is called polyandry. If it is a mixture of men and women, it is a group or communal marriage.

These three basic types of plural marriage have been more or less practiced by different societies in different ages under different circumstances. The most common pattern is polygyny; yet it is still necessarily limited to a very small minority of any given population for various reasons. This is the only pattern permitted by Islam. The other two, plurality of husbands (polyandry) and group marriages are absolutely forbidden in Islam.

However, it is not correct that Judaism and Christianity have always been monogamous or categorically opposed to polygyny, not even today. We are informed by some prominent Jewish scholars, e.g. Goitein (pp. 184-185), that polygynous Jewish immigrants cause the Israeli housing authorities a great deal of both difficulty and embarrassment. The position of the Christian Mormons is well known. So is the view of Afro-Asian bishops who prefer polygyny to infidelity, fornication, and mate swapping. In the United States alone, mate swappers are estimated to number hundreds of thousands.

It will be revealing to examine the high correlation between strict formal monogamy and the frequency of prostitution, homosexuality, illegitimacy, infidelity, and general sexual laxity. The historical record of the Greek-Roman and the Jewish-Christian civilizations is even more revealing in this respect as any standard sociological history of the family will show.[2]

Turning to the case of Islam we find many people in the Western world who think that a Muslim is a man who is possessed by physical passions and himself in possession of a number of wives and concubines, limited or unlimited. Many more among these people show a feeling of surprise when they see a Muslim with one wife or a Muslim who is unmarried. They believe that the Muslim is at full liberty to shift from one wife or a number of wives to another, and

---

[2]S.D. Goitein, *Jews and Arabs: Their Contacts Through the Ages.* (New York: Schoken Books), 1964; L.T. Hobhouse, *Morals in Evolution: a Study of Comparative Ethics.* (London: Chapman and Hall), 1951; E.A. Westermark, *A Short History of Marriage.* (New York: The Macmillan Co.), 1926.

that this is as easy as shifting from one apartment to another, or even as changing one's suit. This attitude is aggravated partly by sensational motion pictures and cheap paperback stories, and partly by the irresponsible behavior of some Muslim individuals. The inevitable result of this situation is that stationary barriers have cut off millions of people from seeing the brilliant lights of Islam and its social philosophy. And it is for such people that an attempt will be made to discuss the question from the Muslim point of view, after which anybody is free to draw his own conclusions.

Polygamy as such has been practiced throughout human history. It was practiced by prophets like Abraham, Jacob, David, Solomon, etc.; by kings and governors; by common people of the East and the West in ancient and modern times alike. Even today, it is practiced among Muslims and non-Muslims of the East and the West in various forms, some of which are legal and some illegal and hypocritical; some in secret and some in public. It does not require much search to find out where and how a great number of married people maintain private mistresses, or stock spare sweethearts, or frequent their beloved ones, or simply go around with other women, protected by common law. Whether moralists like it or not, the point remains that polygamy is in practice and it can be seen everywhere and found in all ages of history.

During the time of Biblical revelations, polygamy was commonly accepted and practiced. It was accepted religiously, socially, and morally; and there was no objection to it. Perhaps this is why the Bible itself did not deal with the subject because it was then a matter of fact, a matter of course. The Bible does not forbid it or regulate it or even restrict it. Some people have interpreted the ten-virgin story of the Bible as a sanction for maintaining ten wives at a time. The stories of biblical prophets, kings, and patriarchs in this regard are incredible.

When Islam was re-presented by Muhammad the practice of polygamy was common and deeply-rooted in the social life. The Qur'an did not ignore the practice or discard it, nor did it let it continue unchecked or unrestricted. The Qur'an could not be indifferent to the question or tolerant of the chaos and irresponsibility associated with polygamy. As it did with other prevailing social customs and practices, the Qur'an stepped in to organize the institution and polish it in such a way as to eradicate its traditional evils and insure its benefits. The Qur'an interfered because it had to be realistic and could not condone any chaos in the family structure which is the very foundation of society. The benevolent intervention of the Qur'an introduced these regulations:

1.   Polygamy is *permissible* with certain conditions and under certain circumstances.   It is a conditional permission, and not an article of Faith or a matter of necessity.

2.   This permission is valid with a maximum of four wives. Before Islam there were no limits or assurances of any kinds.

3.   The second or third wife, if ever taken, enjoys the same rights and privileges as the first one. She is fully entitled to whatever is due to the first one. Equality between the wives in treatment, provisions and kindness is a prerequisite of polygamy and a condition that must be fulfilled by anyone who maintains more than one wife. This equality depends largely on the inner conscience of the individual involved.

4.   This permission is an exception to the ordinary course. It is the last resort, the final attempt to solve some social and moral problems, and to deal with inevitable difficulties. In short, it is an emergency measure, and it should be confined to that sense.

The Qur'anic passage relevant to the subject reads as follows:

If you fear that you shall not be able to deal justly with the orphans (whom you marry or whose mothers you take as wives for you), marry women of your choice, two or three, or four; but if you fear that you shall not be able to deal justly (with them), then only one, or (a captive) that your right hands possess. That will be more suitable to prevent you from doing injustice (4:3).

The passage was revealed after the Battle of Uhud in which many Muslims were killed, leaving widows and orphans for whom due care was incumbent upon the Muslim survivors. Marriage was one way of protecting those widows and orphans. The Qur'an made this warning and gave that choice to protect the rights of the orphans and prevent the guardians from doing injustice to their dependents.

With this background it is apparent that Islam did not invent polygamy, and that by introducing the said regulations it does not encourage it as a rule. It did not abolish it because if it were abolished, that would have been in theory only, and people would have continued the practice as is observed today among other people whose constitutions and social standards do not approve polygamy, Islam came to be enforced, to be lived, to be practised, and not to stay in suspense or be considered a mere theory. It is realistic and its outlook on life is most practicable. And that is why it permits conditional and restricted polygamy; because had it been in the best interest of humanity as a whole to do without this institution, God would have certainly ordered its termination. But who knows better than He?

There is a variety of reasons for which Islam permits polygamy. One does not have to imagine such reasons or make hypotheses. They are real and can be seen every day everywhere. Let us examine some of these reasons.

1.   In some societies women outnumber men: This is especially true of industrial and commercial regions, and also of countries that get involved in wars. Now if a Muslim society is in this category, and if Islam were to forbid polygamy and restrict legal marriage to one wife only, what would the unmarried ones do? Where and how would they find the naturally desirable companionship? Where and how would they find sympathy, understanding, support and protection? The implications of the problem are not simply physical; they are also moral, sentimental, social, emotional and natural. Every normal woman — whether she is in business or in foreign service or in the intelligence department — longs for a home, a family of her own. She needs some one to care for and some one to care for her. She desires to belong socially and familially. Even if we look at it from a strictly physical point of view, the implications are still very serious, and we cannot just ignore them; otherwise, psychological complexes, nervous breaks, social disgust and mental instability would develop as legitimate results of leaving the problem unsolved. Clinical evidence of this is overwhelming.

These natural desires and sentimental aspirations have to be realized. These needs to belong, and to care, and to be cared for, have to be satisfied somehow or other. Women in such a situation do not usually transform their nature or lead an angelic course of life. They feel that they have every right to enjoy life and obtain their share. If they cannot have it in a legal and decent way, they never fail to find other channels, although risky and temporary. Very few women can do without the permanent and assured companionship of men. The overwhelming majority of unmarried women in such a society find their way to meet men. They put up lavish parties, organize social cocktails, attend business conventions, pursue outgoing roads, and so on. The results of this desperate hunting is not always moral or decent. A certain married man may appeal to some woman, and she would try to win him legally or otherwise. Also, some woman may attract a certain man, who might be demoralized or depressed for some reason or other. Such a man will try to have some intimate relationship with her in the open or in secret, in a decent manner or otherwise, in a legal form or just by common law. This would certainly have serious effects on the family life of the married man involved, and would ruin from within the morale and social morality of society. Wives would be deserted or neglected; children would be forsaken; homes would be broken, and so on.

167

The woman who meets a male companion under such circumstances has no security or dignity or rights of any kind. Her male companion or professional lover could be with her, maintain her and frequent her residence with gifts and readiness to shower on her all expressions of passionate romance. But what assurance has she got? How can she stop him from walking out on her or letting her down in times when he is most needed and his companionship is most desired? What will prevent him from calling off this secret romance? Morality? Conscience? The Law? Nothing will help; morality was given a death blow when they started this kind of intimacy; conscience was paralyzed when he indulged in this relationship against all regulations of God and man; the Law of society does not recognize any intimacy except with one's only wife. So, the male can enjoy this easy companionship as long as he wishes, and once his feelings cool off he can go to meet another woman and repeat the same tragedy without regulated responsibilities or obligations on his part.

The woman who has had this experience may still be attractive and appealing, or desirous. She may even look for another man and give it a second trial. But will this give her any security or assurance or dignity or right? She will be running in the same vicious circle all the time hunting or hoping to be hunted. Her burden will grow heavier and heavier, especially if there are children involved. Yet in the end she will be forgotten. That does not befit human dignity or feminine delicacy. Any woman in this situation is bound to become either a nervous wreck or a rebellious revenger and destroyer of morality.

On the other hand, no one can pretend that all married men are happy, successful and satisfied with their marriages. Whether it is his own or his wife's fault, the unhappy husband will look for some other kind of companionship and consolation from somebody else. This is made easy for him when women outnumber men. If he cannot get it through honest channels, he will get it by other means with the result of immoral and indecent intimacies, which may involve illegitimacy, abortion and other endless troubles. These may be ugly and bitter facts, but they are real and acute problems. They have to be solved in a way that will secure the individual, male or female, and protect society.

The solution which Islam offers in this respect is a permission to the unhappy and dissatisfied husband to marry a second wife and live with her openly in a responsible way with equal fulfillment of all obligations to the first wife and to the second. Similarly, it helps unmarried women satisfy their needs, realize their longings and fulfill their legitimate aspirations and natural desires. It gives them a permission to associate with men by marriage and enjoy all the rights and privileges of legal wives. In this way Islam does not try to evade the question or ignore the problem. It is realistic and frank, straightforward and practical. The solution which Islam offers is legal, decent and benevolent. Islam suggests this solution because it can never tolerate hypocrisy in human relations. It cannot accept as legal and moral the attitude of a man who is by law married to one wife and in reality has unlimited scope of intimacies and secret relationships. On the other hand, it is deadly opposed to adultery and cannot condone it. The penalty of adulterers and adulteresses can be as severe as capital punishment, and that of fornicators can be as painful as flogging each of them with a hundred stripes. With hypocrisy, infidelity and adultery forbidden, there is no other alternative except to allow legal polygamy. And this is what Islam has done with the above-mentioned regulations and conditions.

If some people think it unacceptable, they have to resort to the other alternatives which Islam does not accept or particularly favor. And if some other people can control themselves and exercise self-discipline in every aspect, they do not need polygamy. The main concern of Islam is to maintain the dignity and security of the individual, and to protect the integrity and morale of society.

Now anybody can ask himself as to what is better for a society of this kind. Is it commendable to let chaos and irresponsible behavior ruin the very foundations of society, or to resort to and implement the Islamic resolution? Is it in the interest of society to ignore its acute problems, to tolerate hypocrisy and indecency, to condone adultery and secret intimacy? Is it healthy to suppress the legitimate desires and natural longings of man and woman for companionship, the suppression which cannot be effective in reality and which would only drive them to illegal and indecent outlets? Whether the question is considered from a social or moral or humanitarian or spiritual or any other point of view, it will be realized that it is far better for the society to permit its individuals to associate on a legal basis and in a responsible manner, with the protection of the Law and under the supervision of the authorities concerned.

Even if we look at the matter from a feminine point of view, it will be clear that by this very resolution, Islam assures the woman of due respect, secures her rights and integrity, recognizes her legitimate desire for decent companionship, gives her room in society where she can belong, and provides her with opportunities to care for someone dear and to be cared for. This may sound unpleasant to a woman who already has a husband and resents seeing any other woman having access to his companionship and protection, or sharing with her his support and kindness. But what is the feeling of the other women who have no husbands or reliable companions? Should we just ignore their existence and believe that they have no right to any kind of security and satisfaction? And if we ignore them, will that solve their problem or give them any satisfaction? How would this very wife feel and react if she were in a position similar to that of the companionless women? Would she not desire to belong and to be respected and acknowledged? Would she not accept a half cup or a half husband, as it were, if she cannot have it full? Would she not be happier with some protection and security, instead of being deprived of it altogether? What will happen to her and her children, if the dear husband becomes attracted to or by one of those "surplus" women over a social cocktail or a dancing party? What will become of her if he deserts his family or neglects his responsibilities to make time and provision for the new attraction? How would she feel if she comes to know that the only man in her life is having some affairs with other women and maintaining another person in secret or frequenting another spare sweetheart? Such a man is not only a loss but also a menace. He is mean and wicked. Granted! But is this curse going to help anyone involved? It is the woman – the legal wife as well as the illegal companion – who suffers from a state of affairs of this kind. But is it not better for both women involved to equally share the man's care and support, and have equal access to his companionship and be both equally protected by the law? Such a man is no longer, in reality, a husband of one wife. He is a mean hypocrite, but the harm is done, and the soul is injured. It is to protect all parties concerned, to combat unchastity, to prevent such harm and save souls from injuries that Islam benevolently interferes and allows the married man to remarry if there is good reason or justification.

2. In some instances of marriage the wife may not be capable of having any children for some reason or other. To have a family life in the full sense of the word and contribute to the preservation of the human kind, the presence of children is fundamental. Besides, it is one of the major purposes of marriage, and man desires by nature to have children to preserve his name and strengthen the family bonds. In a situation like this a man has one of three ordinary alternatives:

(i) to forget it and suppress his natural desires for children; (ii) to divorce his childless wife through a course of separation, adultery or otherwise; and (iii) to adopt children and give them his name.

None of these alternatives fits the general outlook of Islam on life and nature. Islam does not encourage or approve suppression of anyone's legitimate desires and natural aspirations. It helps to realize those aspirations and desires in a decent and legal way because suppression in such a case is not part of its system. Divorce under these circumstances is not justifiable, because it is not the wife's fault that she cannot have children. Besides, divorce is the most detestible thing in the sight of God and is permissible only when there is no other alternative. On the other hand, the wife may be in need of the support and companionship of her husband. It will be cruel to let her go when she is in need and desperate, and when she has nobody particularly interested in her, knowing that she is unable to give birth.

Adoption is also out of the question, because Islam ordains that every child must be called by his real father's name, and if the name is unknown, he must be called a brother in faith (Qur'an, 33:4-5). This, of course, does not mean that a child who has no known father or supporter should suffer deprivation or lack of care. Far from it. It means that adoption as practiced today is not the way to give that child secure and prosperous life. No one can really and fully substitute for the actual father and mother. The daily course of events, the complicated procedures and cases in courts, and the disputes between families attest that adoption never solves a problem. How many cases are there in courts today where the real parents are demanding the return of their children who have been adopted by strange families and introduced to different environments? How long can a normal mother or father see his child in a strange home? How far can they trust artificial parents to bring up their child in the proper way and give him due care? How will the child himself feel when he grows up to find that his real parents gave him away and that he has had artificial parenthood? How will he react when he discovers that his real parents are unknown, or that his mother gave him up because of fear or poverty or shame or insecurity? How much is the adopted child liked by other members of the adopting family? Do they like a strange child to take their name and inherit the properties to which they are potential heirs? How will the breeders feel when the real parents demand the return of their child, or when the child himself wishes to join his original parents? Many complications are involved. The institution is no doubt unhealthy and may cause much harm to the child, to the parents, artificial and real, to other relations of the adopting family, and to society at large. Adoption is one of the major reasons that encourage many people to indulge in irresponsible activities and intimacies. It is being commercialized nowadays. There are some people who put up their children for "sale" or trade as the news media show. That is not in the African or Asian jungles; it is right here in Canada and America. Because of all that, Islam does not accept the institution or tolerate its practice among Muslims (See Qur'an, 33:4-6).

With these three alternatives discarded for the reasons mentioned, Islam offers its own solution. It permits a man in such a situation to remarry, to satisfy his natural needs and at the same time maintain his childless wife, who probably needs him now more than at any other time. This is, again, a permission, a course that a desperate man may take, instead of adoption or divorce or unnatural suppression of his aspirations. It is another instance where remarriage is the best feasible choice, another way out of a difficult situation to help people to live a normal and secure life in every aspect.

3. There are cases and times where the wife is incapable of fulfilling her marital obligations. She may fail to be as pleasant a companion as she should be or even as she would like to be. She may be in a state where she cannot give the husband all the affection, satisfaction and attention he deserves and desires. All this can and does actually happen. It is not always the wife's fault; it may be nature itself. It may be a long illness, or a period of confinement, or some of the regular periods. Here, again, not all men can endure or exercise self-control or adopt an angelic manner of behavior. Some men do fall into the pit of immorality, deception, hypocrisy and infidelity. There are actual cases where some husbands fall in passionate love with their sisters-in-law or their babysitters or housekeepers who come to look after the family during the illness of the wife or the period of confinement. It has happened many times that while the wives were undergoing the difficult operations of delivery or surgery, their husbands were experiencing fresh romance with other women. The sister or friend of the sick lady is the most frequent character in such a play. With all noble intentions, perhaps, she comes to help her sick sister or dear friend and look after the children or just after the house temporarily, and from there on things develop and get complicated. When there is a sick wife at home or in the hospital, the husband feels lonesome and depressed. The other woman around the house — whether the wife's sister or friend or anybody else, takes it as part of her help to show the husband some sympathy and a bit of understanding, which may be sincere and honest or may be otherwise. Some men and women exploit this simple start of sympathy and use it to the end. The result is a broken heart here or there, and probably a broken home too.

Problems of this kind are not imaginary or even rare. They are common among people. Newspapers deal from time to time with such problems. Court files also bear witness to this fact. The act of man in this respect may be called mean, immoral, indecent, vicious, etc. Granted! But does this help? Does it change the fact or alter human nature? The act is done, an offense is committed repeatedly, and an acute problem is calling for a practicable and decent solution. Should the lawmakers satisfy themselves with an outright condemnation of such a man and his acts? Should they let him ruin his own integrity and destroy the moral foundations of society? Should they allow hypocrisy and immorality to replace honesty and faithfulness? Outright prohibition and condemnation have not stopped some men from committing the offense or quickened their conscience. On the contrary, they have made room for hypocrisy, secret infidelity and irresponsibility in the face of which the law and lawmakers are helpless.

Now Islam cannot be helpless. It cannot compromise on moral standards or tolerate hypocrisy and infidelity. It cannot deceive itself or man by false and pretended satisfactions. Nor can Islam deny the existence of the problem or simply resort to outright condemnation and prohibition, because that does not even minimize the harm. To save a man of this kind from his own self, to protect the woman involved — whether she is the wife or the secret friend — against unnecessary complications, to maintain the moral integrity of society, and to minimize evil, Islam has allowed recourse to polygamy with the reservations and conditions mentioned above. This is to be applied as an emergency measure and is certainly much healthier than nominal monogamy and irresponsible relations between man and woman. Men and women, who find themselves in a desperate state or in a difficult entanglement, may resort to this solution. But if there is any fear of injustice and harm to any party, then monogamy is the rule.

4. Nature itself requires certain things and actions of man in particular. It is man who, as a rule, travels a lot on business trips and stays away from home for various periods of time, on long and short journeys, in his own country and abroad. No one can take the responsibility of ascertaining that all men under such circumstances remain faithful and pure. Experience shows that most men do fall and commit immoral offenses with strange women during the period of absence from home, which may be months or years. Some people are weak and cannot resist even the easily resistible temptations. As a result, they fall into sin, and that might cause a break in the family. This is another case where restricted polygamy may apply. It is much better for a man of this type to have a second home with a second legal wife than to be free in committing immoral and irresponsible offenses. This is even much better for the wife herself; when she knows that her man is bound by legal regulations and moral principles in his intimacy with another woman, she is most likely to be less irritable than when he enjoys the same intimacy otherwise. Naturally she does not like her man to be shared by anybody else. But when she is confronted with a situation wherein

the man has the choice to be either legally responsible and morally bound, or illegally and immorally associated with someone else, she would certainly choose the first alternative and accept the situation. However, if she is harmed or her rights are violated, she can always refer to the law or obtain a divorce if it be in her best interest.

By applying Islamic polygamy to this case, the man's integrity, the second woman's dignity and the moral values of society would be more safeguarded. These cases need no elaboration. They are factual elements in daily life. They may be rare, but rarer is the practice of polygamy among Muslims. Those Muslims who resort to polygamy are much rarer than the infidel husbands and wives who live in monogamous societies.

Although it is risky and contingent on many prerequisites, as explained earlier, polygamy is far better than negligence and infidelity, hypocrisy and insecurity, immorality and indecency. It helps men and women to solve their difficult problems on a realistic and responsible basis. It brings down to a minimum many psychological, natural and emotional complications of human life. It is a precautionary measure to be applied in the best interest of all parties concerned. Yet it is no article of Faith in Islam nor is it an injunction; it is merely a permission from God, a solution of some of the most difficult problems in human relations. The Muslims maintain that legal and conditional polygamy is preferable to the other courses that many people take nowadays, people who pride themselves on nominal marriage and superficial monogamy. The Muslim stand is this: under normal circumstances, monogamy is not only preferable but is the rule. Otherwise, polygamy may be considered and applied if necessary.

To complete the discussion one has to examine the marriages of Prophet Muhammad. These marriages are no problem for a Muslim who understands the ideal character of the Prophet and the circumstances under which his marriages were contracted. But quite often they stand as a stumbling block for non-Muslims to understand the personality of the Prophet, and cause irresponsible and premature conclusions, which are not to the credit of Islam or the Prophet. Here we shall not give any conclusions of our own or denounce the conclusions of others. We shall present certain facts and let the readers see for themselves.

1.   The institution of marriage as such enjoys a very high status in Islam. It is highly commendable and essential for the sound survival of society.

2.   Muhammad never said that he was immortal or divine. Time and again, he emphasized the fact that he was a mortal chosen by

God to deliver God's message to mankind. Although unique and distinguished in his life, he lived like a man and died as a man. Marriage, therefore, was natural for him, and not a heresy or anathema.

3.   He lived in an extremely hot climate where the physical desires press hard on man, where people develop physical maturity at an early age, and where easy satisfaction was a common thing among people of all classes.   Nevertheless, Muhammad had never touched women until he was twenty-five years of age, when he married for the first time.   In the whole of Arabia he was known by his unimpeachable character and called **al-Ameen**, a title which signified the highest standard of moral life.

4.   His first marriage at this unusually late stage in that area was to Lady Khadeejah, an old twice-widowed lady who was fifteen years senior to him.   She herself initiated the contract, and he accepted the proposal in spite of her older age and in spite of her being twice-widowed.   At the time he could have quite easily found many prettier girls and much younger wives, if he were passionate or after things physical.

5.   With this lady alone, he lived until he was over fifty years of age, and by her he had all his children with the exception of Ibraheem.   She lived with him until she passed the age of sixty-five, and in her life he never had any other marriage or any other intimacy with anybody besides his only wife.

6.   Now he proclaimed the message of God, and was well over fifty and she over sixty-five years of age.   Persecutions and perils were continually inflicted on him and his followers.   In the middle of these troubles, his wife died.   After her death, he stayed without any wife for some time.   Then there was Sawdah, who had emigrated with her husband to Abyssinia in the early years of persecutions. On the way back her husband died and she sought a shelter.   The natural course for her was to turn to the Prophet himself for whose mission her husband had died.   The Prophet extended his shelter and married her.   She was not particularly young or pretty and pleasant.   She was an ordinary widow with a quick and loose temper. Later in the same year, the Prophet proposed to a minor girl of seven years, Aishah, the daughter of his dear companion Abu Bakr.   The marriage was not consummated till some time after the migration to Medina.   The motives of these two marriages can be understood to be anything except passions and physical attractions.   However, he lived with the two wives for five to six years, up to his fifty-sixth year of age, without taking any other wife.

7.   From his fifty-sixth year up to the sixtieth year of his life, the

Prophet contracted nine marriages in quick succession. In the last three years of his life he contracted no marriages at all. Most of his marriages were contracted in a period of about five years, when he was passing the most difficult and trying stage in his mission. It was at that time that Muslims were engaged in decisive battles and entangled in an endless circle of trouble from within as well as from without. It was at that time that the Islamic legislation was in the making, and the foundations of an Islamic society were being laid down. The fact that Muhammad was the most dominant figure in these events and the center around which they revolved, and that most of his marriages took place during this particular period is an extremely interesting phenomenon. It invites the serious attention of historians, sociologists, legislators, psychologists, etc. It cannot be interpreted simply in terms of physical attractions and lustful passions.

8. Muhammad lived a most simple, austere, and modest life. During the day he was the busiest man of his era as he was Head of State, Chief Justice, Commander-in-Chief, Instructor, etc., all at once. At night he was the most devoted man. He used to stay one to two-thirds of every night vigilant in prayers and meditation (Qur'an, 73:20). His furniture consisted of mats, jugs, blankets and such simple things, although he was the king and sovereign of Arabia. His life was so severe and austere that his wives once pressed him for wordly comforts but they never had any (cf. Qur'an, 33:48). Obviously, that was not the life of a lustful and passionate man.

9. The wives he took were all widows or divorced with the exception of one minor girl, Aishah. None of these widowed and divorced wives was particularly known for physical charms or beauties. Some of them were senior to him in age, and practically all of them sought his hand and shelter, or were presented to him as gifts but he took them as legal wives.

This is the general background of the Prophet's marriages, and it can never give any impressions that these marriages were in response to physical needs or biological pressures. It is inconceivable to think that he maintained so large a number of wives because of personal designs or physical wants. Anyone, a friend or a foe, who doubts the moral integrity or the spiritual excellence of Muhammad on account of his marriages has to find satisfactory explanations of questions like these: Why did he start his first marriage at the age of 25 after having had no association with any female? Why did he choose a twice-widowed older lady who was 15 years senior to him? Why did he remain with her only until her death when he was over fifty? Why did he accept all those helpless widows and divorcees who possessed no particular appealing qualities? Why did he lead such an austere and hard life, when he could have had an easy and comfortable course? Why did he contract most of his marriages in the busiest five years in his life, when his mission and career were at stake? How could he manage to be what he was, if the harem life or passions overtook him? There are many other points that can be raised. The matter is not so simple as to be interpreted in terms of manly love and desire for women. It calls for a serious and honest consideration.

Reviewing the marriages of Muhammad individually one does not fail to find the actual reasons behind these marriages. They may be classified as follows:

1. The Prophet came to the world as an ideal model for mankind, and so he was in all aspects of his life. Marriage in particular is a striking illustration. He was the kindest husband, the most loving and cherishable partner. He had to undertake all stages of human experience and moral test. He lived with one wife and with more than one, with the old and the young, with the widow and the divorcee, with the pleasant and the temperamental, with the renowned and the humble; but in all cases he was the pattern of kindness and consolation. He was designated to experience all these variant aspects of human behavior. For him this could not have been a physical pleasure; it was a moral trial as well as a human task, and a hard one, too.

2. The Prophet came to establish morality and assure every Muslim of security, protection, moral integrity and a decent life. His mission was put to the test in his life and did not stay in the stationary form of theory. As usual, he took the hardest part and did his share in the most inconvenient manner. Wars and persecutions burdened the Muslims with many widows, orphans and divorcees. They had to be protected and maintained by the surviving Muslim men. It was his practice to help these women get resettled by marriage to his companions. Some women were rejected by the companions and some others sought his personal patronage and protection. Realizing fully their conditions and sacrifices for the cause of Islam, he had to do something to relieve them. One course of relief was to take them as his own wives and accept the challenge of heavy liabilities. So he did and maintained more than one wife at a time which was no fun or easy course. He had to take part in the rehabilitation of those widows, orphans and divorcees because he could not ask his companions to do things which he himself was not prepared to do or participate in. These women were trusts of the Muslims and had to be kept jointly. What he did, then, was his

share of responsibility, and as always his share was the largest and heaviest. That is why he had more than one wife, and had more wives than any of his companions.

3. There were many war prisoners captured by the Muslims and entitled to security and protection. They were not killed or denied any right, human or physical. On the contrary, they were helped to settle down through legal marriages to Muslims instead of being taken as concubines and common mistresses. That also was another moral burden on the Muslims and had to be shouldered jointly as a common responsibility. Here, again, Muhammad carried his share and took some responsibilities by marrying two of those captives.

4. The Prophet contracted some of his marriages for sociopolitical reasons. His principal concern was the future of Islam. He was most interested in strengthening the Muslims by all bonds. That is why he married the minor daughter of Abu Bakr, his First Successor, and the daughter of Umar, his Second Successor. It was by his marriage to Juwairiah that he gained the support for Islam of the whole clan of Bani al-Mustaliq and their allied tribes. It was through marriage to Safiyah that he neutralized a great section of the hostile Jews of Arabia. By accepting Mary the Copt from Egypt as his wife, he formed a political alliance with a king of great magnitude. It was also a gesture of friendship with a neighboring king that Muhammad married Zaynab who was presented to him by the Negus of Abyssinia in whose territory the early Muslims found safe refuge.

5. By contracting most of these marriages, the Prophet meant to eliminate the caste system, the racial and national vanities, and the religious prejudices. He married some of the humblest and poorest women. He married a Coptic girl from Egypt, a Jewess of a different religion and race, a negro girl from Abyssinia. He was not satisfied by merely teaching brotherhood and equality but he meant what he taught and put it into practice.

6. Some of the Prophet's marriages were for legislative reasons and to abolish certain corrupt traditions. Such was his marriage to Zaynab, divorcee of the freed slave Zaid. Before Islam, the Arabs did not allow divorcees to remarry. Zaid was adopted by Muhammad and called his son as was the custom among the Arabs before Islam. But Islam abrogated this custom and disapproved its practice. Muhammad was the first man to express this disapproval in a practical way. So he married the divorcee of his "adopted" son to show that adoption does not really make the adopted child a real son of the adopting father and also to show that marriage is lawful for divorcees. Incidentally, this very Zaynab was Muhammad's cousin, and had been offered to him for marriage before she was

taken by Zaid. He refused her then, but after she was divorced he accepted her for the two legislative purposes: the lawful marriage of divorcees and the real status of adopted children. The story of this Zaynab has been associated in some minds with ridiculous fabrications as regards the moral integrity of Muhammad. These vicious fabrications are not even worth considering here (see Qur'an, 33:36, 37, 40).

These are the circumstances accompanying the Prophet's marriages. For the Muslims there is no doubt whatsoever that Muhammad had the highest standards of morality and was the perfect model for man under all circumstances. To non-Muslims we appeal for a serious discussion of the matter. They, then, may be able to reach sound conclusions.

4. Marriage and Divorce[3]

One of the most distorted concepts of Islam is the real meaning of marriage. In addition to the brief statement made earlier in this survey, a few more remarks may be useful. Marriage in Islam is not a business deal negotiated by two partners, nor is it a secular contract whereby material benefits and obligations are evaluated in contrast to one another. It is something solemn, something sacred, and it would be erroneous to define it in simply physical or material and secular terms. Moral charity, spiritual elevation, social integrity, human stability, peace and mercy constitute the major elements of marriage. It is a contract to which God Himself is the First Witness and the First Party; it is concluded in His Name, in obedience to Him and according to His ordinances. It is a decent human companionship, authorized and supervised by God. It is a Sign of His blessings and abundant mercy as He clearly says in the Qur'an (30:21).

It is evident, therefore, that marriage in Islam is a means of permanent relationship and continuous harmony not only between man and woman but also between those and God. It is also clear that when two Muslims negotiate a marriage contract, they have every intention to make it a lasting success, for good or for bad, for better or for worse.

To insure this result, Islam has laid down certain regulations to give every possible assurance that marriage will serve its purpose fully. Among these regulations are the following:

1. The two parties should acquire a fair knowledge of each other

---

[3]In connection with this point, see the section on "The Family Life" above.

in a way that does not involve any immoral or deceptive and exploitative behavior.

2.   Man in particular is exhorted to choose his female partner on the basis of her permanent values, i.e., religious devotion, moral integrity, character, etc., and not on the basis of her wealth or family prestige or mere physical attractions.

3.   Woman is given the right to make sure that the proposing man is a suitable match, worthy of her respect and love, and capable of making her happy. On this ground, she may reject the proposal of a man whom she finds below her level or unfit, because this may hinder the fulfillment of her obligations as a wife and may even break her would-be marriage.

4.   Woman has a right to demand a dowry from her suitor according to her standards and also according to his means. If she wishes to disregard this right and accept him with a little or no dowry, she may do so. The injunction of dowry on man is to assure the woman that she is wanted, needed, and that the man is prepared and willing to undertake his responsibilities, financially and otherwise. Dowry is also a symbolic gesture indicating that the woman will be secure, and that the man is not looking for any material gains as his motive for entering the marriage. It draws the clear lines between what each party should expect and not expect of the other.

5.   Marriage should be made public and celebrated in a most joyful manner. The free consent of both parties is an essential condition without which marriage is not valid.

6.   Every marriage, in order to be legal, must be witnessed by two adults and registered in official documents.

7.   Complete maintenance of the wife is the husband's duty. She is entitled to that by virtue of marriage. If she happens to have any property or possessions, that will be hers before and after marriage; the husband has no right whatsoever to any portion or share of his wife's property. This is to restrict marriage to its noble purposes and disentangle it from all unworthy objectives.

With all these measures, it can be seen that Islam has given all possible assurances to make marriage a happy companionship and a solid foundation of continuous harmony and permanent peace. But in view of the fact that human behavior is changeable and sometimes unpredictable, Islam takes a realistic outlook on life and makes allowances for all unexpected events. Marriage, as has been said, has decent and noble purposes which must be fulfilled. Islam does not accept or recognize any marriage which is not functional and effective. There can be no nominal or idle marriage. There must be a successful marriage or no marriage at all. Marriage is too solemn a contract to be stationary or non-effective. So if it does not serve its purpose or function properly, it may be terminated by divorce with conservation of all rights of the parties concerned. This is because there is no point in keeping a nominal and worthless contract, and to save human kind from being tied by vows which cannot be honored.

When the Islamic marriage, which is based on the said regulations and governed by the said precautions, does not function properly, there must be some very serious obstacles in the way, something that cannot be overcome by reconciliation. In a situation like this, divorce is applicable. However, it is the last resort because it is described by the Prophet as the most detestable of all lawful things in the sight of God. But before taking this final and desperate step, some attempts must be made in the following order:

1.   The two parties involved must try to settle their disputes and solve their problems between themselves.

2.   If they fail, two arbitrators, one from the husband's relations and the other from the wife's, must be commissioned to try to make peace between them and settle their differences.

3.   If this attempt also fails, divorce might be applied.

In applying divorce to such a difficult situation, Islamic Law requires that it should be agreed upon by both parties, and grants each of them the right of seeking divorce. It does not confine the right of divorce to the man only or to the woman alone. Both can exercise this right. If either one of the two parties does not feel secure or happy with the other who arbitrarily refuses to grant divorce, and if the demand of divorce is found justifiable, the court must interfere and help the wronged party to obtain a divorce. It is the duty of the Law administrators to see to it that all rights are preserved and that harm is minimized.

After the divorce takes place, there is a waiting period — normally three to twelve months — during which the divorcee is completely supported and maintained by her former husband. She cannot marry another man before the expiration of this period. The waiting period is another chance for both to reconsider their attitudes in a more serious manner and deliberate on the reflections of their separation. If they desire during that period to reunite, they are permitted to do so. In fact, they are encouraged to reunite because separation in this way usually helps them appreciate one another more. When the waiting period expires, the divorcee is free to marry another man. They are no longer obligated to one another.

Should there be a reunion between the divorcee and her former husband, their marriage will be just like a fresh one. If their relations do not improve, they can resort to the same solution of divorce, after which they may reunite by a new marriage in case they so desire. But if this second reunion does not succeed, then a final divorce may be applied.

By allowing divorce in the first place, Islam declares its policy that it cannot tolerate unhappy, cold and stagnant marriages which are much more harmful than divorce. By making it twice, one after the other, with the choice of the parties to reunite, it offers every conceivable chance to make marriage effective and purposeful. Here, Islam is prepared to tackle all kinds of problems and cope with all situations. It does not endanger marriage by allowing divorce. On the contrary, it insures it by the very same measure, for the wrong person would know that the wronged one can free himself or herself from injustice and harm by divorce. By realizing that marriage is binding only as long as it is functional and successful, both parties would do their utmost to make their marriage fulfilling before doing anything that might affect the continuance of marriage. It makes each party careful in choosing the other partner before marriage and in treating that partner afterwards.

When Islam makes divorce obtainable by mutual consent or by the interference of the court on behalf of the wronged party, it stands firmly on guard for morality and human dignity. It does not force a person to suffer the injustice and harm of an unfaithful partner. It does not drive people to immorality and indecency. It tells them this: either you live together legally and happily or else you separate in a dignified and decent way. What is morally and humanly most remarkable about Islam in this respect is that it does not force any person to lower his or her dignity and degrade his morality just to obtain a divorce. It is not necessary for a Muslin to "separate" from his or her partner some years before divorce can be granted. Nor is the granting of divorce conditional on adultery. "Separation" as endorsed by many systems can and certainly does involve immoral and indecent actions. In case of "separation" of this kind the person can neither enjoy his rights nor fulfill his obligations of marriage. He or she is officially married, but how much does he enjoy married life? He is tied as tightly as can be, yet he is loose that no restrictions can affect him. He cannot get a divorce or re-marry, but is there any legal limit to his scope of extramarital relationships? He can move with whomever he likes unchecked and unrestricted. These are things which happen every day and need no elaboration. "Separation" of this kind might help someone to finally get a divorce, but how costly it is to morality and how high the price is for society to pay! This is something that Islam can never accept or endorse, because it would violate the whole system of moral values which Islam cherishes.

Considering the case of adultery and its endorsement by some systems as a basis for divorce, we can only say this: it is so humiliating to human dignity and detrimental to morality that a person should commit adultery or pretend to have committed it to obtain a divorce. The viewpoint of Islam on adultery has been already stated above. What happens, however, in most cases is this: people are not divorced because they have committed adultery or pretend to have committed it, but they commit adultery or pretend it in order to obtain divorce decrees, which are not granted otherwise. What a reverse and disgraceful course in human relations!

This is the stand of Islam on the matter. If divorce has to be obtained as a last resort, it must be granted with dignity and due respect. When Islam is applied to married life, there will be no room for "separation" or "adultery" as bases for divorce. Nor will there be that easy Hollywood-type divorce, which sprang as an extreme reaction to an extreme rigidity. Any system dealing with human nature has to be realistic and moderate, making allowances for all circumstances with preparedness to cope with all conditions. Else, it would be self-destructive and groundless, a state of which Islam is absolutely free (see Qur'an, 2:224-232; 4:34-35; 4:127-130).

One final remark will conclude this discussion. In virtually every known society and religion, there are ways to terminate any marriage. The divorce rates in the industrialized world are rapidly rising and divorce laws are increasingly liberalized. However, divorce in Islam remains a remarkable moral act. Mates are commanded by God to be kind and patient and are reminded of how one may dislike something in one's mate in which God has placed much good and virtue. They are assured of God's help if they mean well and stay together. But if they must part by divorce, it is to be sought without intent of injury or harm. If they part gracefully and honorably, God assures them of enrichment of His all-reaching bounty. The whole marital context, from beginning to end, is centered around and oriented to the belief in God. The verses dealing with divorce are not dry legal stipulations; they commence and conclude with moral exhortations of a high order. The moral commitments of the parties extend far beyond the divorce date. Indeed, the entire question is so incorporated into a highly moral system that divorce is rightly regarded as a moral act in the main.

5. The Status of Woman in Islam

The status of woman in Islam constitutes no problem. The attitude of the Qur'an and the early Muslims bear witness to the fact that woman is, at least, as vital to life as man himself, and that she is not inferior to him nor is she one of the lower species. Had it not been for the impact of foreign cultures and alien influences, this question would have never arisen among the Muslims. The status of woman was taken for granted to be equal to that of man. It was a matter of course, a matter of fact, and no one, then, considered it as a problem at all.

In order to understand what Islam has established for woman, there is no need to deplore her plight in the pre-Islamic era or in the modern world of today. Islam has given woman rights and privileges which she has never enjoyed under other religious or constitutional systems. This can be understood when the matter is studied as a whole in a comparative manner, rather than partially. The rights and responsibilities of a woman are equal to those of a man but they are not necessarily identical with them. Equality and sameness are two quite different things. This difference is understandable because man and woman are not identical but they are created equals. With this distinction in mind, there is no problem. It is almost impossible to find two identical men or women.

This distinction between equality and sameness is of paramount importance. Equality is desirable, just, fair; but sameness is not. People are not created identical but they are created equals. With this distinction in mind, there is no room to imagine that woman is inferior to man. There is no ground to assume that she is less important than he just because her rights are not identically the same as his. Had her status been identical with his, she would have been simply a duplicate of him, which she is not. The fact that Islam gives her equal rights — but not identical — shows that it takes her into due consideration, acknowledges her, and recognizes her independent personality.

It is not the tone of Islam that brands woman as the product of the devil or the seed of evil. Nor does the Qur'an place man as the dominant lord of woman who has no choice but to surrender to his dominance. Nor was it Islam that introduced the question of whether or not woman has any soul in her. Never in the history of Islam has any Muslim doubted the human status of woman or her possession of soul and other fine spiritual qualities. Unlike other popular beliefs, Islam does not blame Eve alone for the First Sin. The Qur'an makes it very clear that both Adam and Eve were tempted; that they both sinned; that God's pardon was granted to

184

both after their repentance; and that God addressed them jointly. (2:35-36; 7:19, 27; 20:117-123). In fact the Qur'an gives the impression that Adam was more to blame for that First Sin from which emerged prejudice against woman and suspicion of her deeds. But Islam does not justify such prejudice or suspicion because both Adam and Eve were equally in error, and if we are to blame Eve we should blame Adam as much or even more[4].

The status of woman in Islam is something unique, something novel, something that has no similarity in any other system. If we look to the Eastern Communist world or to the democratic nations, we find that woman is not really in a happy position. Her status is not enviable. She has to work so hard to live, and sometimes she may be doing the same job that a man does but her wage is less than his. She enjoys a kind of liberty which in some cases amounts to libertinism. To get to where she is nowadays, woman struggled hard for decades and centuries. To gain the right of learning and the freedom of work and earning, she had to offer painful sacrifices and give up many of her natural rights. To establish her status as a human being possessing a soul, she paid heavily. Yet in spite of all these costly sacrifices and painful struggles, she has not acquired what Islam has established by a Divine decree for the Muslim woman.

The rights of woman of modern times were not granted voluntarily or out of kindness to the female. Modern woman reached her present position by force, and not through natural processes or mutual consent or Divine teachings. She had to force her way, and various circumstances came to her aid. Shortage of manpower during wars, pressure of economic needs and requirements of industrial developments forced woman to get out of her home—to work, to learn, to struggle for her livelihood, to appear as an equal to man, to run her race in the course of life side by side with him. She was forced by circumstances and in turn she forced herself through and acquired her new status. Whether all women were pleased with these circumstances being on their side, and whether they are happy and satisfied with the results of this course is a different matter. But the fact remains that whatever rights modern woman enjoys fall short of those of her Muslim counterpart. What Islam has established for woman is that which suits her nature, gives her full security and protects her against disgraceful circumstances and uncertain channels of life. We do not need here to elaborate on the status of modern woman and the risks she runs to make her living or establish herself. We do not even need to explore the miseries and setbacks that encircle her as a result of the so-called rights of woman. Nor do we

---

[4]In connection with this discussion, see the Concept of Sin above.

intend to manipulate the situation of many unhappy homes which break because of the very "freedom" and "rights" of which modern woman is proud. Most women today exercise the right of freedom to go out independently, to work and earn, to pretend to be equal to man, but this, sadly enough, is at the expense of their families. This is all known and obvious. What is not known is the status of woman in Islam. An attempt will be made in the following passages to sum up the attitude of Islam with regard to woman.

1.   Woman is recognized by Islam as a full and equal partner of man in the procreation of humankind. He is the father; she is the mother, and both are essential for life. Her role is no less vital than his. By this partnership she has an equal share in every aspect; she is entitled to equal rights; she undertakes equal responsibilities, and in her there are as many qualities and as much humanity as there are in her partner. To this equal partnership in the reproduction of human kind God says:

> O mankind! Verily We have created you from a single (pair) of a male and a female, and made you into nations and tribes that you may know each other...(Qur'an, 49:13; cf. 4:1).

2.   She is equal to man in bearing personal and common responsibilities and in receiving rewards for her deeds. She is acknowledged as an independent personality, in possession of human qualities and worthy of spiritual aspirations. Her human nature is neither inferior to nor deviant from that of man. Both are members of one another. God says:

> And their Lord has accepted (their prayers) and answered them (saying): 'Never will I cause to be lost the work of any of you, be he male or female; you are members, one of another...(3:195; cf 9:71; 33:35-36; 66:19-21).

3.   She is equal to man in the pursuit of education and knowledge. When Islam enjoins the seeking of knowledge upon Muslims, it makes no distinction between man and woman. Almost fourteen centuries ago, Muhammad declared that the pursuit of knowledge is incumbent on every Muslim male and female. This declaration was very clear and was implemented by Muslims throughout history.

4.   She is entitled to freedom of expression as much as man is. Her sound opinions are taken into consideration and cannot be disregarded just because she happens to belong to the female sex. It is reported in the Qur'an and history that woman not only expressed her opinion freely but also argued and participated in serious discussions with the Prophet himself as well as with other Muslim leaders (Qur'an, 58:1-4; 60:10-12). Besides, there were occasions

when Muslim women expressed their views on legislative matters of public interest, and stood in opposition to the Califs, who then accepted the sound arguments of these women. A specific example took place during the Califate of Umar Ibn al-Khattab.

5.   Historical records show that women participated in public life with the early Muslims, especially in times of emergencies. Women used to accompany the Muslim armies engaged in battles to nurse the wounded, prepare supplies, serve the warriors, and so on. They were not shut behind iron bars or considered worthless creatures and deprived of souls.

6.   Islam grants woman equal rights to contract, to enterprise, to earn and possess independently. Her life, her property, her honor are as sacred as those of man. If she commits any offense, her penalty is no less or more than a man's in a similar case. If she is wronged or harmed, she gets due compensations equal to what a man in her position would get (2:178; 4:45, 92-93).

7.   Islam does not state these rights in a statistical form and then relax. It has taken all measures to safeguard them and put them into practice as integral articles of Faith. It never tolerates those who are inclined to prejudice against woman or discrimination between man and woman. Time and again, the Qur'an reproaches those who used to believe woman to be inferior to man (16:57-59, 62; 42:47-50; 43:15-19; 53:21-23).

8.   Apart from recognition of woman as an independent human being acknowledged as equally essential for the survival of humanity, Islam has given her a share of inheritance. Before Islam, she was not only deprived of that share but was herself considered as property to be inherited by man. Out of that transferable property Islam made an heir, acknowledging the inherent human qualities in woman. Whether she is a wife or mother, a sister or daughter, she receives a certain share of the deceased kin's property, a share which depends on her degree of relationship to the deceased and the number of heirs. This share is hers, and no one can take it away or disinherit her. Even if the deceased wishes to deprive her by making a will to other relations or in favor of any other cause, the Law will not allow him to do so. Any proprietor is permitted to make his will within the limit of one-third of his property, so he may not affect the rights of his heirs, men and women. In the case of inheritance, the question of equality and sameness is fully applicable. In principle, both man and woman are equally entitled to inherit the property of the deceased relations but the portions they get may vary. In *some* instances man receives two shares whereas woman gets one only. This is no sign of giving preference or supremacy to man over woman.

The reasons why man gets more in these particular instances may be classified as follows:

First, man is the person solely responsible for the complete maintenance of his wife, his family and any other needy relations. It is his duty by Law to assume all financial responsibilities and maintain his dependents adequately. It is also his duty to contribute financially to all good causes in his society. All financial burdens are borne by him alone.

Secondly, in contrast, woman has no financial responsibilities whatsoever except very little of her personal expenses, the highly luxurious things that she likes to have. She is financially secure and provided for. If she is a wife, her husband is the provider; if she is a mother, it is the son; if she is a daughter, it is the father; if she is a sister; it is the brother, and so on. If she has no relations on whom she can depend, then there is no question of inheritance because there is nothing to inherit and there is no one to bequeath anything to her. However, she will not be left to starve; maintenance of such a woman is the responsibility of the society as a whole, the state. She may be given aid or a job to earn her living, and whatever money she makes will be hers. She is not responsible for the maintenance of anybody else besides herself. If there is a man in her position, he would still be responsible for his family and possibly any of his relations who need his help. So, in the hardest situation her financial responsibility is limited, while his is unlimited.

Thirdly, when a woman gets less than a man does, she is not actually deprived of anything that she has worked for. The property inherited is not the result of her earning or her endeavors. It is something coming to them from a neutral source, something additional or extra. It is something that neither man nor woman struggled for. It is a sort of aid, and any aid has to be distributed according to the urgent needs and responsibilities, especially when the distribution is regulated by the Law of God.

Now, we have a male heir, on one side, burdened with all kinds of financial responsibilities and liabilities. We have, on the other side, a female heir with no financial responsibilities at all or at most with very little of it. In between we have some property and aid to redistribute by way of inheritance. If we deprive the female completely, it would be unjust to her because she is related to the deceased. Likewise, if we always give her a share equal to the man's, it would be unjust to him. So, instead of doing injustice to either side, Islam gives the man a larger portion of the inherited property to help him to meet his family needs and social responsibilities. At the same time. Islam has not forgotten her altogether, but has given her a portion to satisfy her very personal needs. In fact, Islam in this respect is being more kind to her than to him. Here we can say that when taken as a whole the rights of woman are equal to those of man although not necessarily identical (see Qur'an, 4:11-14, 176).

9.   In some instances of bearing witness to certain civil contracts, two men are required or one man and two women. Again, this is no indication of the woman being inferior to man. It is a measure of securing the rights of the contracting parties, because woman, as a rule, is not so experienced in practical life as man. This lack of experience may cause a loss to any party in a given contract. So the Law requires that at least two women should bear witness with one man. If a woman of the witnesses forgets something, the other one would remind her. Or if she makes an error, due to lack of experience, the other would help to correct her. This is a precautionary measure to guarantee honest transactions and proper dealings between people. In fact, it gives woman a role to play in civil life and helps to establish justice. At any rate, lack of experience in civil life does not necessarily mean that woman is inferior to man in her status. Every human being lacks one thing or another, yet no one questions their human status (2:282)[5].

10.   Woman enjoys certain privileges of which man is deprived. She is exempt from some religious duties, i.e., prayers and fasting, in her regular periods and at times of confinement. She is exempt from attending the obligatory congregation of Fridays. She is exempt from all financial liabilities. As a mother, she enjoys more recognition and higher honor in the sight of God (31:14-15; 46:15). The Prophet acknowledged this honor when he declared that Paradise is under the feet of the mothers. She is entitled to three-fourths of the son's love and kindness with one-fourth left for the father. As a wife she is entitled to demand of her prospective husband a suitable dowry that will be her own. She is entitled to complete provision and total maintenance by the husband. She does not have to work or share with her husband the family expenses. She is free to retain, after marriage, whatever she possessed before it, and the husband has no right whatsoever to any of her belongings. As a daughter or sister she is entitled to security and provision by the father and brother respectively. That is her privilege. If she wishes to work or be self-

---

[5]It is interesting that a woman's witness in certain matters is exclusive and her expertise conclusive. No man's witness is accepted and no more than one woman is needed. Furthermore, bearing witness to contracts and business transactions is not a privilege but a duty (Qur'an, 2:282-283) that must be performed. If the woman's share of this duty is lightened by one half, it can hardly be called a denial of her rights; if anything, it is a favor or an exemption.

supporting and participate in handling the family responsibilities, she is quite free to do so, provided her integrity and honor are safeguarded.

11.   The standing of woman in prayers behind man does not indicate in any sense that she is inferior to him.   Woman, as already mentioned, is exempt from attending congregational prayers which are obligatory on man.   But if she does attend she stands in separate lines made up of women exclusively, just as the under-aged children compose separate lines behind the adult men.   This is a regulation of discipline in prayers, and not a classification of importance.   In men's rows the head of state stands shoulder to shoulder to the pauper.   Men of the highest ranks in society stand in prayer side by side with other men of the lowest ranks.   The order of lines in prayers is introduced to help every one to concentrate in his meditation.   It is very important because Muslim prayers are not simply chanting or the sing-a-song type.   They involve actions, motions, standing, bowing, prostration, etc.   So if men mix with women in the same lines, it is possible that something disturbing or distracting may happen.   The mind will become occupied by something alien to prayer and derailed from the clear path of meditation.   The result will be a loss of the purpose of prayers, besides an offense of adultery committed by the eye, because the eye—by looking at forbidden things—can be guilty of adultery as much as the heart itself.   Moreover, no Muslim man or woman is allowed during prayers to touch the body of another person of the opposite sex.   If men and women stand side by side in prayer they cannot avoid touching each other.   Furthermore, when a woman is praying in front of a man or beside him, it is very likely that any part of her dressed body may become uncovered after a certain motion of bowing or prostrating. The man's eye may happen to be looking at the uncovered part, with the result that she will be embarrassed and he will be exposed to distraction or possibly evil thoughts.   So, to avoid any embarrassment and distraction, to help concentrate on meditation and pure thoughts, to maintain harmony and order among worshippers, to fulfill the true purposes of prayers, Islam has ordained the organization of rows, whereby men stand in front lines, children behind them, and women behind the children.   Anyone with some knowledge of the nature and purpose of Muslim prayers can readily understand the wisdom of organizing the lines of worshippers in this manner.

12.   The Muslim woman is always associated with an old tradition known as the "veil".   It is Islamic that the woman should beautify herself with the veil of honor, dignity, chastity, purity and integrity.

She should refrain from all deeds and gestures that might stir the passions of people other than her legitimate husband or cause evil suspicion of her morality. She is warned not to display her charms or expose her physical attractions before strangers. The veil which she must put on is one that can save her soul from weakness, her mind from indulgence, her eyes from lustful looks, and her personality from demoralization. Islam is most concerned with the integrity of woman, with the safeguarding of her morals and morale and with the protection of her character and personality (cf. Qur'an, 24:30-31).

13. By now it is clear that the status of woman in Islam is unprecedentedly high and realistically suitable to her nature. Her rights and duties are equal to those of man but not necessarily or absolutely identical with them. If she is deprived of one thing in some aspect, she is fully compensated for it with more things in many other aspects. The fact that she belongs to the female sex has no bearing on her human status or independent personality, and it is no basis for justification of prejudice against her or injustice to her person. Islam gives her as much as is required of her. Her rights match beautifully with her duties. The balance between rights and duties is maintained, and no side overweighs the other. The whole status of woman is given clearly in the Qur'anic verse which may be translated as follows:

> And women shall have rights similar to the rights against them, according to what is equitable; but man have a degree (of advantage as in some cases of inheritance) over them (2:228).

This degree is not a title of supremacy or an authroization of dominance over her. It is to correspond with the extra responsibilities of man and give him some compensation for his unlimited liabilities. The above-mentioned verse is always interpreted in the light of another (4:34)[6].

It is these extra responsibilities that give man a degree over woman in some economic aspects. It is not a higher degree in humanity or in character. Nor is it a dominance of one over the other or suppression of one by the other. It is a distribution of God's abundance according to the needs of the nature of which God is the Maker. And He knows best what is good for woman and what is good for man. God is absolutely true when He declares:

> O mankind! reverence your Guardian-Lord, Who created you from a single person, and created of like nature his mate, and from them twain scattered (like seeds) countless men and women (4:1).

---

[6]Compare the section on "The Family Life" above.

APPENDIX I
THE QUR'AN AND ITS WISDOM

The Qur'an is the greatest gift of God to humanity and its wisdom is of a unique kind. Briefly stated, the purpose of the Book is to guard the previous revelations and restore the eternal truth of God, to guide humanity to the Straight Path and quicken the soul of man, to awaken the human conscience and enlighten the human mind.

The Qur'an is the Word of God revealed to Muhammad through the Holy Spirit Gabriel, and it is beyond human imagination to produce anything like it. Muhammad's contemporaries were, by acclamation, the greatest masters of the Arabic language with most compelling motives to produce a rival text. But they could not produce anything like the Qur'an in content or style. Muhammad had no formal schooling and he made no secret of it. It is his greatest credit that he was an illiterate man rising from among illiterate people to teach the whole of mankind, literate and illiterate alike, the true message of God. This is the first fact about the Qur'an being the Word of God.

The second fact about this unique Book is the unquestionable authenticity of its contents and order, a quality which no other book of any kind has ever enjoyed or is likely to enjoy. The authenticity of the Qur'an leaves no doubt as to the purity, originality, and totality of its text. Serious scholars, Muslims and non-Muslims alike, have concluded, beyond doubt, that the Qur'an we use today is the very same Book which Muhammad received, taught, lived by, and bequeathed to humanity almost fourteen centuries ago. Some observations may illustrate this unexemplified authenticity of the Qur'an:

1. The Qur'an was revealed in portions and piecemeal, but it was never without some form of order and arrangement. The name of the Qur'an indicates that it was a Book from the very beginning (Qur'an, 2:2; 41:41-42). The arrangements of the Qur'an and the gradual revelation of its passages were the plans and will of God, a will by which Muhammad and his Companions abided (25:32; cf. 75:17).

2. The Arabs were distinguished by their extremely refined literary taste that enabled them to enjoy and appreciate the good pieces of

literature. The Qur'an, by acclamation, was to their taste the most outstanding masterpiece of literature. They were moved by its touching tone and attracted to its extraordinary beauty. They found in it the greatest satisfaction and the deepest joy, and they embarked on a course of recitation and memorization of the Book. It was, and still is, admired, quoted and cherished by all Muslims and many non-Muslims.

3.   It is incumbent upon every Muslim, man and woman, to recite a portion of the Qur'an every day in prayer and during the night vigilance. Recitation of the Qur'an is to the Muslims a high form of worship and a daily practice.

4.   The Arabs were generally illiterate people and had to rely completely on their memories to preserve the poems and passages they liked most. They were distinguished for their sharp memories in which they stored their literary legacy. The Qur'an was acknowledged by all people of literary taste to be inimitable. So they hastened to commit it to their memories but only in the most remarkable and respectful manner.

5.   During the lifetime of Muhammad, there were expert scribes and appointed recorders of the Revelations. Whenever he received a verse or a passage, he immediately instructed his scribes to record it under his supervision. Whatever they recorded was checked and authenticated by the Prophet himself. Every word was reviewed and every passage was put in its right order.

6.   By the time Revelations were completed, the Muslims were in possession of many complete records of the Qur'an. They were recited, memorized, studied and used for all daily purposes. Whenever a difference arose, the matter was referred to the Prophet himself to settle the issue, whether it was connected with the text or the meaning or the intonation.

7.   After the death of Muhammad, the Qur'an was already committed to many Muslim memories and numerous recording tables. But even that did not satisfy Abu Bakr, the First Calif, who was afraid that the death of large numbers of memorizers in battles might lead to serious confusion about the Qur'an. So he consulted the leading authorities and then entrusted Zayd Ibn Thabit, Muhammad's Chief Scribe of Revelations, to compile a standard and complete copy of the Book in the same order as authorized by Muhammad himself. He did that under the supervision of the Companions of the Prophet and with their help. The final and complete version was checked and approved by all Muslims who heard the Qur'an from Muhammad and committed it to their memories and hearts. This was done less than

two years after Muhammad's death. Revelations were still fresh and alive in the minds of scribes, memorizers and other Muslim Companions of the Prophet.

8. During the Califate of 'Uthman, about fifteen years after Muhammad, the compiled copies of the Qur'an were distributed widely in the new territories which came into contact with Islam. Most of the inhabitants did not see Muhammad or hear him. Due to regional and geographical factors, they were reading the Qur'an with slightly different accents. Differences in recitation and intonation began to arise and cause disputes among Muslims. 'Uthman acted swiftly to meet the situation. After mutual consultation with all the leading authorities, he formed a committee of four men made up of the former scribes of Revelations. All the copies in use were collected and replaced by One Standard Copy which was to be used according to the accent and dialect of Quraysh, the very same dialect and accent of Muhammad himself. That dialect was adopted and standardized because it was the best of all dialects and the one in which the Qur'an was revealed. Thus, the Qur'an was again restricted to the accent and dialect of the man who received it. And from that time onwards, the same standardized version has been in use without the slightest change in words or order or even punctuation marks.

From these observations, scholars have concluded that the Qur'an stands today as it first came down, and as it always will be. To it there has never been any addition; from it there was no omission; and in it there occurred no corruption. Its history is as clear as daylight; its authenticity is unquestionable; and its complete preservation is beyond doubt.

The Qur'an is full of unexemplified wisdom with regard to its source, its characteristics and its dimensions. The wisdom of the Qur'an derives from the wisdom of the author who could not have been any other than God Himself. It also derives from the compelling power of the Book which is inimitable and which is a challenge to all men of letters and knowledge. The realistic approach of the Qur'an, the practical solutions it offers to human problems, and the noble objectives it sets for man mark the Qur'anic wisdom as being of a special nature and characteristics.

Dynamism

One of the major characteristics of the Qur'anic wisdom is that it is not the static or dry type. It is a kind of dynamic wisdom that provokes the mind and quickens the heart. In this wisdom there is stirring dynamism and there is moving force attested by historical evidence as well as by the Qur'an itself. When Muhammad first launched the Call of God, his only power was the Qur'an and his only wisdom was the Qur'anic wisdom. The penetrating dynamism of the Qur'an is tremendous and irresistible.

There are numerous examples to show that the most dynamic personalities and the most conclusive arguments could not reach the realm of the dynamic wisdom of the Qur'an. God speaks of the Qur'an as a Rooh or spirit and life, and as a light wherewith the servants of God are guided to the Straight Path (42:52). Again, He says: Had We sent down this Qur'an on a mountain, verily you would have seen it humble itself and cleave asunder for fear of God. Such are the similarities which We propound to men, that they may reflect (59:21). The keywords here are Rooh and Sad', which mean that the Qur'an originates life, quickens the soul, radiates the guiding light and moves the seemingly immobile objects. This is the kind of spiritual dynamism of which the Qur'an speaks.

Practicability

Another significant characteristic of the Qur'an is its practicability. It does not indulge in wishful thinking. Nor do its teachings demand the impossible or float on rosy streams of unattainable ideals. The Qur'an accepts man for what he is and exhorts him to become what he can be. It does not brand man as a helpless or hopeless creature, condemned from birth to death, and drowned in sin from womb to tomb, but it portrays him as a noble, honorable and dignified being.

The practicability of the Qur'anic teachings is established by the examples of Muhammad and Muslims throughout the ages. The distinctive approach of the Qur'an is that its instructions are aimed at the general welfare of man and are based on the possibilities within his reach.

Moderation

A third characteristic is moderation or harmony between the Divine and the human, the spiritual and the material, the individual and the collective, and so on. The Qur'an pays due attention to all facts of life and all needs of man, and deals with them in such a way as to help man to realize the noble objectives of his being. For this approach of moderation, the Qur'an calls the Muslims a Middle Nation (2:143), and with this "middleness" they are called the best people ever evolved for mankind; as they enjoin the right, combat the wrong and believe in God (3:110).

The Qur'anic wisdom functions in three principal dimensions: inwardly, outwardly, and upwardly. Inwardly, it penetrates into the innermost recesses of the heart and reaches the farthest depths of the mind. It is aimed at the healthy cultivation of the individual from within. This inward penetration is different from and far deeper than that of any other legal or ethical system, because the Qur'an speaks in God's name and refers all matters to Him.

The outward function of the Qur'an embraces all walks of life and covers the principles of the entire field of human affairs from the most personal matters to the complex international relations. The Qur'an reaches areas unknown to any secular system of law or code of ethics and inaccessible to any popular doctrine of religion. What is remarkable about the Qur'an in this respect is that it deals with human transactions in such a way as to give them a Divine flavor and a moral touch. It makes the presence of God felt in every transaction and acknowledges Him as the first source of guidance and the ultimate goal of all transactions. It is man's spiritual guide, his system of law, his code of ethics, and, above all, his way of life.

In its upward function the Qur'an focuses on the One Supreme God. Everything that was, or that is, or that will be, must be channeled into and seen through this focus, the active presence of God in the universe. Man is merely a trustee in the vast domain of God, and the sole purpose of his creation is to worship God. This is no pretext for seclusion or passive retirement from life. It is an open invitation to man to be the true embodiment on earth of the excellent qualities of God. When the Qur'an in its upward attention focuses on God, it opens before man new horizons of thought, guides him to unexemplified standards of high morality, and acquaints him with the eternal source of peace and goodness. Realizing God alone as the ultimate goal of man is a revolution against the popular trends in human thought and religious doctrines, a revolution whose objective is to free the mind from doubt, liberate the soul from sin and emancipate the conscience from subjugation.

In all its dimensions the Qur'anic wisdom is conclusive. It neither condemns nor tortures the flesh nor does it neglect the soul. It does not "humanize" God nor does it deify man. Everything is carefully placed where it belongs in the total scheme of creation. There is a proportionate relationship between deeds and rewards, between means and ends. The Qur'anic wisdom is not neutral. It is demanding and its demands are joyfully welcomed by all those blessed with appreciation and understanding.

The wisdom of the Qur'an calls for truth in thought and piety in action, for unity in purpose and goodwill in intent. That is the Book; in it is guidance sure, without doubt . . . (2:2). This is a Book which We have revealed unto you, in order that you might lead mankind out of the depths of darkness into light . . . (14:2).

196

APPENDIX II
MUHAMMAD THE LAST PROPHET

The Muslim's belief that Muhammad is the Last Prophet of God has been misunderstood by many people and, hence, needs an explanation. This belief does not, in any way, mean that God has closed His door of mercy or has retired. It does not impose any restriction on the rise of great religious personalities, or bar the emerging of great spiritual leaders, or obstruct the evolution of great pious men. Nor does it mean that God has done the Arabs, from whom Muhammad was chosen, His Last Favor to the exclusion of everybody else. God is not partial to any race or age or generation, and His door of mercy is ever open and always accessible to those who seek Him. He speaks to man in either of three ways:

(1) by inspiration which occurs in the form of suggestions or ideas put by God into the hearts or minds of pious men;

(2) from behind a veil which occurs in the form of sights or visions when the qualified recipient is asleep or in a state of trance; and

(3) through the Heavenly Messenger Gabriel who is sent down with concrete Divine words to convey to the chosen human messenger (Qur'an, 42:51). This last form is the highest and is the one in which the Qur'an came down to Muhammad. It is confined only to the prophets of whom Muhammad was the Last and the Seal.

But, again, this does not deny the existence or continuance of inspiration in the two other forms to whomever God wills. By choosing Muhammad to be the Seal of the Prophets, God has not lost contact with or interest in man, and man has not been barred from seeking God or obstructed in his aspiration to God. On the contrary, by choosing Muhammad to be the culmination of Prophethood and the Qur'an to be the completion of Revelation, God has established a permanent medium of communication between Himself and man, and has erected an ever-radiating beacon of guidance and light. Besides these general observations, there are other specific points which show why Muhammad is the Last Prophet of God. From among these, a few may be mentioned:

1. The Qur'an states in unequivocal words that Muhammad is sent to all men as the Apostle of God to Whom belongs the dominion of

the heavens and earth (7:158). It also states that Muhammad was sent only as a Mercy from God to all creatures, human and non-human alike (21:107), and that he is the Messenger of God and the Seal of the Prophets (33:40). The Qur'an is the word of God, and whatever it says is the truth of God by which every Muslim abides and on which every man should reflect. The Message of Muhammad was not simply a national revival or a racial monopoly or a temporary deliverance from bondage and oppression. Nor was it an abrupt change or reversion in the trends of history. The message of Muhammad was, and, of course, still is, a universal revival, a common blessing, a supranational heritage and an ever-lasting spiritual deliverance. It is an evolutionary continuance of the previous messages and a well-balanced incorporation of all the former revelations. It transcends all boundaries of race, age, color, and regional features. It is addressed to man of all times and it is precisely what man needs. Thus, a Muslim believes that Muhammad is the Last Prophet because the Qur'an bears true witness to that, and because Muhammad's message has the highest qualities of a truly universal and conclusive faith.

2. Muhammad himself stated that he was the Last Prophet of God. A Muslim, or anyone else for that matter, cannot question the truth of this statement. Throughout his life, Muhammad was known to be most truthful, honest and modest. His integrity and truthfulness were beyond doubt not only in the sights of Muslims but also in the minds of his most staunch opponents. His character, his spiritual accomplishments, and his mundane reforms are unparalleled in the entire history of mankind. And it remains yet to be seen if history could produce any equal to Muhammad. He said that he was the Last Prophet because it was the truth of God, and not because he wanted any personal glory or sought any personal gains. Victory did not spoil him, triumph did not weaken his excellent virtues, and power did not corrupt his character. He was incorruptible, consistent, and inaccessible to any notion of personal gain or glory. His words display dazzling light of wisdom and truth.

3. Muhammad was the only Prophet who fulfilled his mission and completed his work in his lifetime. Before he died, the Qur'an stated that the religion of God has been perfected, the favor of God on the believers has been completed, and the truth of revelation has been guarded and will be safely preserved (Qur'an 5:3 and 10:9). When he died, the religion of Islam was completed, and the community of Muslim believers was well-established. The Qur'an was recorded in his lifetime and preserved in its total and original version. All this means that the religion of God has been completed by Muhammad in

concept as well as in application, and that the Kingdom of God has been established here on earth. Muhammad's mission, his example and his accomplishments have proved the point that the Kingdom of God is not an unattainable ideal or something of the Hereafter only, but it is something of this world too, something that did exist and flourish in the age of Muhammad and can exist and flourish in any age whenever there are sincere believers and men of faith. Thus, if any man was destined to be the culmination of Prophethood, who could it be other than Muhammad? And if any book was designed to be the completion of Revelation, what could it be other than the Qur'an? The actual fulfillment of Muhammad's mission on earth and the authentic recording of the entire Qur'an in his lifetime should leave no trace of doubt in any mind as to the belief that he was the Last Prophet.

4. The decree of God that Muhammad is the Last Prophet is based on the original and pure authenticity of the Qur'an, on the conclusive and unique accomplishments of Muhammad, on the universality of Islam, and on the applicability of the Qur'anic teachings to every situation, every age, and every man, This is the religion which transcends all borders and penetrates far beyond all barriers of race, color, age and status of wealth or prestige. It is the religion which assures men, all men, of equality and brotherhood, freedom and dignity, peace and honor, guidance and salvation. This is the pure essence of God's religion and the kind of aid He has always extended to man from the beginning of history. With Muhammad and the Qur'an has come the culmination of religious evolution. This, however, does not mean the end of history or the termination of man's need for Divine guidance. It is only the beginning of a new approach, the inauguration of a new era, wherein man has been sufficiently provided with all the Divine guidance and the practical examples he needs. This Divine guidance is contained in the Qur'an, the most authentic and incorruptible Revelation of God, and these practical examples are found in the personality of Muhammad. If there were to come a new prophet or a new revealed book, what could this add to the quality of prophethood or to the truth of the Qur'an? If it is to preserve the word of God or guard the truth of Revelation, this has been done through the Qur'an. And if it is to show that the Law of God can be implemented in history or that the Kingdom of God can be established on earth, all this has been shown by Muhammad. And if it is to guide man to God and the Right Way of life, this has been well-established by the Qur'an and Muhammad. Man does not need new revelations or new prophets. What he needs most is to wake up, to open his mind and to quicken his heart. What he needs now is to make use of the already available Revelations, to utilize his existing

resources and to draw from the inexhaustible treasures of Islam which has incorporated, preserved and perfected the purity of the previous revelations.

5.   God decreed that Muhammad would be the Last Prophet and so he was.   No prophet before Muhammad had done or accomplished or bequeathed so much as he did.   And no one after him, of those who have claimed prophethood, has done anything comparable to what he did.   However, this Divine decree was in anticipation of the great historical events which have followed.   It heralded good news for man that he would enter a new stage of intellectual maturity and spiritual heights, and that he would have, from then on, to do without new prophets or new revelations, to be on his own, aided by the rich legacies of prophethood and revelations as found in Muhammad and his predecessors.   It was in anticipation of the fact that the cultures, races and regions of the world would become closer and closer to each other, and that mankind could do well with one universal religion in which God occupies His rightful position and man realizes himself.   It was a solemn witness to the great role which advanced knowledge and serious intellectual undertaking would play in terms of bringing man to God.   And it is true that if man can combine his advanced knowledge and his sound intellectual potential with the spiritual and moral teachings of the Qur'an he cannot fail to recognize the existence of God and adapt himself to God's Law.

The historical stage of prophethood has ended with Muhammad to give man the evidence that he can mature on his own initiative, to give science an opportunity to function properly and explore the vast dominion of God, and to give the mind a chance to reflect and penetrate.   The nature of Islam is such that it has a great deal of flexibility and practicability and can cope with any arising situation. The nature of the Qur'an is such that it is universal and ever-revealing, and in it guidance is sure, without doubt.   The nature of Muhammad's message is such that it is addressed to all men and directed to all generations. Muhammad was not merely a racial leader or a national liberator.   He was, and still is, a man of history and the best model of him who seeks God.   In him every man can find something to learn, and excellent examples of goodness and piety to follow.   And in him every generation can find its lost hope.

APPENDIX III

THE ISLAMIC CALENDAR

The Muslim Era began with the Great Event of the Hijrah from Mecca to Medina or the Emigration of Prophet Muhammad and his Companions from Mecca to Medina. The adoption of this Event as the beginning of the Muslim Era took place in the Caliphate of 'Umar Ibn Al-Khattab, the second Caliph after Muhammad. We are now in the year 1395 after Hijrah (1395 A.H.).

The Muslim calendar is Lunar, and its months are determined by the various positions of the moon. In every year there are twelve months, and each month is either thirty or twenty-nine days depending on the position of the moon. These months are: Muharram, Safar, Rabee' Al-Awwal, Rabee' Al-Thani, Jumada Al-Oola, Jumada Al-Thaniyah, Rajab, Sha'ban, Ramadan, Shawwal, Thul-Qa'dah, and Thul-Hijjah.

Every week has one special day to remember and observe. This is Friday, and its significance stems from the noon congregational prayers which must be observed by every Muslim who can attend. There are other significant occasions which should be remembered with a special observance.

1. The Hijrah which falls on the Eve of the first day of Muharram.
2. The Prophet's Birthday which falls on the Eve of the twelfth day of Rabee' Al-Awwal.
3. Ramadan, the Month of Fasting, in which the Qur'an was revealed.
4. The Night of Power of Qadr which may be celebrated on the eve of the twenty-third or the twenty-fifth or the twenty-seventh of Ramadan.
5. 'Eedul-Fitr (Feast of Breaking the Fast of Ramadan) which falls on the First day of Shawwal.
6. 'Eedul-Adha (Feast of Sacrifice) which falls on the tenth day of Thul-Hijjah.

INDEX